WOMEN, FAMILY, AND WORK

For Avery and Halsey, who make the balancing act worthwhile.

Women, Family, and Work

Writings on the Economics of Gender

EDITED BY

Karine S. Moe
Macalester College

Blackwell
Publishing

© 2003 by Blackwell Publishing Ltd
except for editorial material and organization © 2003 by Karine S. Moe

350 Main Street, Malden, MA 02148-5018, USA
108 Cowley Road, Oxford OX4 1JF, UK
550 Swanston Street, Carlton South, Melbourne, Victoria 3053, Australia
Kurfürstendamm 57, 10707 Berlin, Germany

First published 2003 by Blackwell Publishing Ltd

Library of Congress Cataloging-in-Publication Data

Women, family, and work: writings in the economics of gender/edited by
Karine S. Moe.
        p. cm.
Includes bibliographical references and index.
    ISBN 0–631–22576–5 (hbk: alk. paper)—ISBN 0–631–22577–3 (pbk: alk. paper)
    1. Work and family. 2. Sex role—Economic aspects. 3. Women—Employment. 4. Family—
Economic aspects. 5. Sexual division of labor. I. Moe, Karine S.

    HD4904.25 .W654 2003
    330′ .082—dc21

                                                                    2002008974

A catalogue record for this title is available from the British Library.

Set in 10/12.5 pt Galliard
By Newgen Imaging Systems (Pvt.) Ltd.
Printed and bound in the United Kingdom
by TJ International, Padstow, Cornwall

For further information on
Blackwell Publishing, visit our website:
http://www.blackwellpublishing.com

Contents

Contributors

Debra Barbezat is Associate Professor of Economics at Colby College where she teaches courses on labor, health, and the economics of gender. She received an AB from Smith College and a PhD in economics from the University of Michigan. She has published mainly in the area of labor economics with an emphasis on the academic labor market. Her scholarly publications have focused on trends in male–female salary differentials, gender differences in career development, academic collective bargaining, and the salary effects of mobility and job market experience.

Robert Cherry is a Professor of Economics at Brooklyn College and the Graduate Center of the City University of New York. He has published extensively on the economics of discrimination. His most recent works include *Prosperity for All? The Economic Boom and African Americans*, which he coedited for Russell Sage, and "Impact of Tight Labor Markets on Black Employment" in *Review of Black Political Economy*. He is currently working on a book for Rutgers University Press on the history of exclusionary employment barriers and the effectiveness of affirmative action in combating them.

Cheryl Doss is the Director of Graduate Studies of the MA program in International Relations at Yale University. In addition, at Yale she is the Associate Chair of the International Affairs Council and a Lecturer in Economics. Previously, she was an Assistant Professor at Williams College, where the courses she taught included Feminist Economics and the Economics of the Household. She earned an MA from Yale University in International Relations in 1986 and a PhD in Applied Economics from the University of Minnesota in 1996. Her research has focused on understanding economic decisions made within households, especially in Africa. Her work has been published in *Economic Development and Cultural Change*, and the *American Journal of Agricultural Economics, Agricultural Economics, and World Development*.

Marianne A. Ferber obtained her PhD at the University of Chicago. She is Professor of Economics and Women's Studies, Emerita, University of Illinois, Urbana-Champaign, and during 1993–95 was Horner Distinguished Visiting Professor at the Radcliffe Public Policy Institute. She is co-editor with Brigid O'Farrell of *Work and Families: Policies for a Changing Work Force*, 1991; with Julie A. Nelson of *Beyond Economic Man: Feminist Theory and Economics*, 1993; with Jane W. Loeb of *Academic Couples: Problems and Promises.* 1997; and of *Women in the Labor Force*, 1998. She is also co-author with Francine D. Blau and Anne Winkler of *The Economics of Women, Men, and Work*, 3rd edition. In addition she has published in economics, education, sociology and women's studies journals, and continues to serve on the editorial board of several journals. She was president of the Midwest Economic Association; president of the International Association for Feminist Economics, and received the McMaster University 1996 Distinguished Alumni Award for the Arts. Most recently, she was awarded the 2002 Carolyn Shaw Bell Award for furthering the status of women in the economics profession.

Lisa Giddings is an Assistant Professor of Economics and Women's Studies at the University of Wisconsin-La Crosse. She studied mathematics and institutional economics at the University of Nebraska, and received her PhD in economics from American University. Her main scholarly interests are on the effects of the transition in Central and Eastern Europe on women and ethnic minorities in the labor market. Her work has been published in such journals as *Feminist Economics,* the *Eastern Economic Journal,* and the *International Journal of Manpower.*

Joni Hersch is a Lecturer on Law at Harvard Law School where she teaches a course on empirical methods for lawyers. Her research interests include gender differences in the labor market, the economics of home production, and the economics of risky behavior such as job injury risk and smoking. Her work has been published in journals including the *American Economic Review, Review of Economics and Statistics, Journal of Human Resources, Industrial and Labor Relations Review,* and *Duke Law Journal.* Most of her professional career was spent at the University of Wyoming, where she was Professor of Economics until December 1999. Hersch has also taught at CalTech, Duke, Northwestern, and Harvard College. She has served on the Board of the American Economic Association Committee on the Status of Women in the Economics Profession (CSWEP) and was a recipient of the National Science Foundation Visiting Professorship for Women grant. Hersch received her PhD in Economics from Northwestern University.

Joyce P. Jacobsen is Professor of Economics at Wesleyan University in Middletown, Connecticut. She received an AB in economics from Harvard, an MSc in economics from LSE and a PhD in economics from Stanford. She has published mainly in the area of labor economics, including articles on sex segregation, migration, and the effects of labor force intermittency on women's earnings. She is the author of *The Economics of Gender* (2nd edition, 1998).

Jean Kimmel is Associate Professor of Economics at Western Michigan University in Kalamazoo, Michigan. She is a labor economist whose research interests include child-care, welfare-to-work, employment-related health and disability issues, and multiple-job holding. New research projects include a study of the wages of childcare workers and the motherhood wage penalty. Her research papers have been published in such academic journals as the *Review of Economics and Statistics*, the *Journal of Monetary Economics*, *Labour Economics*, and *Industrial Relations*. She has received research funding from the National Science Foundation and the Joint Centers for Research on Poverty. Professor Kimmel is currently serving as board member and Midwest representative to the Committee on the Status of Women in the Economics Profession (CSWEP), a subcommittee of the American Economics Association. Kimmel earned her BA in economics from the George Washington University in 1982, her MA in economics at the University of Delaware in 1984, and her PhD in economics from the University of North Carolina at Chapel Hill in 1990. Prior to joining the faculty at WMU in August 2001, she was Senior Economist at the W. E. Upjohn Institute for Employment Research, where she was a researcher for 12 years.

Diane Macunovich is a Professor of Economics at Barnard College, Columbia University, following ten years as Assistant and Associate Professor at Williams College in Massachusetts. She specializes in demographic and labor economics, with a particular focus on the effects of the Baby Boom on the economy, and the effects in turn of changing economic conditions on the Boomers' life cycle demographic decisions. Prior to her academic career she spent 17 years as an economic and demographic consultant in the US, UK, Canada and Iran, after having completed undergraduate work at MIT. She received her PhD in economics in 1989 from the University of Southern California. In addition to numerous scholarly articles, she is the author of *Birth Quake: The Baby Boom and Its Aftershocks*, published by the University of Chicago Press (2002).

Karine S. Moe is an Associate Professor of Economics at Macalester College in Saint Paul, Minnesota. She also teaches regularly in the Women and Gender Studies Program at Macalester. She earned a PhD and MA in economics at the University of Minnesota, a Master of Public Policy at Harvard University's JFK School of Government, and a BA in economics from Saint Olaf College. Her main scholarly interests are in economic demography, the informal sector, and labor economics. In particular, she is interested in how the use of time (especially for women and girls) affects labor market outcomes. Her work has been published in such journals as *Feminist Economics*, the *Journal of Developing Areas*, the *Review of Economic Dynamics*, and *World Development*.

Julie A. Nelson is currently at Tufts University, Massachusetts, with the Global Development and Environment Institute. Formerly an Associate Professor of Economics at the University of California-Davis, she has also served at the U.S. Bureau of Labor Statistics, Brandeis University, Harvard University, and the University of Massachusetts Boston. She is author of *Feminism, Objectivity, and Economics* (London: Routledge, 1996) and co-edited *Beyond Economic Man: Feminist Theory and Economics* (Chicago: University of Chicago Press, 1993). Her articles on household behavior, and on feminist theory and economics, have appeared in many journals including the *Journal of Economic Perspectives, Econometrica, Journal of Labor Economics, Feminist Economics,* and *Signs: Journal of Women in Culture and Society.* She holds a PhD degree (1986) in Economics from the University of Wisconsin, Madison.

Irene Powell is an Associate Professor of Economics at Grinnell College, and has also taught at Mount Holyoke and Smith Colleges. Before coming to Grinnell she was an economist with the Human Resources Division of the U.S. General Accounting Office. She received her BA at the University of Delaware and her MA and PhD at the University of Wisconsin. Her primary areas of research are industrial organization, labor economics, and the economics of health care. Her work has been published in such journals as the *Review of Economics and Statistics, The Journal of Human Resources, Industrial Relations, Child and Youth Care Forum,* and others. She is married and has two children.

Leslie S. Stratton is an Associate Professor of Economics at Virginia Commonwealth University in Richmond, Virginia where she teaches labor economics and econometrics at both the undergraduate and graduate level. She earned her PhD in economics at the Massachusetts Institution of Technology and her BA in both mathematical economics and government from Wesleyan University in Middletown, Connecticut. Her research has centred on how individuals make choices regarding the allocation of time and how those choices influence labor market-related outcomes. To this end she has explored the decision to work part-time, the decision to seek no employment, and the effect these choices have upon wages. As the decision to work less than full-time is often made because individuals are taking on more household based responsibilities, this work has led her to examine the interaction between market and home production activities. Her research has been published in such journals as the *Industrial and Labor Relations Review,* the *Journal of Human Resources,* and *Economic Inquiry.*

Preface

During recent decades, economists' interest in gender-related issues has generated interesting research. Along with this expanded research agenda came the introduction of relevant courses in economics departments at colleges and universities across the United States: courses carrying titles such as Economics of the Family, Economics of Gender, Women in the Economy, and Feminist Economics. Typically, instructors aim to show how economic theory can be applied to topics such as marriage and divorce, fertility, and the division of work and leisure in the household, as well as labor market outcomes. *Women, Family, and Work* is a collection of 12 original essays written specifically for these courses.

A survey of such courses offered at both colleges and universities indicates that instructors typically supplement one or two texts with readings from journals and books. I have taught such a course for the past 8 years, both at the University of Minnesota and at Macalester College in exactly this way. This manner of teaching the course creates two challenges for the instructor: (1) locating appropriate readings for undergraduates and (2) making those articles available to the students. *Women, Family, and Work* eases both of these challenges.

Locating appropriate readings for undergraduates is a difficult process. Typically journal articles are too sophisticated and specific for undergraduates. Overviews, on the other hand, tend to be too general. This anthology provides a good overview of the issues as well as economic models. The economics background required of the reader is either one course in introductory microeconomics or a mini-unit by the instructor to cover the basics of consumer choice theory. While several of the articles present regression results, the results are clearly interpreted in the essay, and the Powell chapter gives a brief overview of basic regression analysis. Other technical information is relegated to two appendices. Thus despite the minimal prerequisites, the range of topics covered, the sophistication of the arguments, and the technical appendices make the book an appropriate choice as a reader for more advanced courses as well.

The second task of making the readings accessible raises issues of copyright (especially at institutions that do not provide an office to secure permission to create course packs), accessibility, and convenience for students. The challenges associated with locating appropriate readings for undergraduates and then making them available to the students convinced me of the need for an anthology of readings in the Economics of Gender.

This anthology is a comprehensive set of essays written by leading thinkers in the field. The book provides an invaluable resource for instructors by compiling current, original articles from a variety of perspectives and works well either as a stand-alone text to accompany lectures or as a supplementary reader. It offers in one text recent scholarship on gender-related economics, which is now accessible only through a variety of sources.

First, I want to thank all the contributors, who devoted their time and considerable talent to creating this book. I also want to acknowledge Karen Warren, who encouraged me to undertake this project and provided invaluable advice along the way. Thanks to Al Bruckner, who saw potential in my idea, and to Elizabeth Wald, Seth Ditchik, and Linda Auld at Blackwell Publishing. This was my first editing project, and the professionals at Blackwell made the process a smooth one. Thanks also to Megan Johnson for editing assistance and to the Macalester students who served as "classroom testers." Finally, thanks to Paul Moe, my husband and my best friend.

Karine S. Moe

Setting the Stage

Setting the Stage: An Introduction and Overview

Karine S. Moe

Love, commitment, work. As we begin the twenty-first century, women in the United States increasingly must make tradeoffs in order to balance love, commitment, and work. In 2000, 60.2 percent of women in the United States worked in the labor force, as did 62.8 percent of married women with children under the age of six (U.S. Bureau of the Census 2001: Tables 568 and 577). Along with labor market work, women continue to act as primary caregivers of their children and perform the bulk of household tasks. In this book, economists contribute to the understanding of this balancing act, through the application of economic theory to gender, work, and family.

While men and women interact as economic agents, both within families and in the marketplace, historically, economists have modeled the behavior of *men* interacting in the *marketplace*. Women and families were virtually ignored in economic thought before the 1960s, and many argue that they continue to be marginalized in economic theory today. As women have increased their labor force attachment, however, economists have generated research on how gender differences lead to different economic outcomes for women and men, both within families and in the marketplace.

As you read this book, you will find that most of the authors apply traditional, or neoclassical, economic theory to topics not traditionally considered part of the economic realm, such as the decision to marry and/or have children. Yet at the same time, the authors stretch and bend neoclassical economic thought to provide a better model of economic interactions. The chapters in this volume challenge our assumptions of the family as a loving unit that is separate from the marketplace. Connecting the domain of home, family, and care to the domain of labor market work, income, and achievement requires economists to reach beyond the traditional economic models of self-interested agents interacting in free markets.

This anthology is a collection of 12 original essays, written specifically for undergraduates, on topics related to the economics of gender, work, and family. The remainder of this introduction describes these chapters, which are organized into five parts: Setting the Stage; The Economics of Marriage; The Division of Work in the Household; The Economics of Childbearing and Childcaring; and The Gender Gap in Earnings.

Part I: Setting the Stage

Following this introduction, Marianne Ferber provides a feminist critique of the neoclassical economic theory of the family, as described by Gary Becker (1981). While much of the applied microeconomic research on the economics of the family uses Becker's framework as a theoretical basis for empirical work, feminist economists have criticized Becker's work, as overly simplistic at best and sexist at worst. Barbara Bergmann, for instance, writes that Becker's theory of the family restricts "itself to looking at a dominating male married to subordinated female(s), with safely subordinated children" (1995: 142). Becker's simplifications and sexist assumptions lead to unrealistic conclusions. Ferber presents the main feminist critiques of the neoclassical perspective. She begins with a brief overview of the neoclassical model, and then discusses the major criticisms laid against it by feminist economists. Ferber concludes with the challenges researchers face in the field of economics of the family, especially with respect to policy.

Part II: The Economics of Marriage

The chapters of Part II introduce the reader to the two mainstream frameworks for analyzing the economics of marriage: rational choice and bargaining. These chapters demonstrate the major advantages and disadvantages of using the various types of marriage models for addressing issues of power and bargaining in an economic framework.

In chapter 2, Robert Cherry presents a rational choice model of marriage to explain the price of marriage determined in the marriage market. Cherry develops the concept of an equitable marriage in which the allocations of time and income are determined by the individual's preferences. The equilibrium marriage price, then, is defined as the measure of the welfare lost because the individual must provide services in excess of what would be expected in an equitable marriage. Patriarchal policies, such as male control over resources or female inability to own land, therefore, will affect the marriage price. Cherry concludes his chapter with an explanation for the persistence of the marriage price in the United States.

Bargaining theory provides an alternative framework in which to analyze the economics of marriage. In a bargaining framework, the model explicitly recognizes that individuals come to a marriage with separate utility functions and that individuals retain those separate functions even after the marriage takes place. The individuals decide whether or not to marry based on the returns to marriage versus the returns to remaining single.

In chapter 3, Cheryl Doss explains how economists typically conceptualize bargaining power, either through cooperative or non-cooperative bargaining models. She then discusses the challenge of finding appropriate measures of bargaining power. Making reference to measures in both more- and less-developed contexts, she explores factors that are critical to bargaining outcomes, such as social norms, cultural contexts, and institutions, but are often taken as exogenous in the standard bargaining models. Doss concludes with a case study in Ghana to explore how bargaining power affects household decisions.

Part III: The Division of Work in the Household

Housework in the United States continues to require a large fraction of time, especially for women. Recent data indicate that men spend roughly six to 14 hours per week on housework, while women spend between 20 and 30 hours per week (Hersch and Stratton 1994). In addition, there is evidence that time spent on non-market activities, such as housework, has a negative effect on wages. As such, the disproportionate amount of time women spend on housework may contribute to the gender gap in earnings. The essays in this section analyze the relationship between gender and the division of work within households for both heterosexual and homosexual couples.

Leslie Stratton investigates how heterosexual, married couples allocate their time between housework and labor market work in the United States. Drawing upon the human capital literature and the bargaining literature, Stratton motivates a theory of time allocation, and then presents empirical evidence of gender differences in market and household work. She concludes with an analysis of household and market work interactions, finding that wives do more housework, and that housework reduces wages. These interactions suggest a vicious cycle where women do relatively more housework because their wages are lower, and then their wages are reduced because they are doing more housework.

Same-sex couple households provide an interesting case for investigating the relationship between gender and the division of work and leisure. Feminist economists are interested in knowing how much gender factors into the division of labor and leisure in the household. Are gay and lesbian households less likely to exhibit gendered patterns of specialization? Or do same-sex couples suffer from the same gendered patterns as heterosexual couples?

Lisa Giddings tackles these questions in chapter 5. She applies the theory of time allocation outlined by Stratton to same-sex couples. Giddings explores how gay and lesbian couples allocate time among market and household work and discusses possible reasons for the choices these couples make. Same-sex couples face institutional and biological structures that constrain their choices with respect to market and household work. In her conclusion, Giddings outlines the current legal structure protecting gays and lesbians and argues that further protections are needed in order to level the playing field between heterosexual and same-sex couples.

Part IV: The Economics of Childbearing and Childcaring

Part IV is devoted to the economics of fertility and of childcare. After Thomas Malthus (1803), economists largely ignored childbearing as an economic phenomenon, in part because it was difficult to explain why fertility falls with income if we believe that children are normal goods. It was only in the 1960s with Becker's notion of the child quantity–quality tradeoff that the economics of fertility was brought into the mainstream of economic discourse. As women enter (and remain in) the labor force in greater numbers, the issues of fertility and childcare have become increasingly important. In particular, as the opportunity cost of time spent on family care rises, so does a distributional question as to whether society or the individual should pay for such care.

In chapter 6, Diane Macunovich reviews the economic theories of fertility from a utility-maximizing framework. This overview covers both the Beckerian, "price of time" model and the Easterlin relative income hypothesis. She argues that while neither of these theories adequately models observed fertility behavior, a hybrid of the two can explain United States fertility patterns since World War II. She shows that the combined "relative income and price of time" model can also explain differences between African-American and white marriage and fertility patterns since 1950. Macunovich concludes with a discussion of the applicability of these theories to less-developed economies.

As women increasingly move into the labor force, concerns of childcare quality and affordability become critical, both to families and to society. Childcare workers earn relatively low wages, which helps on the affordability end, but worsens quality. Julie Nelson frames this problem in chapter 7. She discusses the standard economic explanations for low wages in the childcare sector, and investigates the extent to which this framework helps to analyze the connections among quality, affordability, and wages in the childcare sector. Nelson concludes her essay with a call for an expansion of economic theory to encompass a connected view of self-esteem combined with care for others.

Jean Kimmel turns from the supply-side to the demand-side in chapter 8, where she explores the quality–availability–affordability problem facing working families with children in the United States. After describing the economic circumstances facing poor working families and their childcare utilization patterns, Kimmel applies economic choice theory to explain the childcare decisions and employment decisions. She summarizes the empirical literature on the relationship between childcare cost and the employment behavior of mothers in the United States. Kimmel argues for government intervention in the market for childcare and makes policy recommendations to ease the "childcare crunch" facing low-income working families.

Part V: The Gender Gap in Earnings

Part V investigates the earnings gap between men and women. Human capital differences, occupational segregation, and discrimination constitute three standard economic explanations of the gender gap in earnings. Each of the four chapters in this part addresses one of these three explanations, with two chapters devoted to discrimination. (A fourth explanation, compensating differentials, is discussed by Nelson in chapter 7.)

Most economists believe that human capital can explain a substantial portion of the gender gap in earnings. In chapter 9, Joyce Jacobsen analyzes the human capital explanation for the gender gap in earnings. She presents evidence of differences in amounts and types of human capital, both in the United States and around the world, and evaluates the contribution of human capital gender differences to the gender gap in earnings. Jacobsen concludes with a discussion of alternative explanations for why human capital varies by gender and what causes the gender gap in pay.

In chapter 10, Deborah Barbezat investigates the degree of occupational segregation by gender. Barbezat reviews the theoretical explanations of occupational segregation. She then presents evidence of occupational segregation for a cross-section of countries from all the major regions of the world and from different stages of economic development. Barbezat argues that in addition to reinforcing and perpetuating gender stereotypes, occupational segregation has a negative effect on a variety of economic outcomes, including labor market inefficiencies and rigidities, elevated fertility levels (particularly in developing countries), and male–female wage differentials. Thus, occupational segregation is an important topic that extends beyond the desire to improve the economic situation of women.

Irene Powell explores the economics of gender discrimination in the labor market in chapter 11. She describes the major neoclassical theories of discrimination and introduces multiple regression analysis, the primary statistical method used by economists to identify discrimination. Evidence indicates women are more likely than men, on average, to leave their jobs during childbearing years. Since it is impossible to discern which women will leave their jobs, employers may use gender as a signal for the higher costs associated with hiring and training replacement workers. In order to illustrate how economists use multiple regression analysis to identify discrimination, Powell presents a case study of professional women with MBAs to test whether receipt of an MBA offsets the negative signal of being female.

In chapter 12, Joni Hersch explores the role of economics in discrimination litigation. A vast number of statutes regulating equal opportunity in employment have been passed since the landmark Title VII of the Civil Rights Act of 1964. Not surprisingly, a staggering amount of litigation has resulted from alleged non-compliance with Equal Employment Opportunity laws. Hersch surveys the relevant laws that prohibit employment discrimination. Connecting economics and the legal context, she uses noteworthy cases to illustrate the arguments employed in the courtroom to establish a legal finding of discrimination.

Love, commitment, work. The essays in this book illustrate how economics can lead to a better understanding of the balancing act in women's lives. The authors help beginner readers of economics to understand how economics can be applied to realms outside of the marketplace. The essays also challenge more advanced readers to think critically about how women connect the domain of family and care to the domain of labor market work.

REFERENCES

Becker, Gary. 1981. *A Treatise on the Family*. Cambridge, MA: Harvard University Press.
Bergmann, Barbara R. 1995. "Becker's Theory of the Family: Preposterous Conclusions." *Feminist Economics* 1: 141–50.
Hersch, Joni and Leslie S. Stratton. 1994. "Housework, Wages, and the Division of Housework Time for Employed Spouses." *American Economic Review* 84: 120–5.
Malthus, Thomas. 1803. *An Essay on the Principle of Population*. London: T. Bensley.
U.S. Bureau of the Census. 2001. *Statistical Abstract of the United States*, 121st edition. Washington, DC: U.S. Government Printing Office.

Chapter 1

A Feminist Critique of the Neoclassical Theory of the Family

Marianne A. Ferber

Gary Becker's *A Treatise on the Family* (1981) was published about 20 years ago, a culmination of much of his previous work.[1] It has remained the centerpiece of neoclassical economic theory of the family ever since, and Becker has widely, albeit not entirely accurately, been considered "the father" of what is also widely referred to as the "new home economics."[2] Actually, the honor of pioneering research on and analysis of the household as an economic unit properly belongs mainly to Margaret Reid (1934), who in turn gave a great deal of credit to Hazel Kyrk, her teacher and mentor.[3] Interestingly, both Kyrk and Reid were also on the faculty of the University of Chicago, which makes Becker's (and the profession's) failure to acknowledge their work all the more surprising.[4]

Reid was the first to recognize explicitly that the household is the locus of production as well as consumption. She specifically defined housework (that is, those unpaid tasks performed by family members that could be replaced by market goods or services), as productive. Mary Hirschfeld (1994) argues that Reid's work, despite lacking Becker's elegant mathematical models, is far more realistic and, in many respects, considerably more progressive from the feminist point of view. While, like Becker, she assumes rational economic agents and a single family utility function, she follows Charlotte Perkins Gilman (1903) in rejecting the isolation of the domestic sphere from the public sphere of the market and government. Reid even appeals to the state to recognize the economic value of women's role in the home and to find ways of supporting their family responsibilities. Becker, on the other hand, does not appear altogether serious about considering homemaking as real work, given his assertion that married women "work" much less than single women. His description of a very poor society as one "where adult males manage only a few hours of leisure" (Becker 1996: 3) points toward the same conclusion.

Even so, Becker brought economic analysis of the family into the mainstream and developed a model that sheds a good deal of light on the evolution of the family as an economic institution. While objections have been raised to what some perceive to be undue emphasis on the market aspect of marriage[5] there is no question that economic considerations have always played an important role in this institution. Historically, in many societies dowry or bride price were the norm, and it was common for parents to hire marriage brokers, matchmakers, or place advertisements in newspapers, in order to find suitable partners for their sons and daughters. Acquisition through marriage of parcels of land by peasants, of territories by aristocrats, of guild or union member-ships by working men, and of businesses by capitalists has long been common and widely accepted.

It is, however, ironic that the neoclassical theory, which emphasizes the advantages of what is widely regarded as "the traditional family"[6] came to the fore just at the time when women and men were increasingly opting for alternative arrangements,[7] often more egalitarian relationships that emphasize sharing rather than specialization. Becker himself acknowledges that there need not be complete specialization. In a family where demand for money income is high, the wife may take a job in addition to fulfilling her household responsibilities. Similarly, he suggests that in case of high demand for household services, the husband may do some housework. Yet, he went so far as to develop a formal theorem that shows it would never be worthwhile for both spouses to share in both types of work. This presumably proves that an egalitar-ian couple could not maximize their wellbeing. At the same time, there has been a clear, albeit slow trend toward this pattern. For instance, between 1966 and 1999, the labor force participation rate of married women with husbands present in the United States rose from 35.4 percent to 61.6 percent (Francine Blau et al. 2002: 102). Meanwhile, the number of hours employed women spent on housework work declined from 24.3 in 1966 hours to 20.8 hours per week in 1994, while their hus-bands' increased from 6.4 hours to 7.8 hours per week (Blau 1998: 152–3). Thus, to the extent that the purpose of theory is to assist in understanding and interpreting observed events, Becker's theory, whatever its merits in other respects, was rather untimely, and certainly is not helpful in providing guidance towards the future of the family.

The Neoclassical Model of the Family

Neoclassical economists use the new home economics model to analyze marriage, births, division of labor in the household, and divorce. In the family, as elsewhere, individuals are presumably rational maximizers. Each spouse specializes in the work s/he does best in order to attain the largest income and hence the greatest amount of satisfaction. A simple example serves to illustrate this point. Assume that the man can earn $20 an hour or produce a dinner during the same period of time, while the woman can produce a better dinner, or earn $15; it is obvious that he should work in the market, and the woman should stay home and cook dinner. Or, assume that both could earn $15 an hour, but the woman would cook a better dinner; the rational decision still is that she should stay at home.

While Becker claims that his designation of the wage earner as "he" and the home-maker as "she" is purely for convenience, it happens to coincide with the popular view that the man will specialize in market work, the woman in housework. Presumably, since women bear children, they are better suited for raising them, and by extension also better suited to homemaking in general. Obviously this is not a convincing argu-ment. Alternatively, some argue that women devote more time and effort to child rearing because they can only have a relatively small number of children and hence have a greater stake in the quality of children, while men can "father" a very large number. This, of course, ignores that in a monogamous society men are deprived of this opportunity, except if they have multiple sequential marriages and/or children outside of marriage.

At first glance it might appear that a stronger case can be made for the traditional male and female roles on the grounds that men are more productive in the market since, on average, they continue to earn considerably more than women. There is, however, a problem with this argument as well. While many neoclassical economists reject the explanation that women's lower earnings are the result of discrimination, most are not prepared to claim that women are inherently less productive in the labor market than men. Instead, they fall back on the explanation that women acquire less human capital because they expect to spend less time in the labor market, accumulate less labor market experience, and have less energy for work in the labor market because they expend so much effort on housework. Of course, this is a flagrant case of circular reasoning.[8] For this essentially amounts to arguing that women spend more time in the household because men have a relative advantage in the labor market, and men have a relative advantage in the labor market because women spend more time in the household.

In addition to efficiency, neoclassical economists argue that in the traditional family specialization minimizes competition and conflict between husband and wife, and maximizes mutual dependence. Consequently there is more reason for couples to avoid getting divorced. Becker even goes one step further and argues that when divorce is difficult there is more incentive to "nurture love," so that marriages will actually be better.

Finally, although Becker rejects the assumption of a consensus on preferences within the family,[9] he too manages to avoid facing the disagreements about allocation of resources that often exist in real families where individuals have different tastes and different preferences. The new home economists avoid such problems by assuming that all decisions are made by the altruistic head of the family (who, once again, is referred to as "he") and that these decisions are accepted by all other family members as in their own best interest.[10]

A Feminist Critique

A careful reading of Becker's work rightly elicits admiration for its ambitious scope, for the application of the powerful tools of economic analysis to the family, which provides a number of original useful insights. At the same time, the model invites critical examination of the basic assumptions that underlie the analysis,[11] of the concepts used and, most importantly, some of the conclusions reached. Such an examination reveals surprising omissions, oversimplifications, and misunderstandings that inevitably lead to ill-founded conclusions. Yet, these have received remarkably little attention outside of feminist circles.

Feminists have challenged many aspects of Becker's view of the family, none more so than the notion of the altruistic head of the household who ensures that everyone's interests are equally safeguarded. By way of contrast, radical feminists see the family as the true locus of women's oppression (Heidi Hartmann 1981; Nancy Folbre 1994). While recognizing both that there are emotional ties and, to some extent, unified interests within the family, they also see it as the locus of struggle.[12] Further, they do not believe that these problems are merely the result of private decisions of individuals within each family. In this view, when Jane is responsible for taking care of the household and the children, while John "helps her," by clearing the table, taking out the garbage, and putting the children to bed, this is substantially influenced by patriarchal tradition and, in turn, serves to perpetuate this tradition. Hence the slogan "the personal is political."

Before going on to focus on specific aspects of Becker's model of the family, it may be useful to note some of the general flaws in this body of work.

First, indiscriminate citations of sources lend support to the proposed conclusions, without regard to their legitimacy. Thus one may be surprised to find a reference to George Bernard Shaw (a brilliant author who is not, however, noted for his understanding of women), on the subject of women's preferences for husbands (Becker 1981: 48–9). The most flagrant example, however, is the use of a quotation from the Ayattollah Khomeini in support of the contention that favoritism among wives in a polygamous family is not a problem (Becker 1981: 562). Second, sweeping conclusions are drawn in spite of conflicting evidence. One example of this is the assertion that women have always relied on men to provide them and their children with food and shelter.[13] Third, Becker occasionally "hedges his bets" so that no conceivable outcome would falsify the proposition offered. For example, he argues that both the mating of "likes" and of "unlikes" maximizes aggregate commodity output.

What is a family?

In view of the central role of the family in the new home economics, one would expect that considerable attention would have been devoted to the question of just what constitutes a family. Actually, there has been practically no discussion of this subject in the mainstream. Most neoclassical economists simply assumed that it is a nuclear family, comprised of a husband, a wife, and usually one or more children or, at times, of a single parent with a child or children.[14] The new home economics virtually ignores unmarried heterosexual couples, gay and lesbian couples, cooperative groups, and even extended families.[15] These households clearly deserve attention; moreover, applying the same model to them would clarify the extent to which the assumptions underlying the model are based on traditional stereotypes. For instance, would anyone really expect many homosexual couples (even those with children) to adopt a division of labor where one partner is the "housespouse" while the other one specializes in market work and is the "head of the household," although that would presumably be efficient and maximize household income? For more discussion of comparative advantage and same-sex households, see chapter 5 by Lisa Giddings in this volume.

Polygamous families represent the only exception to this neglect of other family types. Becker (1981) as well as others, such as Shoshana Grossbard-Shechtman (1976) argue that polygamy is good for women because it increases demand for them and hence improves their bargaining position. Barbara Bergmann (1995) asked, if polygamy is so beneficial for women, why is it almost invariably men who advocate it while women oppose it? The answer is that the more favorable terms, where they exist, often benefit fathers or brothers rather than women themselves. Often the girls, who tend to marry at a very young age, do not choose to do so but are rather "given in marriage" by a man in their birth family (Frances Woolley 1996). Thus, it is not surprising that neither women's economic nor their social position is favorable in countries where polygamy is permitted nor, for that matter, in countries where there are more men than women (Marianne Ferber and Helen Berg 1991). This may explain why men generally had to use force or threat of force to establish polygamous societies (William Goode 1974).

Rationality

The most serious problem with the neoclassical model is the crucial assumption that people are rational,[16] without a clear definition of rationality. Essentially Becker's view amounts to assuming that anyone is rational as long as s/he maximizes utility, but utility can be defined as whatever is being maximized. Thus, he says in *Accounting for Tastes* (1996) that he "retains the assumption that individuals behave so as to maximize utility, while extending the definition of individual preferences to include personal habits and addictions, peer pressure, parental influences on the tastes of children, advertising, love and sympathy, and other neglected behavior" (Becker 1996: 4). In other words, people's current preferences are not only influenced by their own past decisions, which people presumably do take into account at all times, but are also influenced by others. At the same time, these admissions do not resolve the fundamental question as to what rationality means.

The following example illustrates this point. It is reasonable, for instance, to assume that people consider the effect current decisions will have on future wellbeing – say that smoking cigarettes now will lead to addiction and ill health later – but that how much this recognition affects their current behavior is largely determined by the extent to which they discount the future. Yet, Becker has nothing to say concerning the rationality of various discount rates. In other words, if some teenagers give virtually no weight to what will happen tomorrow, let alone a year from now or ten years from now, they are perfectly rational, as long as their behavior is consistent with their discount rate.

Specialization

Becker concludes that specialization and exchange result in maximum family wellbeing at a particular point in time. Complete specialization in homemaking, though never universal, was widespread in earlier days, and did make a good deal of sense at one time. When fertility was high and life expectancy short, so that women were pregnant or nursing most of their adult lives, and while most necessities and amenities of life were produced in the household, homemaking was a full-time job for most or all of a woman's life. The situation is very different now. Today, with a life expectancy of about 79 years and the average number of children less than two, the wife who specializes in housework is not likely to maximize her income in the long run, even if she does in the short run. Over the years, her value as a homemaker will decline as her market skills atrophy. Only a very high discount rate of the future can justify such behavior.

The model also leads to the conclusion that in order to maximize income at least one partner must specialize completely in either housework or market work. The assumption of fixed proportions production functions guarantees that an additional hour spent on the production of each type of output will be the same, independent of how much of that output each partner has already produced. This is entirely possible, particularly in the case of market work, but is not very likely when it comes to housework, mainly because it includes a great many different types of tasks. Therefore, the husband's first few hours of housework are likely to make a larger net contribution to total output than the wife's last few hours of housework, even if his market wage is higher than hers. Consequently, complete specialization is unlikely. Both casual observation and a large array of data on sharing of housework suggest that this conjecture corresponds to reality. For more discussion on specialization in heterosexual households, see chapter 4 by Leslie Stratton in this volume.

Utility and disutility of work

Even if specialization were to result in maximum income, the family's utility is not necessarily maximized, because the model ignores the utility or disutility associated with work itself. Nor does it recognize that there is most likely diminishing marginal utility for each type of work. Yet, an individual who enjoys doing a particular type of work will enjoy it less as s/he does increasingly more of it; and if s/he disliked the work to begin with, this dislike will become more intensive. In addition, the partner who specializes in homemaking is at a serious disadvantage because, with the exception of childcare, people tend to prefer all other work to housework (Thomas Juster 1985).[17] One way to alleviate the boredom and isolation of housework would be for the partners to do it together, but the model does not allow for this possibility.

Assortative mating

The disutility for wives associated with specialization would likely be mitigated if men whose skills are highly valued in the labor market were to marry women who have little interest in doing paid work and have few marketable skills. Therefore, the ideal match would presumably be between a highly educated and well-trained man and a woman with the kind of education and background in domestic skills that would make her a good homemaker and a capable hostess. Conversely, a woman who has acquired human capital that is highly rewarded in the labor market would do best to marry a man with no relative advantage in market work who would therefore be expected to do a good deal of housework. Instead, we find that highly educated men and women tend to marry each other. This is, no doubt, in part the result of such young people being more likely to meet each other, but also suggests that men and women are more interested in enjoying the company of individuals with interests, tastes, and concerns similar to their own, rather than merely maximizing economic gains from marriage.

Uses of time

The new home economics model fails to recognize leisure as an alternative to both market work and housework. Reuben Gronau (1977) discussed this subject several decades ago, but focused mainly on the dominance of the substitution effect when a person's own wages increase, resulting in less time spent on leisure, while the income effect will dominate when the partner's earnings increase resulting in more time spent on leisure. There are, however, other issues related to leisure that deserve attention. Most important, partners must not only decide who should do which kind of work, but also how much time each should spend on work, and how much leisure each will have. Assuming that most people enjoy their own leisure more than their partner's, this question is likely to be considerably more contentious, for it inevitably involves interpersonal comparisons of utility. An inveterate optimist might assume that the altruistic head of the household gives due weight to his spouse's desire for leisure. Not everyone is an inveterate optimist, however, and a woman might do better to rely on other means to enhance the chances that her husband will do a larger share of housework.

Altruism

The subject of altruism also deserves more general consideration. The selfless head of the household is introduced as a kind of "*deus ex machina*" in this model who assures the equitable division of both responsibilities and benefits within the family.[18] This was a rather convenient solution for economists who, as Theodore Bergstrom (1996) noted, have often found family relationships an embarrassing nuisance because they are accustomed to modeling society as a set of interactions among self-interested individuals. Instead, as long as the family is dominated by a benevolent dictator, bargaining power is not, of course, an issue.

The question arises, however, whether such dictators, should they exist, are entirely benevolent. Is it reasonable to assume that "rational economic man," so dear to the hearts of neoclassical economists, who is concerned only with maximizing his own utility in his dealings with others, will turn from the selfish Mr. Hyde in the larger world into the benevolent Dr. Jekyll inside the family?[19] In recent years, economists who apparently found this an unlikely scenario, have developed a variety of bargaining models that do not rely on this assumption. Actually, Becker thinks of altruism as not being entirely selfless or devoid of calculations involving the individual's own interests. This is clear when he says "Altruistic parents choose fertility and consumption by maximizing a dynastic utility function. The maximization implies an arbitrage condition for consumption across generations, and equality between the benefit from an extra child and the child-rearing cost" (Becker 1988: 1). Thus there is a substantial literature by economists who find this split personality scenario to be unlikely, and have developed a variety of bargaining models that do not rely on this assumption.[20] Cheryl Doss explores the application of bargaining models to the family in chapter 3 in this volume.

Interdependence

As already mentioned, specialization is often considered desirable not only because it is thought to be efficient, but also because it is believed to result in interdependence and hence would presumably reduce the divorce rate. In truth, however, specialization does not so much lead to interdependence as it makes the full-time homemaker dependent on the wage earner. If a couple divorced, the non-employed wife could not expect to be able to earn an adequate income, nor can she count on finding another wage earner to support her. This is all the more true if she is middle aged or older, because most men consider such women less attractive than younger ones, perhaps in part because they are no longer able to bear children. Men, on the other hand, are considerably more likely to remarry quickly than are women, and even among those who do not, all but the very poor can afford to hire some help to replace the services of the homemaker. Nor are older men at a special disadvantage. The great majority can still father children, their earnings are often at a peak, and furthermore, in that age group women substantially outnumber men. Thus, men are far less likely to face serious problems in case of dissolution of the marriage, and consequently have sub-stantially more bargaining power if they are willing to use it as a threat. Generous alimony awards and strict enforcement of payments would tend to level the playing field, but neither of these appears to be common. The fact that even so many house-wives seek a divorce is evidence that they prefer a divorce on unfavorable terms to what they apparently consider an unsatisfactory marriage. It would, therefore, clearly be preferable to reduce the divorce rate by finding ways to make marriages better, rather than by making divorce more difficult.[21]

Policy Implications

Why, after all these years – Becker's first paper on marriage appeared in 1973 – does his work on the family continue to inspire such strong feelings, positive and negative? On the one side are his disciples who admire his originality, his competence, and his success in applying economic analysis to new areas of human behavior.[22] On the other side are the critics who are chagrinned that Becker uses his considerable talents and ingenuity to demonstrate that the traditional family, a flawed institution at best, and one that is clearly not well suited to present day conditions, is efficient and serves everyone's best interests. Passion was added to the debate because, although both sides have produced a voluminous literature ever since Becker first published *A Theory of the Allocation of Time* (1965), for the most part neither Becker himself, nor his disci-ples have as much as acknowledged the questions and objections raised by feminist economists.[23] Nor have the new home economists taken much notice as to what extent the real world increasingly deviates from their models. Thus for instance, although women, who are (or plan to be) full-time homemakers all their married lives while they and their children are supported and protected by the benevolent head of the family, have virtually become an endangered species, they continue to populate the neoclas-sical literature. Inevitably, this leaves the critics thoroughly frustrated.[24]

The main reason for this frustration, however, is that the views of the two groups differ radically concerning policies. As Bergmann (1995: 141) pointed out, Becker's "kind of theorizing leads, as does almost all neoclassical theory, to a conclusion that the institutions depicted are benign, and that government intervention would be use-less at best and probably harmful." In other words, while feminists see the traditional family as a major obstacle in the way of movement toward greater gender equality, members of the Becker school continue to see its preservation not as the problem but as the solution. As long as this is the case, the clash between these two groups is inevitable. The remainder of this chapter outlines some of the major policy reforms advocated by feminist economists.

1. All public support for the needy should go to individual adults,[25] not families. This will not only result in a considerably different distribution of resources within

families,[26] but will also obviate problems concerning inequities between people who live in families, as opposed to those who live in households that are not recognized as families.

2.   Tax inequities between one-earner and two-earner couples should be remedied. At present, families with a full-time homemaker have a substantial advantage as compared to those where both spouses are employed, because they need not pay taxes on the real income produced at home. Such preferential treatment not only fails to satisfy the generally accepted norms of "horizontal equity," but also provides a substantial incentive to keep the secondary wage earner, usually the wife, out of the labor market. This is especially true if her potential earnings are rather low, but are nonetheless taxed at the marginal rate that applies to the husband's earnings. Yet, this issue has received virtually no attention. It is admittedly difficult to determine the value of home production,[27] but the main reason for not even trying to solve this problem most likely is the continued high regard many people have for the traditional family.[28]

3.   The Earned Income Tax Credit (EITC), a refundable tax credit based on household earnings, mainly intended to benefit low-income families, raises similar issues. In 2000, a family with two children and earnings of less than $9,720, was subsidized at the rate of 40 percent, but the subsidy declined with rising income, and was fully phased out at $31,152. This program has been widely acclaimed as helping the poor, presumably without reducing their incentive to work in the labor market. Yet, it causes some secondary earners to leave the labor force because the additional earnings often place the family's income in the range where the credit is gradually phased out. This problem also would be remedied if refunds were based on individual rather than family earnings.

4.   Except for leaves of very limited duration for childbirth, both parents should be entitled to all other leaves for infant and childcare. Further, in order to provide maximum incentive for the father to take his share, the time he is entitled to should not be transferable. To the extent that this works and also creates stronger attachments between fathers and their children, this approach might even have effects well beyond the duration of the leave.

5.   Subsidized childcare for low-income families, perhaps with fees on a sliding scale, depending on the number of children and on the parents' income, would be a way to make more and better childcare available, most notably for children with parents who can not afford adequate care under present conditions. This would be of far more help to two-earner couples with low incomes than tax deductions, which are most helpful to couples in higher tax brackets. For a further discussion of the effects of childcare subsidies, see chapter 8 in this volume by Jean Kimmel.

These policies, in addition to the advantages already mentioned, would officially endorse the egalitarian view that fathers can and should take on their share of domestic responsibilities, and would amount to putting an official stamp of approval of both parents working for pay. Because this would be an important step toward breaking the hold of the patriarchal traditions, many neoclassical economists oppose, and most feminists support these policies. As long as these ideological differences remain, Beckerians are likely to continue developing their models, whether they are relevant to the real world or not, and feminist economists will continue to attack them, whether or not mainstream economists pay any attention to them.

NOTES

1 This critique of Becker's model of the family draws heavily on Ferber and Birnbaum (1977).

2 His earlier work on allocation of time (Becker 1965) and on marriage (Becker 1973 and 1974) laid the groundwork. A later "enlarged edition" of the Treatise, published in 1991, includes some discussion of more recent contributions by other scholars as well as responses to some criticisms of his work. The fundamental approach, however, has remained the same.

3 Kyrk also studied the family in a broader context, but her own work largely focused on consumption (see Kyrk 1923, 1953).

4 This is in sharp contrast to the fact that both Milton Friedman and Franco Modigliani (the latter in his Nobel address) acknowledged Reid's contribution to their life cycle model and permanent income hypothesis.

5 Non-economists, particularly, are often taken aback by the term "marriage market." On the other hand it may be the close analogy with the market economy that has made this model so attractive to many economists.

6 In fact, the male breadwinner, female homemaker family came into existence relatively late in history, and was never universal in all societies, or among all classes in any society.

7 Humphries (1999: 516) puts it more strongly than that: "in the late twentieth century [the traditional family] is more than creaking. It is falling off its hinges! Increasingly, those activities that the family traditionally coordinated take place outside it."

8 This was pointed out many years ago by Sawhill (1977) and her view has never been adequately refuted.

9 The consensus model was proposed earlier by Samuelson 1956.

10 Just in case there is someone in the family who is selfish and fails to act in everyone's best interest, Becker introduces the "rotten kid theorem." This demonstrates that the altruist can adjust transfers of income to other family members so as to remove all incentives for even the "rotten kid" to behave selfishly.

11 Friedman (1953) argued that it does not matter if assumptions are unrealistic, as long as they generate satisfactory predictions, but as Kuhn (1970) pointed out, this is not convincing when the same results may be consistent with more than one theoretical construction. Further, Solow (1956) suggested that when theoretical results are directly derived from a crucial assumption, that assumption should be reasonably realistic.

12 Interestingly, Marxian economists, who share few other views with members of the neoclassical school, have few differences with them concerning the family, which they also see as an almost wholly cooperative unit.

13   Even a casual review of the relevant anthropological literature leaves no doubt that in many societies women produced much or most food and clothing, and participated in providing shelter for themselves and their families.

14   This assumption is not entirely realistic in economically advanced countries, but less so in many developing countries, most notably Africa, where kinship structures and household forms are particularly diverse (Blumberg 1986).

15   An exception to this is when Becker (1981) claims that because [men's and women's] time is complementary in sexual enjoyment and the production of children households with men and women are more efficient than those with only one sex, and that this is the reason why there is less sexual division of labor in homosexual households. As Badgett (1995), however, points out, not only can sexual pleasure be produced by individuals of the same sex, but lesbians can produce children by obtaining sperm. Further, homosexual relationships are more efficient for couples who do not want any children and, arguably, for those who want only one or two.

16   This is, of course, an assumption shared by neoclassical economics in general, but it is perhaps particularly inappropriate in this context. For instance, Becker even assumes that the number of children couples have to be the result of rational decisions, in spite of overwhelming evidence of large numbers of unplanned pregnancies.

17   This is not surprising in light of the fact that Bird and Ross (1993) found that unpaid domestic work is more routine, provides less intrinsic gratification and fewer extrinsic rewards, than paid work.

18   Interestingly, here again, no question is raised as to just who is included in that "family." Is it only the head's wife and their children? Or does it include members of his birth family, grandparents, uncles and aunts? And what about his wife's family? Further, do most people not have some friends who are closer to them than many of their relatives? Merely asking these questions is sufficient to make clear that this is by no means a simple issue.

19   In fact, there is considerable evidence that it is the wives rather than husbands who most often are the altruists. For instance, they tend to spend a larger share of their income on their children's nutrition and education than their husbands do (Blumberg 1988; Lundberg and Pollak 1996; and Thomas 1990). Also, Kumar (1977) specifically found that in Kerala, India, a child's nutritional level was correlated positively with the mother's but not with the father's income. In addition, Sen (1992; 1993) showed that women and men do not have the same access to health care and nutritious food within families. During famines in India women had to become sicker before they were taken to the hospital and they were more likely to die after being taken there. Women were also given less adequate supplies of food.

20   For an excellent review of this literature see Lundberg and Pollak (1996).

21   It is possible that the recent modest decline in the divorce rate is the result of the growing number of more egalitarian marriages being more satisfactory, or at least that husbands are more likely to be resigned to such arrangements.

22   It has, however, also been suggested that some of Becker's admirers may be attracted by "his validation of sexist assumptions and ... the pro-market anti-interventionist flavor of many of his conclusions" (Woolley 1996: 117).

23   For example, in the nineteen pages of bibliography in Becker's *Treatise* (1981), there is not a single reference to a scholar who has been critical of the author's work. A relatively recent

exception to this is that in his Nobel lecture (1993: 297) he claimed that "Contrary to allegations in many attacks on the economic approach to the gender division of labor (see, for example Boserup 1987), this analysis does not try to weight the relative importance of biology and discrimination." Actually, Becker is right about that. The problem is not that Becker has tried to determine the relative importance of biology and discrimination, but rather that he simply ignored discrimination as a cause of the domestic division of labor.

24 In addition, as Woolley (1996) points out, Becker and his followers have made gratuitously offensive and needlessly provocative statements. Two of the examples she provides are sufficient to illustrate her point. Girls who are oriented toward market work rather than housework are described as "deviant" (Becker 1991: 40). Also, we are told that "the average divorced person can be presumed to be more quarrelsome and in other ways less pleasant than the average person remaining married" (Becker 1981: 339).

25 Support for children would go to their adult guardians.

26 As already noted, there is evidence that who within the family receives welfare payments makes a considerable difference (Lundberg and Pollak 1996).

27 Both the opportunity cost and the market cost approach present problems; nonetheless in recent years a growing number of countries are providing estimates of the value of home production in their data on national product. Further, it is surely reasonable to assume that almost any estimate would be more accurate than, in effect, assuming that it has no value.

28 Interestingly, the higher taxes two individuals with relatively equal earnings have to pay when they are married rather than single, a burden that falls most heavily on high income couples, has received a great deal of attention. As of the beginning of the year 2001, Congress was hard at work trying to remedy this situation.

REFERENCES

Badgett, M. V. Lee. 1995. "Gender, Sexuality, and Sexual Orientation: All in the Feminist Family." *Feminist Economics* 1(1): 121–39.

Becker, Gary S. 1965. "A Theory of the Allocation of Time." *Economic Journal* 75(299): 493–517.

——. 1973. "A Theory of Marriage: Part I." *Journal of Political Economy* 81(2): 813–46.

——. 1981. *A Treatise on the Family*. Cambridge, MA: Harvard University Press, enlarged edition 1991.

——. 1988. "A Reformulation of the Economic Theory of Fertility." *The Quarterly Journal of Economics* CIII(1): 1–25.

——. 1993. "Nobel Lecture: The Economic Way of Looking at Behavior." *Journal of Political Economy* 101(3): 385–409.

——. 1996. *Accounting for Tastes*. Cambridge, MA and London, UK: Harvard University Press.

Bergmann, Barbara R. 1995. "Becker's Theory of the Family: Preposterous Conclusions." *Feminist Economics* 1(1): 141–50.

Bergstrom, Theodore C. 1996. "Economics in a Family Way." *Journal of Economic Literature* 34(4): 1903–34.

Bird, Chloe and Catherine Ross. 1993. "Houseworkers and Paid Workers: Qualities of the Work and Effects on Personal Control." *Journal of Marriage and Family* 55(4): 913–25.

Blau, Francine D. 1998. "Trends in the Well-Being of American Women, 1970–1995." *Journal of Economic Literature* 36(1): 112–65.

Blau, Francine D., Marianne A. Ferber, and Anne E. Winkler. 2002. *The Economics of Women, Men, and Work*. Upper Saddle River, New Jersey: Prentice Hall.

Blumberg, Rae L. 1986. "A Women-in-Development Natural Environment in Guatemala: The Alcosa Agribusiness Project in 1980 and 1985." Unpublished paper.

——. 1988. "Income Under Female versus Male Control. Hypotheses From a Theory of Gender Stratification and Data from the Third World." *Journal of Family Issues* 9(1): 51–84.

Boserup, Ester. 1987. "Inequality Between the Sexes," in John Eatwell, Murray Milgate, and Peter Newman (eds.) *The New Palgrave: A Dictionary of Economics*, pp. 824–7. New York: Stockton.

Ferber, Marianne A. and Helen M. Berg. 1991. "Labor Force Participation of Women and the Sex Ratio: A Cross-Country Analysis." *Review of Social Economy* 49(1): 2–19.

Friedman, Milton. 1953. *Essays in Positive Economics*. Chicago: University of Chicago Press.

Gilman, Charlotte P. 1903. *The Home: Its Work and Influence*. New York: McClure, Phillips.

Goode, William. 1974. "Comment: The Economics of Nonmonetary Variables." *Journal of Political Economy* 82(Part II): S27–S33.

Gronau, Reuben. 1977. "Leisure, Home Production, and Work – The Theory of the Allocation of Time Revisited." *Journal of Political Economy* 85(6): 1099–123.

Grossbard-Shechtman, Shoshana. 1976. "An Economic Analysis of Polygamy: The Case of Maiduguri." *Current Anthropology* 17(4): 701–7.

Hartmann, Heidi I. 1981. "The Family as the Locus of Gender, Class and Political Struggle: The Example of Housework." *Signs: Journal of Women in Culture and Society* 6(3): 366–94.

Hirschfeld, Mary. 1994. "Antecedents of the New Home Economics." Presented at 1994 ASSA Meetings.

Humphries, Jane. 1999. "Special Issue on the Family: Introduction." *Cambridge Journal of Economics* 23(5): 515–17.

Juster, F. Thomas. 1985. "Preferences for Work and Leisure," in F. Thomas Juster and Frank P. Stafford (eds.) *Time, Goods and Well-Being*, pp. 333–51. Ann Arbor: Institute for Social Research, University of Michigan.

Kuhn, Thomas. 1970. *The Structure of Scientific Revolution: Second Edition*. Chicago: University of Chicago Press.

Kumar, Shubh. 1977. "Composition of Economic Constraints in Child Nutrition: Impact from Maternal Incomes and Employment in Low Income Households." PhD dissertation, Cornell University 1977.

Kyrk, Hazel. 1923. *A Theory of Consumption*. Boston/New York: Houghton Mifflin.

——. 1953. *The Family in the American Economy*. Chicago: University of Chicago Press.

Lundberg, Shelly and Robert Pollak. 1996. "Bargaining and Distribution in Marriage." *Journal of Economic Perspectives* 10(4): 139–58.

Reid, Margaret. 1934. *Economics of Household Production*. New York: Wiley and Sons.

Samuelson Paul. 1956. "Social Indifference Curves." *Quarterly Journal of Economics* 70(1): 1–22.

Sawhill, Isabel V. 1977. "Economic Perspectives on the Family." *Daedalus* 106(2): 115–25.

Sen, Amartya K. 1993. "The Economics of Life and Death." *Scientific American* 268(5): 40–7.

——. 1992. "Missing Women." *British Medical Journal* 304(6827): 587–8.

Solow, Robert M. 1956. "A Contribution to the Theory of Economic Growth." *Quarterly Journal of Economics* 41(1): 65–94.

Woolley, Frances. 1996. "Getting the Better of Becker." *Feminist Economics* 2(1): 114–20.

The Economics of Marriage

Chapter 2

Rational Choice and the Price of Marriage

Robert Cherry

One of the most discussed family trends in the United States has been the substantial decline in the share of women who are married. Between 1970 and 1998, the percentage of women aged 18 or older who are married declined from 68.5 to 57.9 percent; among African-American women, it declined from 61.7 to 38.9 percent.[1] (US Department of Commerce 1994: Table 59; Terry Lugailia 1998: Table 1). Departing from their libertarian stance on most public policy issues, virtually all US politicians pronounce that the government should encourage heterosexual marriages. Historically, this position was rooted in a breadwinner model of family life where men specialized in market production while women specialized in home production. Building on the work of Gary Becker (1973, 1981), neoclassical economists also contend that marriage is efficient because it enables partners to specialize in what they do best.

Most feminists reject this idyllic vision of marriage. In the not so distant past, women were often forced to marry or remain under the authority of a father or brother. Constrained access to well-paying jobs and societal pressure against unwed mothers had created a "reserve army" of women willing to marry at virtually any price. Elaine McCrate (1987: 79) writes, "Men's power, much like capitalists', enable them to extract economic benefits from the dependent group." According to Heidi Hartmann (1981: 10), these economic benefits include a disproportionate share of "luxury goods, leisure time, and personal services." While during the second half of the twentieth century the situation changed substantially, these feminists continue to believe that in the marriage market, women pay a patriarchal price.

In this chapter, I develop a rational choice model that systematically assesses this changing situation. It builds on Becker's work but departs from his narrow focus on income allocation.[2] Instead, the model assumes that the allocation of income is but one dimension of the marriage contract. However family income is allocated, women might be forced to conform to the demands and desires of their husbands. These qualitative losses may be more important than the quantitative income changes.

This model defines a marriage price that measures the excess services provided by wives to their husbands and identifies factors that change this price and the number of marriages. In particular, I show how government policies that provide incentives for women to marry and/or limit their earnings potentials invariably increase the marriage price. Finally, this paper enumerates the reasons why women continue to face a substantial marriage price despite the legal and social changes that have occurred since World War II.

The Marriage Model

Let us define an equitable marriage as one in which sexual behavior and the allocation of household time and income are determined completely by comparative advantage and each individual's preferences. A marriage is equitable even if the wife does the bulk of household services as long as this allocation reflected genuine altruism or an acceptable compensation for services rendered. The actual services provided by each spouse in the typical marriage can deviate from those that should be provided in equitable marriages. The *marriage price* is defined as the dollar measure of the lost welfare of wives due to their provision of services beyond those that should be provided in an equitable marriage. These excess services may include ceding control of an excessive share of household income to the other spouse, requiring the dominated spouse to do an excessive share of household production, and/or ceding to the dominating spouse excessive influence over the choice and frequency of sexual activities.

Once the marriage price is defined, I use marriage offer curves to analyze the marriage decision. For each gender, the marriage offer curve is the relationship between the marriage price and the quantity willingness to marry. Marriage offer curves are culturally specific, and we would expect to find considerable variation in them across countries. In the following discussion, I will focus on circumstances in the United States.

A number of factors other than the marriage price influence female and male marriage decisions. The male marriage offer curve is influenced by male preferences and the number of men available. In addition, some studies (Frances Goldscheider and Linda Waite 1986) indicate that marriage is a normal good for men so that they will be more willing to marry as their earnings increase.

Female marriage offer curves are influenced by the income of men. If male income declines, men may be perceived as less valuable so that fewer women seek marriage (Valerie Oppenheimer 1988; Francine Blau et al. 2000). Becker suggests that the female–male earnings ratio also influences female marriage offer curves. He (1981: 248) contends that an increase in the female–male earnings ratio reduces the gains from the sexual divisions of labor so that the value of marriage to husbands is reduced.

Female marriage offer curves are also influenced by female income potentials. Independent of male incomes, as female earnings rise, fewer women may seek marriage. Blau et al. (2000) find that as women's earnings increase, marriage rates decline. McCrate (1987) finds that her measure of female economic independence is inversely related to marriage rates.[3]

Female marriage offer curves are influenced by the viability of alternatives to marriage available to women. By living alone, many gains from joint production and joint consumption are lost. If, however, some of these losses are compensated for by society – such as through the provision of childcare services – alternatives to marriage become more viable. Joint production, joint consumption, and sexual intimacy can also be provided by alternatives to marriage, including other forms of collective living arrangements among unmarried adults. As the price and access to these alternatives vary, the female marriage offer curves will shift. Finally, since childrearing responsibilities limit many women's ability to function independently, changes in the preference for children also influences female marriage offer curves.[4]

Let us begin by assuming that in the absence of patriarchal policies, F_0 and M in figure 2.1 reflect the initial female and male marriage offer curves respectively. At a very high marriage price, p_2, the quantity of men willing to marry equals s_2, while at p_1, the quantity of women willing to marry equals s_1. The male marriage offer curve is positively related to the marriage price. As the marriage price declines *ceteris paribus*, a smaller quantity of men are willing to marry. The female marriage offer curve is inversely related to the marriage price. As the unequal services provided by women declines, the quantity of women willing to marry rises.

At negative prices, the quantity of females willing to marry is greater than the quantity of males willing to marry so that the marriage price rises. At positive prices, the quantity of females willing to marry is less than the quantity of males willing to marry so that the marriage price declines. Let us assume that the marriage market is efficient so that its price adjusts until equilibrium is established.[5] These initial offer curves are drawn so that the marriage price equals zero; no excess services would be paid to either spouse.

Now let us introduce patriarchal policies that limit women's alternatives to heterosexual marriages and/or lower their earnings potential. Since at each marriage price more women would be willing to marry, these policies would shift the female offer curve to F_1. Now when the marriage price equals zero, the quantity of women willing to marry is greater than the quantity of men willing to marry. In this case, the marriage price rises until a new equilibrium price is attained at p^*, reflecting excessive services provided to husbands in the typical marriage.

This outcome reflects the price paid by women in the typical marriage. The actual marriage price will deviate around this market-determined price according to the bargaining power of individual women.[6] This mirrors the pattern in labor markets where the wage paid to individual workers deviates around the market-determined wage according to their bargaining power.

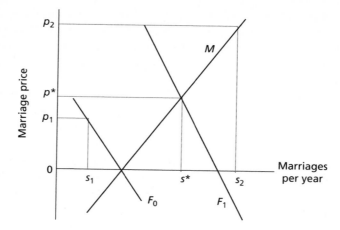

Figure 2.1   Marriage market

In capitalist societies, market forces could generate this outcome. Men do not formally have to control the decision making of women. Yet, as Nancy Folbre (1982: 324) points out, "Lacking access to some independent means of livelihood, [women] are likely to continue to cooperate within a patriarchal family despite its inequalities." Unlike output markets, however, there are no potential self-regulating mechanisms that could eliminate inequitable marriage outcomes. No new male "firms" will automatically enter the market. As contestable market theory suggests, the "monopoly" power of men can be eroded by the development of alternative living arrangements. There is no reason to believe, however, that these alternatives would be close enough substitutes to cause the marriage price to reach zero, especially when societal institutions enforce patriarchal policies.

The framework developed here can help explain the differential degree of inequities experienced by different groups of women and how the level of inequities changes over time. It also indicates that *equitable* relationships may be unattainable simply through changes in market parameters since institutions, culture, and male power can perpetuate patriarchal policies. Marcia Guttentag and Paul Secord (1983: 26) contend, "[M]en use their superior power [over political, economic, and legal structures] to limit women's marital and familial options."[7]

Evidence of the critical role of patriarchal policies is provided by Teresa Amott's and Julie Matthaei's (1991) discussion of the experience of Chinese women in California. The United States Chinese Exclusion Act of 1882 created a severe shortage of Chinese women in the United States; 13 men for every woman. Becker-type models would predict that nineteenth century Chinese women living in the United States would be in a highly favorable situation. Few of these women, however, benefited from their scarcity. Almost all of these women were forced into prostitution and the payments they received were controlled by Chinese men. It was the patriarchal policies enforced by

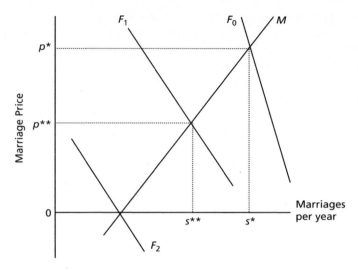

Figure 2.2 Marriage market

Chinese cultural institutions, not supply and demand factors, which primarily determined the marriage price.

Similarly, west of the Mississippi River there was generally a shortage of women during the nineteenth century. In a few cases, this enabled white women to escape some of the limitations of patriarchy. For example, some western states were among the first to allow women to vote. The shortage of women, however, did not necessarily lower the marriage price. Instead, cultural institutions often enabled men to import women. Dorothy Smith (1987: 29) notes that in Canada, growing competition lowered the price farmers received for their output. To lower their labor costs, women's labor was substituted for hired labor, compensating "for the lack of money at every possible point in the enterprise.... Women were virtually imported into Canada in this period to serve these functions."

When marriage was a social and/or economic necessity, the female marriage–offer curve F_0 in figure 2.2 was price inelastic. With male marriage offer curve M, the equilibrium price p^* reflected a high level of excess services provided to husbands and a high marriage rate, s^*. In recent years, however, patriarchal polices have lessened, reducing these constraints on female behavior. Changes in divorce laws, abortion laws, maternity leave policies, and welfare regulations have tended to provide women with more substitutes to the traditional family so that *at a given marriage price*, some women are no longer willing to marry. This shifts the female offer curve to the left, eventually lowering both the marriage price and the number of marriages.

The marriage price and marriage rate also depend on the responsiveness of men to the changing environment they face. John Kenneth Galbraith (1973) has argued that men seek marriage for the material benefits they receive, pointing out that patriarchal social norms enabled men to obtain domestic services at much more favorable prices through marriage than if purchased in the marketplace. However, as the excess marriage services obtained by men declined, there would be a movement downward along their marriage offer curve. Supporting this notion, McCrate (1987: 83) notes, "Men may be abandoning marriage rather than adjusting to women's new demands." Eventually, equilibrium is reestablished at a marriage price, p^{**}.

A number of US government policies have further extended female choice in recent years. City governments have begun passing legislation to extend fringe benefits including medical insurance and parental leave to significant others. The federal government's Earned Income Tax Credit now provides substantial income transfers to low-income working women. Women with two dependent children can receive up to $4,000 annually to supplement their wages, reducing the necessity of marriage. In theory, these changes could eventually shift the female marriage offer curve to F_2 so that truly equitable marriages would become the norm.

Persistence of the Marriage Price

Unfortunately, the theoretical ideal has not been realized; the marriage price remains substantial. Recent studies (Karen Seccombe 1986; Maureen Perry-Jenkins and Karen Folk 1994; Beth Manke et al. 1994) find that in households where both husbands and wives are full-time year-round workers, over 70 percent of these household tasks are done by wives, and the number of hours husbands spend on them has been unchanged since the 1960s.[8]

Other researchers also argue that the direct power men exert over their wives is an important component of inequality within the family. Jan Stets (1995) finds evidence among college daters that men compensated for lack of power in other areas by seeking greater control over the behavior of their girlfriends. This control is especially important in areas Folbre and Ann Ferguson (1981) characterize as sex-affective production. Besides childrearing activities, these areas include the fulfillment of human needs for affection, nurturance, and sexual expression. Patriarchal power often enables men to dictate the forms of intimacy allowed or the beauty styles that are acceptable. This section enumerates the reasons why equality in marriage remains the exception rather than the norm.

The persistence of patriarchal social norms

Social norms continue to constrain women. This was most visible after World War II. As a result of the war effort, female labor was needed in industry. Ruth Milkman (1976) found that articles and stories championed the value of day-care and the benefits of paid work for women. Firms provided day-care and a willingness to hire women in non-traditional occupations – "Rosie the Riveter." With the ending of the war and the return of men, opinion changed. Suddenly absent mothers were responsible for juvenile delinquency and certain jobs detracted from femininity. Firms eliminated day-care facilities and again refused to hire women for certain jobs. Men began to reinforce their desire for women to be full-time mothers and housewives. Not surprisingly, many women left the work force, resigning themselves to becoming "happy homemakers."

While not as powerful, a similar movement arose in the 1970s. Led by Phyllis Schafly (1978), this movement reaffirmed that the preferred way to raise well-adjusted children was for mothers to be full-time homemakers. Her efforts were supported by 1977 survey data that indicated a majority of women believed "married women's paid work was discretionary and should not come at the expense of men's paid work" (Edward McCaffery 1997: 77).

The ambivalence society feels towards married women working when they have children is still significant. McCaffery (1997: 210) documents that in 1991, 88 percent of working mothers felt that "if I could afford it, I would rather be home with my children" while 82 percent of the American public believed it is best for "young children to be cared for by one or more parents or by extended family members." During the 1990s, the Moral Majority continued to decry the decline of traditional family values while the Promise Keepers promoted the reestablishment of patriarchal families, led by caring and sensitive men.

The latest wrinkles on this theme have been recent studies (Jeffrey Gray 1997) that seek to explain variations in the earnings of men. Holding productivity factors constant, husbands with working wives earned on average 10 percent less than those whose wives were full-time homemakers. Husbands with working wives were somewhat less willing to relocate, to work overtime, or take on special projects. These studies reinforced traditional notions that career women sacrifice the interest of all members of their families – husbands and children. Not surprisingly, this stigma continues to burden women in ways that limit their earnings and independence; in ways that enable men to maintain patriarchal relations within the family.

Policies to increase female willingness to marry

Many traditionalists believe that the marriage rate decline is due to changing female behavior. If women are the culprits, government should undertake social policies that increase female willingness to marry. One such policy, known as Bridefare, was enacted by the Wisconsin legislature in 1994. It allowed the welfare department to raise monthly benefit from $440 to $531 for recipients who marry. To the extent this policy increased the willingness of unwed mothers to marry, it increased the marriage price they offered. Fearing this harmful outcome, Wisconsin state representative Gwendolyn Moore stated:

> The Bridefare program . . . may place battered women in more danger . . . Aid to Families with Dependent Children (AFDC) has traditionally been one way that women could escape from abusive situations that were dangerous for them or their children. Let us not

begin telling battered women that if they do not marry, they and their children will be thrust deeper into poverty. (Cherry 1997: 42)

Dismissing the seriousness of the harm bad marriages can do to poor women, traditionalists blame welfare for the decline in marriage rates among poor women. As welfare became more generous, they maintain, women increasingly traded dependence on man for dependence on the government. The problem with this thesis is that the growth in welfare caseloads occurred during the 1980s when welfare became less generous. However, there is no question that as more women have been refused welfare in the 1990s, many have been forced to seek male partners, raising the marriage price they must pay.

Changes in male preferences for marriage

As has been noted, in response to the lowering of the excess services they obtain, the number of men willing to marry declines. However, some observers argue that there has been a more fundamental change in male marriage behavior – fewer would now choose marriage even if the excess services provided to them remained the same. Emphasizing this point, McCrate (1990) notes that among African-American men with stable employment, almost one-half of those 25 to 34 years old were unmarried; for those 16 to 24 years old, more than 80 percent were unmarried.

Barbara Ehrenreich (1983) traces the change in male marriage preferences to the 1950s. Historically, male self-image was derived from their ability to be the family breadwinner. Men were expected to marry young and focus on providing for their family. Patriarchy allowed men to be "king of their castle" but it required them to seek fulfillment through financial support provided, not personal activities. For many men, this social norm was a heavy burden. Trapped in joyless marriages, sacrificing their happiness for the family good, these men did not feel that these patriarchal rules served their interests.

Ehrenreich believes that this explains the meteoric rise in circulation of *Playboy* magazine. It now became more acceptable for middle-class men to seek gratification outside of marriage, to no longer suppress their personal desires. Rather than marrying their high school or college sweethearts, more men began to delay marriage until they had spent time being free of familial responsibilities. This new male attitude, she maintains, was one of the reasons that the Frank Sinatra, Las Vegas "Rat Pack" had such mass appeal. After all, these were men who rejected the "home life" and instead, sought hedonistic pleasures. Through them, middle-class men could live vicariously.

Ehrenreich believes that the 1960s counterculture movement accelerated this "flight from commitment." Women were attracted because it allowed them to rebel against oppressive sexual mores. Men were attracted because it freed them from traditional male responsibilities: getting a steady job so that they could marry and support a family. Indeed, Ehrenreich believes that female rejection of patriarchal sexual mores, however justifiable, reinforced male devaluation of marriage. These changing male values help explain why the marriage price has remained.

The growing scarcity of marriageable men

William Wilson (1987) emphasizes that low marriage rates among poor women reflect the declining number of marriageable men available. This is particularly the case in the black community. Cherry (1999) notes that as a result of the fourfold increase in incarceration rates between 1970 and 1990, there were as much as 20 percent more black women than black men in the non-institutionalized population in some regions. In addition, since the mid-1970s, the wages of low-skilled men have not kept pace with inflation so that the share of male workers who work full-time year-round but do not earn enough for a family of four to escape poverty rose from 9 to 13 percent between 1979 and 1994 (Lawrence Mishel et al. 1999).

Not surprisingly, Kathryn Edin (2000) finds that poor black women were very conscious of the employment record of the men they were considering partnering with. The reluctance to marry available black men, however, went well beyond income calculations. Just as our model predicts, given the scarcity of available men, these women realize that they face a high marriage price. As one respondent states, "There's a shortage of men so that they think, 'I can have more than one woman. I'm gonna go around this one or that one, and I'm gonna have two or three of them'" (Edin 2000: 29). Many of these women fear that they would become their husband's personal slave, cooking their meals, cleaning their house, and doing their laundry. They lament, "A man gets married to have somebody to take care of them 'cause their mommy can't do it anymore'" (Edin 2000: 31). These women also expect that their husbands would feel free to spend money on personal leisure activities rather than on family necessities.

Unfortunately, the price that many of these vulnerable women pay includes domestic violence. From a wide variety of mid-1990s studies, Jody Raphael and Richard Tolman (1999) find that 15 to 20 percent of women on welfare experienced physical abuse during the most recent 12 months and about 60 percent at sometime in their past. Current abuse is about 20 percent higher among recipients who were currently involved in a relationship with a man. In a New Jersey study, Raphael and Tolman (1999: 14) find that "three times as many abused women as nonabused women (39.7 percent as compared with 12.9 percent) report that their intimate partner actively prevents their participation in education and training."[9] Even if partners do not overtly sabotage their efforts, more abused recipients than non-abused recipients have symptoms of depression, which itself creates a barrier to sustaining employment or educational efforts.[10]

The tax system

While paid work is not sufficient to end patriarchy in the home, for many women it is a precondition. As a working-class Mexican woman recounts:

> Of course it is important because if you can earn your own money, you yourself distribute it and you do not have to beg for it. You buy food or a dress for your daughter, the socks for your son. He used to tell me, "You must wait, because I do not have enough

money this month." But he would never do it, neither today, nor tomorrow. Now I want to buy it, I buy it. If he gives me money, fine. If not I buy it myself. And one feels fine and useful with one's own money. Also, in case of an emergency, an accident, if I have my own money I can fetch a taxi and take the child to the hospital. And it is money well spent *because I earned it myself.* Otherwise he would tell me, why didn't you take a bus, why did you spend on a taxi. (Roldan 1988: 229)

Traditionalists have consistently used the federal tax system to discourage middle-class women from working. Beginning in 1948, except in special situations, married couples have been required to file joint returns that continue to be a major impediment to the ability of married women to gain from paid employment. A numeral exercise adapted from McCaffery (1997) will demonstrate this point.

Let us assume a simple married tax schedule with rising marginal tax rates: The first $15,000 of adjusted gross income is untaxed; the next $25,000 is taxed at 15 percent; while any subsequent income is taxed at 30 percent. Now let us look at the situation of over 80 percent of married couples where husbands earn more than their wives. Specifically, let us assume that the husband earns $40,000 while his wife earns $25,000. In this situation, it is reasonable to assume that the wife is considered the secondary wage earner in the household.

Let us look at the economic consequences of the wife's decision to work. If she chooses not to work, household income is $40,000 and its tax liability is $3,750 – 15 percent of the last $25,000 the husband earns. If the wife chooses to work, her income is added on and is taxed at the higher 30 percent rate. Thus, $7,500 – 30 percent of $25,000 – of her income would go to federal taxes. If we add on social security and state taxes, close to one-half of her income would be lost to taxes. If we then add on the childcare and business expenses incurred, the net additional income to the household could be quite small. Not surprisingly, this could easily discourage the wife from working, resulting in a strengthening of the patriarchal family.

The simplest way to solve the secondary wage earner problem is to eliminate joint returns, forcing all households to file individually. (This would also solve the marriage-penalty problem many households face.) Eliminating joint returns is unpopular with traditionalists for two reasons. First, by raising their net earnings, it would induce more married women to work. Second, it takes away the current benefits accruing to households where one spouse has very little income. Indeed, the reason that the joint return was instituted in 1948 was to enable middle and upper income married households with one wage earner to reduce their tax liabilities by having the husband's income taxed at the joint rate that was lower than the single rate.

The secondary wage earner bias could also be reduced if the highest tax rate is lowered. Since this is the tax rate at which the wife's income is taxed, it would increase the net income she receives. With more net income, more married women would find it profitable to work. This was exactly the outcome in the 1980s when the highest tax rate was reduced from 70 to 28 percent. Married women, especially those whose husband's earnings placed them in the 70 percent tax bracket, had little to benefit financially from working before the rate reductions. Once rates were lowered, many entered the labor force (Nadia Eissa and Jeffrey Liebman 1996).

A more direct method is to reduce the tax rate on secondary wage earners. This can be accomplished by eliminating a certain percentage of the wife's income from taxation. In our example above, suppose that only 60 percent of the wife's income is taxable. In that case, she would only add $15,000 – 60 percent of $25,000 – to the household's taxable income. Thus, the household's taxes would rise by only $4,500 – 30 percent of the $15,000; a tax savings of $3,000.

Traditionalists strongly oppose this method. They argue that it would undermine the notion that households with the same income should be taxed the same. In particular, households with adjusted gross income of $65,000 but where wives have no income would not benefit from this proposal and would be paying $3,000 more taxes than household where husbands earn $40,000 and the wives earn $25,000. When Congress legislated this method of reducing the marriage penalty in 1981, traditionalists were taken by surprise but were able to incorporate its repeal into the 1986 tax reform bill.

A final way to increase the benefits to married women who work is through child-care credits. Federal taxes could be reduced to offset childcare expenses. If the credit is 40 percent, the household's taxes would be reduced by $2,400 if $6,000 is spent on childcare, again improving substantially the benefits from work.

Traditionalists have responded by reducing the link between child-related benefits and the employment of married women. First, they made sure that the childcare credit is available to households with taxable income, whether or not both spouses are working. More importantly, traditionalists have fought attempts to increase the generosity of childcare policies. Instead, they have lobbied for tax relief through a child credit program. This program was a centerpiece of the Republican *Contract with America*, and was enacted in 1998. When benefits of the 2001 tax legislation are fully phased in, households will be able to subtract $1,000 from their tax liabilities for each dependent child. Since this shifts income to households with children whether or not the secondary wage earner is working, it has no affect on their benefits from work. Married women still face higher marginal tax rates and still are discouraged from working, sustaining patriarchal relations within the family.

Special needs of women

As long as women have primary responsibility for childrearing, they will not attain labor market equality. Many jobs are structured by patriarchal notions of the family. Employees are expected to sacrifice household responsibilities if they conflict with corporate needs. If employers require overtime, unexpected rescheduling of work hours, or other sudden changes, spouses are expected to adjust their schedules. As long as many jobs are structured in this way, job applicants who do not have spouses willing to accommodate to employers' prerogatives are at a disadvantage. Patriarchy posits that women be the accommodating spouse. Thus, even if employers are genuinely non-discriminatory, without a change in job requirements, women will continue to be at a disadvantage.

The most visible example of the dilemma professional women face has been their experience in major law firms. As Jennifer Kingson (1988) notes, these firms pay high salaries but also require long hours. Moreover, to gain partnership, junior lawyers have to further extend themselves by networking in order to demonstrate an ability to draw customers to the firm. This networking can often require attendance at professional and social events on top of the long hours at the office. Not surprisingly, many women find it impossible to balance these demands with those of their families. In recognition, law firms began developing what became known as "mommy" tracks. Women would have the option of working shorter hours but would sacrifice upward mobility within the firm.

For these reasons, there should be a greater focus on public policies that limit the conflict between work and home faced by working mothers. There are two models that can accomplish this. The *universal* breadwinner model emphasizes providing services, particularly quality childcare, which free women from childrearing responsibilities. The *caregiver* model emphasizes policies, such as flextime and family leaves, that allow women to fulfill their childrearing activities without sacrificing their earnings potential. In the past decade, many companies have adopted one or more of these policies and it has enabled women to break through previous glass ceilings. However, as long as these policies are not universally required, many women will be unable to compete on an equal basis with men, reinforcing the patriarchal family.

Concluding Remarks

The neoclassical model developed by Becker assumes away the possibility that marriages can be inequitable. The unequal allocation of time for household activities is simply a matter of specialization and domestic violence or sexual coercion has nothing to do with the workings of the marriage market. In contrast, the model developed here assumes that the marriage market has biases similar to the labor market. In capitalism, workers and owners do not necessarily negotiate from an equal position. As long as there is substantial unemployment, workers must adapt to the desires of capitalists if they wish to avoid poverty. Similarly, men and women do not necessarily enter the marriage market from equal positions. Only if women have equality in the labor market, can they bargain effectively. As long as women cannot earn a decent living, many must adapt to male desires if they wish to avoid poverty.

To promote equality in the labor market, pay equity policies for working class women must be promoted. In addition, the economic experience since 1997 has demonstrated the importance to low-waged women of tight labor markets, and any attempt by the Federal Reserve to soften labor markets should be resisted. Finally, tax policies should be adjusted so that single heads can more easily attain economic independence.[11]

This marriage model emphasizes how market forces, not inherent traits, determine behavior. When we find capitalists paying their workers starvation wages, we don't argue that those who become capitalists have inherently different values than those who remain workers. Instead, we focus on the market forces that compel capitalists to act that way. Similarly, men take advantage of the marriage market by extracting the available patriarchal price from their spouses. We should not consider men to be inherently different from women – men are from Mars, women are from Venus. Instead, we should realize that they are simply responding to the market outcomes available to them. Change the marriage price and men will respond differently.

Movements toward equality would be accelerated if men rejected the benefits they can obtain from market forces. Charles Dicken's *Christmas Carol* and Frank Capra's film *Its a Wonderful Life* promote the view that an individual's ethical values can overcome market forces. Historically, ethical values were embedded in religious dogma. Since most religions are strongly patriarchal, however, this vision of transformation does not seem realistic. As a result, we may be forced to focus on secular solutions to patriarchy that rely on changing market relationships. Women must have the same alternatives as men, which, at a minimum, require full gender equality in the labor market.

Finally, there is a downside to this secular solution to patriarchy. It risks dramatically devaluing children. They are increasingly viewed as burdens, diminishing the ability of men to partake in hedonistic activities and constraining the occupational mobility of women. Michael Males (1996: 1) captures this danger:

> Maybe America, for all its prating about family values, hates its children. What else can explain the cruel abandonment of so many kids to such wretched circumstances: bad schools, poor health care, deadly addictions, and crushing debts – and utter indifference.

Unless market systems find a way to socialize the cost of childrearing, harming children may be one unfortunate legacy of the quest for gender equity within capitalist societies.[12]

NOTES

1   In 1998, among black and white women aged 35 to 44 years old, 30.0 and 9.8 percent, respectively, were never married; 38.5 and 70.9 percent, respectively, were married spouse present (Lugailia 1998: Table 1).

2   Frances Woolley (1996: 115) criticizes Becker for the "offensive" nature of some of his assertions: (1) girls oriented toward market rather than household activities are deviant; (2) the average divorced person can be presumed to be more quarrelsome and in other ways less pleasant than the average person remaining married; and (3) more beautiful, charming, and talented women tend to marry wealthier and more successful men. For other feminists criticisms of Becker, see Diana Strassman (1993), Paula England (1993), Julie Nelson (1994), Barbara Bergmann (1995), and chapter 1 by Marianne Ferber in this volume.

3   For an additional measure of female economic dependency, see Annamette Sorensen and Sara McLanahan (1987).
4   For evidence of changing preferences, see Goldscheider and Waite (1986).
5   It should be noted that the actual number of marriages could be different than the equilibrium quantity, s^*, due to search behavior and locational mismatches. Oppenheimer (1988) has explicitly used a search model to analyze changes in the timing of marriage.
6   For surveys of bargaining models, see Janet Seiz (1992), Theodore Bergstrom (1996), and Shelly Lundberg and Robert Pollak (1996).
7   For a critique of this view, see Scott South and Kim Lloyd (1995).
8   George Stigler (1946) found that households increased dramatically the share of expenditures going to domestic servants as family income increased; this was especially true for working-class households. This suggests that easing the wife's burden was a priority expenditure.
9   In a Massachusetts study, Mary Ann Allard et al. (1997) find that 15.5 and 1.6 percent of non-abused and abused welfare mothers, respectively, reported that their present or former partner would not like it if they had a job or enrolled in a job-training program.
10 Allard et al. (1997) find 40 and 27 percent of abused and non-abused recipients, respectively, suffered symptoms of mental depression. Raphael and Tolman (1997) report a New Jersey study where 31 percent of all recipients but 54 percent of those currently in an abusive relationship indicated that they were currently depressed. See also Cherry (2001c).
11 For details of how pay equity and more rigorous enforcement of Equal Employment Opportunity policies can aid working-class women, see Cherry (2001a); for evidence of the benefits of tight labor markets, see Cherry (2001b); and for tax proposal to benefit single heads and working-class families, see Cherry and Sawicky (2001).
12 For a discussion of the need for government involvement, see Nancy Folbre (2001). For proposal to improve accessibility to quality childcare, see Bergmann and Suzanne Helburn (2001) and Isabell Sawhill and Adam Thomas (2000).

REFERENCES

Allard, Mary Ann, Mary Colten, Randy Albelda, and Carol Cosenza. 1997. *In Harm's Way*. Boston: McCormack Institute.
Amott, Teresa and Julie Matthaei. 1991. *Race Gender and Work*. Boston: South End Press.
Becker, Gary. 1981. *A Treatise on the Family*. Chicago: University of Chicago Press.
——. 1973. "A Theory of Marriage: Part I." *Journal of Political Economy* 81(4): 813–46.
Bergmann, Barbara. 1995. "Becker's Theory of the Family: Preposterous Conclusions." *Feminist Economics* 1(1): 141–50.
Bergmann, Barbara and Suzanne Helburn. 2001. *The Future of Child Care*. New York: St. Martins Press.
Bergstrom, Theodore. 1996. "Economics in a Family Way." *Journal of Economic Literature* 34(4): 1903–34.
Blau, Francine, Lawrence Kahn, and Jane Waldfogel. 2000. "Understanding Young Women's Marriage Decision." National Bureau of Economic Research Working Paper 7510.
Cherry, Robert. 2001a. *Who Gets the Good Jobs? Combating Race and Gender Disparities*. New Brunswick, NJ: Rutgers University Press.

——. 2001b. "Social Benefits of Tight Labor Markets." *Working USA* 5 (Fall): 106–18.

——. 2001c. "Sexual Coercion and Limited Choices: Their Link to Teen Pregnancy and Welfare," in Merril Smith (ed.) *Sex Without Consent*. New York: NYU Press, pp. 265–83.

——. 1999. "Impact of Tight Labor Markets on Black Employment." *Review of Black Political Economy* 27(2): 27–41.

——. 1997. "Rational Choice and the Price of Marriage." *Feminist Economics* 4(1): 27–49.

Cherry, Robert and Max Sawicky. 2001. "And Now for Something Different: Progressive Tax Policies Republicans Can Support." *Challenge* 44(May/June): 43–60.

Edin, Kathryn. 2000. "Few Good Men." *The American Prospect* 11(Jan): 42–3.

Ehrenreich, Barbara. 1983. *The Hearts of Men: American Dreams and Their Flight from Commitment*. Garden City, NY: Anchor Press.

Eissa, Nadia and Jeffrey Liebman. 1996. "Labor Supply Response to the Earned Income Tax Credit." *Quarterly Journal of Economics* 111(2): 605–37.

England, Paula. 1993. "The Separate Self: Andocentric Bias in Neoclassical Assumptions," in Marianne Ferber and Julie Nelson (eds.) *Beyond Economic Man*, pp. 37–53. Chicago: University of Chicago Press.

Folbre, Nancy. 2001. *The Invisible Heart*. New York: New Press.

——. 1982. "Exploitation Comes Home: A Critique of the Marxian Theory of Family Labour." *Cambridge Journal of Economics* 6(4): 317–29.

Folbre, Nancy and Ann Ferguson. 1981. "The Unhappy Marriage of Patriarchy and Capitalism," in Lydia Sargent (ed.) *Women and Revolution*, pp. 313–38. Boston: South End Press.

Galbraith, John K. 1973. *Economics and the Public Purpose*. Boston: Houghton Mifflin.

Goldscheider, Frances and Linda Waite. 1986. "Sex Differences in the Entry into Marriage. *American Journal of Sociology* 92: 91–109.

Gray, Jeffrey. 1997. "The Fall in Men's Return to Marriage." *Journal of Human Resources* 32(3): 481–504.

Guttentag, Marcia and Paul Secord. 1983. *Too Many Women? The Sex Ratio Question*. Beverly Hills, CA: Sage.

Hartmann, Heidi. 1981. "The Unhappy Marriage of Marxism and Feminism," in Lydia Sargent (ed.) *Women and Revolution*, pp. 1–41. Boston: South End Press.

Kingson, Jennifer. 1988. "Women in the Law Say Path is Limited by 'Mommy Track.'" *New York Times*, August 8.

Lundberg, Shelly and Robert Pollak. 1996. "Bargaining and Distribution in Marriage." *Journal of Economic Perspectives* 10(4): 139–58.

Lugailia, Terry. 1998. "Marital Status and Living Arrangements." *Current Population Report* P20–514. Washington DC: U.S. Printing Office.

Males, Michael. 1996. *The Scapegoat Generation: America's War on Adolescents*. Monroe, ME: Common Courage Press.

Manke, Beth, Brenda Seery, and Ann Crouter. 1994. "The Three Corners of Domestic Labor: Mothers', Fathers', and Children's Weekday and Weekend Housework." *Journal of Marriage and the Family* 56: 657–68.

McCaffery, Edward. 1997. *Taxing Women*. Chicago: University of Chicago Press.

McCrate, Elaine. 1990. "Labor Market Segmentation and Relative Black/White Teenage Birth Rates." *Review of Black Political Economy* 18(4): 37–53.

——. 1987. "Trade, Merger, and Employment: Economic Theory on Marriage." *Review of Radical Political Economy* 19(1): 73–89.

Milkman, Ruth. 1976. "Women's Work and the Economic Crisis: Some Lessons from the Great Depression." *Review of Radical Political Economy* 8(1): 73–97.

Mishel, Lawrence, Jared Bernstein, and John Schmitt. 1999. *The State of Working America, 1998–99.* Ithaca, NY: ILR Press.

Nelson, Julie. 1994. "I, Thou, and Them: Capabilities, Altruism, and Norms in the Economics of Marriage." *American Economics Review* 84(2): 126–31.

Oppenheimer, Valerie. 1988. "A Theory of Marriage Timing." *American Journal of Sociology* 94: 63–91.

Perry-Jenkins, Maureen and Karen Folk. 1994. "Class, Couples, and Conflict." *Journal of Marriage and the Family* 56: 165–80.

Raphael, Jody and Richard Tolman. 1997. *Trapped by Poverty, Trapped by Abuse.* Chicago: Taylor Institute.

Roldan, Martha. 1988. "Renegotiating the Marriage Contract," in Daisy Dwyer and Judith Bruce (eds.) *A House Divided: Women and Income in the Third World*, pp. 228–47. Stanford, CA: Stanford University Press.

Sawhill, Isabel and Adam Thomas. 2000. A Hand Up for the Bottom Third. Washington DC: The Urban Institute.

Seccombe, Karen. 1986. "The Effects of Occupational Conditions upon the Division of Household Labor." *Journal of Marriage and the Family* 48: 839–48.

Seiz, Janet. 1992. "The Bargaining Approach and Feminist Methodology." *Review of Radical Political Economy* 22(2): 22–9.

Schafly, Phyllis. 1978. *The Power of the Positive Women.* New York: Harcourt-Brace.

Smith, Dorothy. 1987. "Women's Inequality and the Family," in Naomi Gerstel and Harriet Gross (eds.) *Family and Work*, pp. 23–54. Philadelphia: Temple University Press.

Sorensen, Annamette and Sara McLanahan. 1987. "Married Women's Economic Dependency, 1940–1980." *American Journal of Sociology* 93: 659–87.

South, Scott and Kim Lloyd. 1995. "Spousal Alternatives and Marital Dissolution." *American Sociological Review* 60: 21–35.

Stets, Jan. 1995. "Modeling Control of Relationships." *Journal of Marriage and the Family* 57: 489–501.

Stigler, George. 1946. "Domestic Servants in the United States, 1900–1940." Occasional Paper #24, National Bureau of Economic Research.

Strassmann, Diana. 1993. "Not a Free Market: The Rhetoric of Disciplinary Authority in Economics," in Marianne Ferber and Julie Nelson (eds.) *Beyond Economic Man*, pp. 54–68. Chicago: University of Chicago Press.

U.S. Department of Commerce. 1994. *Statistical Abstract of the United States, 1994.* Washington DC: U.S. Printing Office.

Wilson, William J. 1987. *The Truly Disadvantaged.* Chicago: University of Chicago Press.

Woolley, Frances. 1996. "Comment." *Feminist Economics* 2(1): 114–20.

Chapter 3

Conceptualizing and Measuring Bargaining Power within the Household

Cheryl Doss

People engage in a wide variety of economic activities. People are producers – they produce goods for sale and for home consumption and sell their labor in the marketplace. People are consumers – they buy goods and services in the market and consume goods that they produce themselves. People invest in physical capital, such as houses, and in human capital, such as health and education. People typically live with others in households and make all of these decisions within this context. Thus, it doesn't make sense to think of these decisions as being made completely by individuals. In particular, it would not usually be appropriate to consider each individual's expenditures as only for himself or herself. One person typically does the grocery shopping for the entire household. Decisions about how income should be earned and who should do the household work are often made collectively.

Because many of these decisions are made within households, economists have traditionally modeled households as the smallest unit of analysis. In these unitary models of the household, the household is treated as though it were an individual, taking advantage of the tools of microeconomics. The household is assumed to make production and consumption decisions, maximizing a single utility function subject to a single budget constraint.

There is increasing evidence, however, that this approach to modeling household decisions may lead to incorrect conclusions. A number of studies have demonstrated empirically that households do not behave as if they were individuals. Instead, the dynamics among individuals within the household influences the outcomes of economic decisions. Policies based upon a unitary model of the household may have unexpected consequences, including consequences that mitigate or reverse the intended effects of the policy. For example, policies that are designed to increase household income may have different effects, depending on which individuals in the household receive the income. In some instances, one household member may be worse off, both in relative terms and in absolute terms, when additional income accrues to another household member.

Unitary models of the household do not take into consideration that individual household members may have the power to influence the outcomes of household decisions in their own favor. This chapter demonstrates that this bargaining power may be an important determinant of household decisions. In this chapter, we examine how bargaining power can be conceptualized and measured. Both economic and institutional factors that affect bargaining power are discussed with reference to examples from the US and developing countries, especially in Africa. A detailed analysis of how asset ownership in Ghana affects bargaining power is used as a case study. Finally, we look at how these factors should affect policy making at all levels.

Conceptualizing Bargaining Power

Bargaining power is anything that allows a particular individual to influence household decisions. It is the *relative* amount of influence that one individual has compared to other individuals within the household. Many people are uncomfortable with the idea that household members "bargain." There are two reasons for this. The first is that many people expect household members to share common interests and concerns. The notion of "bargaining" brings up images of individuals striving for a bigger share of the household pie, trying to get more and give other household members less. While this may be the case, bargaining may also involve issues where there is less of a clear winner and loser. Individuals may bargain over whether to buy a new car or save the money, where to live, or where to send the kids to school. Each adult may have a different preferred outcome that they think will be the best for everyone.

The second reason that people are often uncomfortable with the notion of bargaining is that they think of bargaining as the decision-making *process.* Bargaining among household members suggests that they sit down at the kitchen table to negotiate over a decision. Again, this may be the case. Imagine an example of a dual career couple with children in the United States. They may sit down frequently to discuss how responsibilities will be allocated – who will take the kids to soccer practice on a given day or stay home with a sick child. On the other hand, the decision-making process may be implicit. It may be that one person always stays home when a child is sick and no discussion takes place. In either case, an economist would view the outcome as the result of a bargaining process, whether explicit or implicit.

Economists use two broad categories of models to describe household bargaining: cooperative and non-cooperative bargaining models. Unfortunately, the terms, "cooperative" and "non-cooperative" have very different meanings in common usage than they do in this context. Non-cooperative models do not imply that the parties involved sit sullenly across the table from each other as they discuss the issues or that the

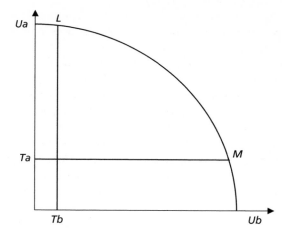

Figure 3.1   Utility possibility frontier for two-person household
Ua and *Ub* are the utility for individuals *a* and *b*.
Ta and *Tb* are the threat points for individuals *a* and *b*.
Pareto efficient households will always choose a point on the utility possibility frontier between
   L and *M*. Moving the threat points by increasing or decreasing outside options will affect the
   range of possible outcomes.

individuals no longer speak to each other after the decision has been reached! Instead, a cooperative model is one in which binding contracts can be negotiated. Non-cooperative models are ones in which those involved cannot negotiate binding and enforceable contracts.

Cooperative bargaining models often use a Nash-bargaining framework. They suggest that the "threat point" or "outside option" of each individual determines bargaining power. The threat point is the amount of utility that an individual would be able to attain outside of the household. This result is important because it claims that any factors that affect an individual's wellbeing outside of the household will affect his or her bargaining power within the household.

A simple graph illustrates the concepts of threat points and possible outcomes. Figure 3.1 shows the utility possibilities frontier for the two members of the household. Every point on the frontier is a possible combination of utility received by each of the two individuals. All of the points on the frontier are Pareto efficient since there are no possible points where one person could gain utility without the other person losing utility. The lines *Ta* and *Tb* indicate the threat points. *Ta* is the amount of utility that individual *a* would have if he or she left the household. *Tb* is the similar point for individual *b*. In the graph, individual *A* has a higher threat point than individual *B*. In a cooperative model, it is assumed that only the points between *L* and *M* on the utility possibility frontier are possible outcomes. When *Ta* and *Tb* shift, the range of possible outcomes also changes.[1] For example, increasing the earning ability of women by decreasing discrimination in the workplace would shift out *Ta* for all women, including married women who do not work outside the home, because it improves their outside options.

There are numerous non-cooperative bargaining models, each designed to address a specific question and each of which defines bargaining power appropriately for that question and the context. Generally, bargaining power is based on the individual's ability to contribute to the household and on the "conjugal contract" or the agreement reached when the household was formed about how resources and responsibilities would be allocated. These models typically leave greater scope for defining bargaining power within a particular context and often explicitly model how decisions about shared goods in the household are made. Many of the factors discussed above affect bargaining power in these models, especially the ability of an individual to contribute to the household.

One key difference between the two sets of models is that cooperative models assume that the outcome will be Pareto efficient – in other words, they assume that neither person could be made better off without making the other person worse off. They assume that the outcome is on the utility possibilities frontier. Non-cooperative models explicitly allow for the possibility that the outcomes are not Pareto efficient. In other words, the outcomes may be a point within the utility possibilities frontier. Each type of model has a different focus, but many of the implications for looking at bargaining power within the household are the same.

In the discussion below of particular factors affecting bargaining power, the focus is on how these factors will affect an individual's well being outside of the household and how they affect an individual's contribution to the household. For a discussion of the specific models, see Cheryl Doss (1996).

Measuring Bargaining Power

Since bargaining power is the ability to influence the outcomes of household decisions, to show that bargaining power is relevant in household decision-making, we must show that a measure of bargaining power has a direct effect on a particular outcome. If we can demonstrate this relationship, we can also reject unitary models of the household in favor of models that include the power dynamics within households. We need both a measure of bargaining power and some outcome to examine the relationship of bargaining power to the outcome. Finding appropriate measurements has been one of the biggest challenges for researchers interested in these issues.

A number of outcomes of household decisions have been used to demonstrate these relationships. The intrahousehold allocation of resources, especially consumption among household members are frequently used outcome measures. Investments in education and health are also used. In poor countries, the allocation of food among household members is an important economic decision that can be measured. Expenditure patterns also are used as measures of economic outcomes.

Researchers have used a number of measures of bargaining power to understand the effect of bargaining power on household economic decisions. Many of the ones that are easy to determine are difficult to interpret. Both economic factors, such as income and wealth, and institutional factors, such as laws and social norms, may be sources of bargaining power.

Income

The most obvious economic measure to consider when looking at bargaining power of individual members of the household is income. Income affects bargaining power by influencing the threat point or outside option of individuals. In addition, some of the non-cooperative bargaining models suggest that the individual's contribution to the household affects bargaining power.

A simple way to look at the relationship between income and bargaining power is to assume that the person who earns the most money has the most influence on household economic decisions. Thinking of this in terms of a stylized American nuclear family where one parent works outside the home and the other stays home taking care of the children, we would expect to find that the income-earner decides where to live and how to allocate the resources across major expenditure items. The stay-at-home parent may make many (or most) of the day to day economic decisions, such as what to purchase for dinner, but within the context set by the income earner. As long as the two adults agree on the decisions, then we may not see any effects of bargaining power, but when they disagree, the one who earns the wages may determine the outcome.

Bargaining models suggest that the relationship may be more complicated. Cooperative bargaining models suggest that the ability of the stay-at-home parent to earn an income will affect his or her bargaining power. Thus, someone who gave up a job as a lawyer to stay home with children – and could return to a high salary position – will have more bargaining power within the household than a stay-at-home parent with few labor market skills. Non-cooperative bargaining models suggest that all production should be included, so that a stay-at-home parent who contributes significantly to the wellbeing of the household will have more bargaining power than one who simply sits in front of the television.

Economists who have used income as a measure of bargaining power often use potential income of each individual rather than their actual income. Potential income is estimated based on the individual's characteristics, including age, gender, education, and work experience. There are two reasons for this. The first was discussed above – the cooperative bargaining models suggest that the potential income is what matters, since it is the best measure of an individual's threat point.

The second reason to use potential income is that actual income may be related to bargaining power in other ways. For example, imagine that an individual's income had no effect on his or her bargaining power. We might still see a correlation between income and household economic decisions under the following circumstances. Suppose that the person with more bargaining power was able to insist that they wanted to hold a particular job, even though that meant that the other person could not work. The job could involve living overseas or making frequent moves which severely limited the options for the other person. We would see a relationship between income and household decisions, but the underlying relationship is that bargaining power determines both income and economic outcomes. The same underlying relationship could produce the opposite relationship between income and household decisions. The individual with more bargaining power could decide not to work or could decide only to work limited hours. This same person would also have the greatest influence on other major household decisions.

Several studies have shown that household expenditure patterns do differ, based on potential earnings. For example, using 1986 data from Canada, Shelley Phipps and Peter Burton (1993) demonstrate that even for households where both the husband and wife worked full-time, the sources of income made a difference in the level of expenditure on eight of 12 categories of consumption goods. In addition, John Hoddinott and Lawrence Haddad (1995) find that the percentage of female income significantly affects budget share for a number of goods in Cote d'Ivoire. Benjamin Senauer et al. (1988) find that potential wages affect the distribution of food within households.

Yet even using potential income has a disadvantage as a measure of bargaining power. If we conclude that increasing income, or potential income, affects household expenditure patterns, we cannot necessarily conclude that income is a measure of bargaining power. From household expenditure data, it is difficult to determine whether the increase in expenditures simply corresponds to changes in an individual's marginal productivity or to changes in bargaining power within the household. For example, Benjamin Senauer et al. (1986) found that in Sri Lanka, an increase in women's earnings resulted in higher expenditures on the "convenience" food of bread rather than on rice. This could be attributed either to changes in the relative prices due to the increased value of women's time – women who work for wages have less time available for cooking – or to women's increased bargaining power within the household or both.

A related problem is that often inputs are needed to earn income. We can see this clearly in the context of a poor farm household in a developing country. The person who earns the income may receive a larger allocation of food, not because they have more bargaining power, but because they require the additional energy in order to be able to work to earn the income. Food would be allocated to the person with the highest marginal returns from it. Similarly, the wage earner may require clothing or transportation in order to work to earn an income. Higher allocations of expenditure on women's clothing in households where women work may not necessarily indicate that these women have more bargaining power. It is difficult to disentangle these relationships between earnings and bargaining power.

One way to resolve this latter issue is to use income that is not earned as a measure of bargaining power. The bargaining models suggest that any source of income that accrues to an individual would be a source of bargaining power. Sources of non-labor income include government transfer payments (such as Social Security), gifts, pensions, or interest income. If income is not a source of bargaining power, then we would not expect that it matters which person receives non-labor income.

A number of studies have used non-labor income as a measure of bargaining power. Duncan Thomas (1993) finds that non-labor income controlled by women in Brazil is associated with larger increases of the household budget share being devoted to human capital and leisure. Mary Jean Horney and Marjorie McElroy (1988) find that individual non-labor income is significant in determining levels of labor supply. Paul Schultz (1990) demonstrates that women's unearned income affects the amount of wage labor that they provide, but he does not find the same result for men. In addition, he finds that only the unearned income of women – not men's unearned income nor men's or women's earned income – is associated with higher fertility levels.

Another interesting example comes from a study by Shelly Lundberg, Robert Pollak and Terence Wales (1997) where they take advantage of a shift in policy to examine this issue. In the United Kingdom, a child tax allowance that was primarily realized as a tax credit in paychecks (primarily men's paychecks) was shifted to a child benefit scheme that primarily accrued as a direct payment to women. Thus, the only thing that the policy changed was which household member received the benefit. They found that expenditures on women's and children's clothing increased relative to expenditures on men's clothing as a result of this policy. This suggests that allocating the money to women gave them more power to decide how it should be spent.

Wealth

Similar to income, wealth may affect an individual's bargaining power. Wealth may involve both a stock of assets, that may be sold, and a flow of income resulting from the assets. Wealth may provide prestige or social status. All of these reasons imply that a wealthier individual may have more bargaining power. One study using assets as a measure of bargaining power in Ghana is discussed in detail below.

Using current assets as a measure of bargaining power has some of the same drawbacks as using income. The ability to acquire assets may reflect bargaining power. Individuals may use their bargaining power to build up their own assets. Thus, some researchers have used the assets brought to the marriage as a measure of bargaining power. This sidesteps the problem that current assets may be derived from decisions made within the household. Using data from Bangladesh, Indonesia, Ethiopia and South Africa, Quisumbing and Maluccio (2000) find that assets controlled by women have a positive and significant effect on expenditure allocations towards the next generation, such as education and children's clothing.

Education

Another measure of bargaining power may be levels of education. Formal education may increase an individual's bargaining power in two ways. First, people with more formal education usually can earn a higher income. Second, especially in parts of the world with low literacy rates, it is expected that individuals with higher education will be more comfortable in dealing with the formal economy and political structures and thus will have more bargaining power both in terms of the community and within the household. These individuals will be more likely to have access to formal markets, credit, and government services than those with less education.

One study that specifically looks at education as a measure of bargaining power finds that in the United States, Brazil, and Ghana, women with higher education have daughters who are taller. Height is often used as an indicator of health and nutritional status. Similarly, men with more education have taller sons. Thomas interprets these results to claim that the relative levels of parent's education are an indication of power in household decisions and that men and women have different preferences in childrearing (Thomas 1994).

Laws

Moving beyond measures of bargaining power that are easily quantified at an individual level, there are a number of factors that affect bargaining power at the communal and institutional levels. The legal system is one set of institutions that can have a powerful affect on household decision-making. Here, we focus on three types of laws and how they may affect household bargaining power: labor law, property rights, and marriage law.

Labor laws affect bargaining power through their effect on individuals' ability to work and earn an income. Any anti-discrimination law, whether based on gender or on physical disabilities such as the Americans with Disabilities Act (July 26, 1990) will increase the bargaining power of individuals affected. Restrictions on women working outside the home will limit their bargaining power within the home. Thus, in a country like Afghanistan, where women are prohibited from holding employment outside the home, women's outside options are very limited and this will be reflected in their ability to influence decisions at home. The Americans with Disabilities Act will increase the outside options of people in the US with disabilities, thus improving their outside options and increasing their bargaining power within households.

Laws regarding property rights may also affect the distribution of bargaining power among household members. Laws may limit the ability of some individuals to hold any or all property, based on age, gender, race, or class. If only men can own property, this will clearly limit women's outside options. Laws that do not overtly discriminate may do so inadvertently. For example, in many parts of Africa, programs to grant formal land titles to households are being undertaken. These programs give farmers individual rights to the land that they farm and allow the land to be used as collateral. Concern is being expressed, however, that in practice, much of the land is titled in the name of the household head, who is usually male, even if he is not the farmer or the one who had rights to the land under customary practice. By consolidating land titles under one individual within the household, the process of land registration also consolidates bargaining power within the household.

Divorce law also affects the bargaining power of household members. Divorce laws determine the availability of divorce, and in the event of a divorce, determine the distribution of household property and the custody of the children. When divorce is prohibited, neither individual's outside option includes remarriage. In addition, the division of household property upon divorce will affect an individual's outside option. Bargaining power will be more evenly divided when household assets are evenly divided in the case of divorce. Custody of children will also be an important determinant of wellbeing after divorce. If a man can leave the household and take the children with him, women will have relatively little bargaining power within the household. If a woman's outside option involves not seeing her children again, the value of this option may be low. When women are automatically granted legal custody of children, this affects bargaining in another way. Women's outside options will be improved because they will have custody of the children, but they may also incur all of the costs of raising the children themselves.

Thus, legal institutions affect the range of outside options that are available to different individuals, and they affect individuals' ability to contribute within the household.

Social norms

Social norms interact with legal institutions to affect the outside options for individuals. For example, social norms often dictate what types of jobs are considered appropriate for certain individuals. These may vary by gender, age, class, and race or ethnicity. Simply changing the legal structure does not mean that individuals will move into jobs from which they had previously been banned. For example, gender norms prescribe which jobs are appropriate for men and for women. Although men and women may cross these lines, the level of occupational segregation is still relatively high in many places, including the US. This affects bargaining power when it limits the availability of opportunities or the potential wages of individuals. Similarly, social norms may prescribe which professions are appropriate for members of different social classes. Some well-paid jobs in the trades may be seen as inappropriate for individuals coming from upper-class backgrounds; whereas lower paid positions, such as teaching, may be considered appropriate.

Even within the US, women from different backgrounds face different constraints when considering employment options, especially when they have young children. In some communities, women are expected to work and there is a strong network of support to take care of children when they are ill or when the mother has to work late. In other communities, women face strong community disapproval when they combine motherhood with a job or career. These women may still be expected to do all of the things within the household and community that they would do if they weren't employed. Instead of providing support, the community provides additional difficulties and costs. These social norms make it more difficult for a woman to earn an income. Social norms also affect men's roles. Although it is slowly changing in the US, employers often expect men to be able to work late and travel without considering family responsibilities. These expectations limit the options available to men.

Similarly, social norms affect individual opportunities to own assets. Social norms may prescribe how assets should be allocated among sons and daughters. For example, in the Philippines, it is common for sons to be given land as their inheritance while daughters are given an education. Land and education may affect bargaining power differently.

Social norms interact with laws to affect the outside option of divorce. Even when divorce is legal, social sanctions may affect individuals differently. It may be seen as more of a disgrace for women to be divorced than it is for men. In addition, it may be easier for divorced men than divorced women to remarry. Thus from within marriage, men and women may see their options outside of marriage differently.

A set of norms regarding the access to other formal institutions will affect the opportunities for individuals within households. In rural areas, these institutions may include cooperative farmers' associations or credit associations. To the extent that resources, such as farm inputs or credit, are only made available to members of these organizations, memberships will provide benefits to individuals. Women may be excluded from these organizations, either officially or *de facto*. This may mean that they have to rely on male relatives to obtain these inputs for their farms or to sell their produce.

Similarly, there may be social norms that affect an individual's ability to obtain other services. Extension services and other sources of information may only be available to some individuals, based on age, gender or educational background. Many formal organizations, such as government offices or banks, are more responsive to some types of individuals than to others.

Another set of social norms that will have a large effect on the outcomes of household decisions are those related to the acceptance of violence against women, especially within the household. In many parts of the world, it is widely accepted that a man has the right to beat his wife. Even where violence is not considered acceptable, it may be widespread. For example, in the United States, the National Institute of Justice estimates that there are 4.8 million rapes and physical assaults perpetrated against women annually by intimate partners. Many women are killed when attempting to leave their husband or boyfriend who is a batterer. In India, although issues of violence against women have recently received national attention, the majority of men and women agree that it is appropriate for a husband to beat his wife under some circumstances. Thus, there are not social sanctions against a man for beating his wife, but there are social sanctions against a wife who protests or leaves her abusive husband.

Violence within the household has several effects on economic decision-making. First of all, if one person can beat or threaten to beat another household member, this clearly gives them power over the other person in a wide realm of household decisions. It is difficult to influence household decisions when your spouse has the right to beat you. Second, violence has psychological consequences that will affect the perceived options of the victim.

In all of these ways, social norms affect the range outside options actually available or perceived as available to individuals. They also affect the cost and utility received from these outside options.

Assets and Household Decisions in Ghana

Using a detailed example from Ghana, we examine how bargaining power affects household decisions. We measure women's bargaining power by the share of assets owned by women in the household. The effects of asset ownership on household decision are examined and then we discuss the strengths and weaknesses of this approach. Finally, we explore other factors that may affect bargaining power.

Bargaining models suggest that each individual's assets or wealth will affect their bargaining power within the household. An individual who owns farmland will be better off if the household dissolves than the person who owns no farmland. Similarly, the individual who owns a small business will be better off than a person who does not. Thus, the share of assets owned by women in the household can serve as a measure of women's bargaining power.

Ghana is a relatively small country in West Africa. About two-thirds of the population lives in rural areas. Along the coast, fishing is an important occupation, but the majority of people are farmers. Women are involved in a wide range of economic activities, including farming, manufacturing and processing, trading, and working for wages.

The World Bank and the Government of Ghana carried out a detailed survey of Ghanaian households in 1991–2 (The Ghana Living Standards Survey). They interviewed people in 4,552 households, and the survey involved asking individuals detailed questions about their income and assets as well as asking about household expenditures. Many surveys simply ask about household income and household assets but do not disaggregate this information to provide information on individual earnings and asset ownership. The households in this survey range in size from one to 30 members. The mean household size is 4.5 individuals. Six percent of the households are polygamous, with most of them reporting two wives. Women are the heads of 32 percent of the households.

The most important asset that Ghanaians own is farmland. Depending on the region of the country, farmers grow maize, cassava, and yams as staple crops. In addition, fruit and vegetables are grown. Most farmers produce for both home consumption and market sale. Men and women may own and farm their own plots of land.

In addition, many households are involved in small businesses. Fifty-seven percent of the businesses are in retail trade and 18 percent are in food manufacturing. Of businesses controlled by women, 67 percent were in retail trade and 21 percent were in food manufacturing. Business assets include buildings, land, equipment, bicycles, and carts. Finally, information is available on savings accounts. The amounts of money in savings are relatively small and are held by relatively few individuals. These data are also the least reliable, since individuals are likely to underreport their savings.

Many more men than women reported owning land and having savings accounts, while many more women reported having business assets. The mean value of each of the three types of assets, however, is significantly higher for men than for women. The value of the assets owned by all women in the household was added together, as was the value of the assets of all of the men in the household. Thus, we use the share of assets owned by all women in the household as a measure of women's bargaining power. (We could have instead used the share of assets owned by all men and the net results would be the same.)

To explore whether assets are a source of bargaining power, we examine how individual asset ownership affects the outcome of household expenditure decisions. The outcomes examined are the allocations of household consumption across eight categories of goods: food, alcohol and tobacco, education, medical expenses, recreation, clothing, housing and durable goods, utilities and household goods, and the remaining miscellaneous expenses. To capture the consumption across each of these eight categories, we include both the cash expenditure on each category plus the value of the goods that were produced and consumed within the household. Thus, food consumption is the expenditure on purchased food plus the value of food grown and consumed by the household. Housing consumption is the monthly value of the house in which the household resides (roughly speaking, it is either the rent that they pay or the amount of rent that they would have to pay for their dwelling).

For many household expenditures, it is impossible to determine which household member received the goods, especially for shared goods such as housing and utilities. Thus, to understand how bargaining power affects the allocation of resources among household members, we look at whether differences in household expenditure patterns across households vary based on patterns of asset ownership. The data do not allow us to determine that when an individual owns more assets, he or she individually receives more or better food or clothing.

A number of factors in addition to women's bargaining power are expected to affect household expenditure patterns, including household structure (the number of boys, girls, men and women in the household), location (by region and urban/rural), seasonality (date of interview), education levels, household income and wealth. These factors have been taken into account in order to isolate the effect of women's bargaining power. Table 3.1 presents the results of the econometric estimations of the effects of women's bargaining power on household expenditures.[2] The results indicate that women's bargaining power is an important factor in household decision-making.

In households where women own a greater share of the assets, a greater proportion of household expenditure is on food. Thus, for two households with similar characteristics and income and wealth levels, more money is spent on food in the household where women own a greater share of household assets. The mean expenditure on food for urban households is 31,578 cedis (the exchange rate was approximately 400 cedis/dollars during the period of the survey) and the budget share for food is 48.5 percent. For urban households that own some assets, a 1 percent increase in the share of assets held by women increases the budget share spent on food to 51.3 percent. Thus a 1 percent increase in the amount of assets owned by women would result in a increased monthly expenditure of 909 cedis on food. This is approximately one extra day's worth of food per month for the household. For rural households, food is 42 percent of the household budget, with an average monthly expenditure of 15,616 cedis. Thus, a 1 percent increase in the amount of assets owned by rural women would result in an increased monthly expenditure on food of 290 cedis.

Other factors that affect food consumption are consistent with findings in other studies. Household monthly income has a negative effect on the budget share on food, which is consistent with Engel's Law. (Engel's Law says that as incomes rise, people will spend more money on food, but that food as a share of the total household budget will decrease.) As households become richer, they may spend more money on food, but the share of their budget on food decreases. Although the education levels of the male and female heads of household are included since they may shift preferences, economic theory does not give us any *a priori* expectations about the direction of the change in expenditures for food relative to other goods. Women's education is often found to be associated with increased nutritional status of children; however, it is not necessarily associated with an increased *share of the budget* spent on food, holding total income or expenditure constant. Women with better education may be able to provide better nutrition for their children with the same levels of spending on food. In Ghana, increasing education levels results in decreased budget shares on food. This suggests that in Ghana an increase in education shifts preferences in favor of spending on nonfood items more than it shifts preferences in favor of additional spending on food. Finally, households with more men in the household have lower budget shares on food but the number of women or children does not affect the budget share on food.

Both urban and rural households where women own more of the assets spend a lower share of their budget on alcohol and tobacco. The level of household income did not affect the consumption share on these goods. Additional girls and women in the household also reduce the budget share. Households that were female headed

Table 3.1 Effects of women's asset ownership on household budget shares, Ghana 1991–2

	Food	Alc. & Tob.	Education	Medical	Recreation	Clothing	Durables	Household
Urban × **PFA**[a]	**0.0288****	**−0.0176****	**0.0028**	**0.0009**	**−0.0072***	**0.0026**	**0.0035**	**0.0098****
	0.0090	0.0040	0.0026	0.0033	0.0028	0.0042	0.0043	0.0037
Rural × **PFA**	**0.0186***	**−0.0288****	**0.0055***	**−0.0030**	**−0.0121****	**0.0033**	**0.0175****	**−0.0043**
	0.0074	0.0033	0.0021	0.0027	0.0023	0.0034	0.0036	0.0030
Income	**−2.0E-08****	9.96e-10	6.9E-11	−1.8E-10	**4.4E-09***	1.8E-09	**6.3E-09***	3.3E-09
	5.6e-09	2.48e-09	1.6E-09	2.1E-09	1.8E-09	2.6E-09	2.7E-09	2.3E-09
Assets	−6.9E-10	3.74e-11	−9.5E-11	−2.4E-11	−2.2E-10	**6.0E-10***	−3.5E-10	**−6.3E-10****
	5.1E-10	2.28e-10	1.5E-10	1.9E-10	1.6E-10	2.4E-10	2.5E-10	2.1E-10
Asset **Dummy**[b]	**−0.0251****	**0.0138****	−0.0025	0.0004	**0.0044***	−0.0046	**0.0104****	−0.0027
	0.0057	0.0025	0.0017	0.0021	0.0018	0.0027	0.0028	0.0023
M Educ 1[c]	**−0.0485****	0.0057	0.0024	0.0005	**0.0134****	**0.0082***	0.0045	−0.0038
	0.0076	0.0034	0.0022	0.0028	0.0024	0.0035	0.0037	0.0031
M Educ 2	**−0.0367****	**−0.0074***	0.0042	0.0004	−0.0005	0.0031	**0.0099****	0.0010
	0.0079	0.0035	0.0023	0.0029	0.0025	0.0037	0.0038	0.0032
M Educ 3	**−0.0674****	0.0067	**0.0099****	**−0.0076***	−0.0026	**0.0167****	**0.0244****	−0.0049
	0.0101	0.0045	0.0029	0.0037	0.0032	0.0047	0.0049	0.0041
F Educ 1	**−0.0229****	**−0.0142****	**0.0064****	0.0036	−0.0023	**0.0113****	**0.0096****	0.0031
	0.0057	0.0025	0.0016	0.0021	0.0018	0.0026	0.0028	0.0023
F Educ 2	**−0.0458****	0.0043	**0.0096****	0.0011	**−0.0093****	**0.0169****	−0.0029	−0.0046
	0.0100	0.0044	0.0029	0.0037	0.0031	0.0046	0.0048	0.0041
F Educ 3	**−0.0801****	0.0050	**0.0215****	−0.0078	0.0004	0.0170	0.0211	**−0.0268****
	0.0200	0.0089	0.0057	0.0074	0.0063	0.0093	0.0097	0.0082
Boys	0.0034	−0.0015	**0.0043****	0.0004	**−0.0030****	0.0011	−0.0014	−0.0010
	0.0019	0.0008	0.0005	0.0007	0.0006	0.0009	0.0009	0.0008
Girls	−0.0007	**−0.0026****	**0.0050****	0.0002	**−0.0015***	**0.0032****	0.0003	**−0.0023****
	0.0020	0.0009	0.0006	0.0007	0.0006	0.0009	0.0010	0.0008
Men	**−0.0115****	0.0006	**0.0122****	−0.0014	−0.0012	−0.0012	0.0004	**−0.0037****
	0.0025	0.0011	0.0007	0.0009	0.0008	0.0012	0.0012	0.0010

Women	−0.0008	−0.0055**	0.0094**	0.0013	−0.0048**	0.0015	0.0016	−0.0013
	0.0026	0.0012	0.0008	0.0010	0.0008	0.0012	0.0013	0.0011
MF	0.0139*	0.0125**	−0.0145**	−0.0040	−0.0050**	0.0102**	0.0047	−0.0095**
	0.0059	0.0026	0.0017	0.0022	0.0018	0.0027	0.0028	0.0024
Heads[d]								
Date 1	0.0328	0.0074	−0.0086	−0.0064	−0.0076	−0.0068	−0.0067	0.0111
	0.0176	0.0078	0.0050	0.0065	0.0055	0.0081	0.0085	0.0072
Date 2	0.0412*	−0.0008	−0.0053	−0.0051	−0.0072	0.0046	−0.0164*	−0.0027
	0.0173	0.0077	0.0050	0.0064	0.0055	0.0080	0.0084	0.0071
Date 3	0.0523**	−0.0043	−0.0077	−0.0059	−0.0120*	0.0028	−0.0121	−0.0113
	0.0173	0.0077	0.0050	0.0064	0.0055	0.0080	0.0084	0.0071
Date 4	0.0135	−0.0070	−0.0041	0.0005	−0.0087	0.0057	0.0016	−0.0013
	0.0174	0.0077	0.0050	0.0064	0.0055	0.0080	0.0084	0.0071
Forest	−0.0240**	−0.0109**	−0.0053**	0.0139**	0.0020	0.0192**	−0.0148**	−0.0115**
	0.0053	0.0023	0.0015	0.0019	0.0017	0.0025	0.0026	0.0022
Savannah	0.0319**	0.0119**	−0.0131**	0.0028	0.0028	−0.0118**	−0.0176**	−0.0139**
	0.0067	0.0030	0.0019	0.0025	0.0021	0.0031	0.0032	0.0027
Rural	−0.0918**	0.0273**	−0.0063**	0.0183**	0.0196**	0.0251**	−0.0214**	0.0470**
	0.0061	0.0027	0.0017	0.0022	0.0019	0.0028	0.0029	0.0025
Constant	0.5317**	0.0341**	0.0065	0.0262**	0.0545**	0.0451**	0.0839**	0.1165**
	0.0183	0.0081	0.0053	0.0068	0.0058	0.0085	0.0089	0.0075
F-statistic	47.48	31.64	56.86	11.18	27.06	23.47	22.92	30.32

* Indicates significance at .05 level.

** Indicates significance at .01 level. Standard errors are below.

[a] Percentage of household assets owned by women in the household.

[b] Dummy variable indicating whether the household owned any assets that can be assigned by gender.

[c] Dummy variables indicating level of education of male and female heads – completed 4 years of primary education, attended secondary school, and completed "O" level (high school) exams.

[d] Dummy variable indicating whether both a male and female head of the household are present (head and spouse).

also have a lower budget share on alcohol and tobacco. Similar results were found for recreation expenses. Increasing women's share of assets and increasing household income decreased the budget share on recreation.

Alcohol, recreation, and tobacco are considered, in Ghana, to be items that men purchase and consume, and thus we might expect that as women have more influence in household decision-making, the proportion spent on these categories would decrease. The results are consistent with this expectation.

For rural households, but not for urban households, the share of assets held by women increases the budget share on education. In addition, the budget shares on education are increased when the male head of household has completed his "O" level exams (high school level exams) and for each level of education of the female heads of household. These results suggest that women's education may be more important in determining the budget share spent on education than women's asset ownership.

When asked who paid their education expenses, 61 percent of the respondents who had attended school in the past year said their father, while only 17 percent said their mother. Thus, it is surprising that for rural households the bargaining power of women increases the expenditures on education. This may reflect that women use their bargaining power to encourage men to increase education expenses.

Medical expenses (including over-the-counter type treatments and visits to clinics, hospital, or traditional healers) are not significantly affected by women's share of assets for either rural or urban households. Medical expenses are primarily for curative care. Thus, any increase in health care provided due to women's increased bargaining power might be offset by increased preventive care and thus less need for curative care. These offsetting effects may cancel each other out.

Finally, it is worth noting that the share of the budget on clothing was not significantly affected by women's asset ownership. Clothing purchases cannot be disaggregated to categories of men's, women's and children's clothing, so it is not possible to determine whether the composition of the clothing budget differs depending on women's control of assets.

Overall, the results indicate that for urban households, four of the eight categories of expenditure are significantly affected by women's asset holdings. Food and household expenditure (including utilities) are positively related to the percent of assets held by women in urban households, while alcohol and tobacco and recreation are negatively related to the percent of assets held by women in urban households.

For rural households, five of the eight categories of goods are influenced by women's asset holdings. Food, education, and the use value of durable goods (including housing) are positively related to women's asset holdings. Alcohol, tobacco and recreation are again negatively related to women's asset holdings.

A number of things should be noted about the findings regarding bargaining power and household expenditures in Ghana. First, there is no information about individual preferences. So we can't say that when an individual owns a bigger share of the assets, they have more power in determining the outcomes. All we can show is that when women have more bargaining power, the outcomes are different than when men have more bargaining power. We infer that men and women are systematically different in their preferences. If there were no systematic differences in preferences between men and women, we would not observe any effects of bargaining power, even when bargaining power is an important determinant of outcomes.

There are both advantages and disadvantages of using current assets as a measure of bargaining power. The advantage is that asset ownership represents one indicator of individuals' outside options and is relatively straightforward to calculate. The problem with asset ownership as a measure of bargaining power is that assets may be acquired while living within the household. Thus, the underlying relationship may not be that assets are a measure of bargaining power that affect household decisions. For example, if assets are acquired by hard work, then it may be the ability to work hard that gives one bargaining power, not the ownership of assets itself. The ability to work hard affects both asset ownership and bargaining power. Similarly, if the flow of income accruing from the assets is important, then again, it may not be the ownership of assets that is influencing economic decisions.

There is some reason to believe that in Ghana assets are relatively good measures of bargaining power. Much of the asset ownership is relatively stable. Only 25 percent of all business reported purchasing any assets during the year prior to the survey and only 0.4 percent reported selling any assets during this period. Land is even less likely to be bought and sold. No household reported selling land in the year prior to the survey and only 15 households reported purchasing land. If bargaining power is measured as the share of farmland owned by women, rather than the share of all three assets, similar effects on household budget shares are found.

Conclusion and Policy Implications

There is significant evidence that the distribution of power within households affects the outcomes of household decisions. In spite of the difficulties with demonstrating empirically the effects of bargaining power on household decisions, the evidence that bargaining power matters is growing. Hence, it should be expected that any policy that affects the distribution of resources among household members or changes the outside options of some household members will have an effect on other household decisions. Although policy makers may be uncomfortable with the idea of redistributing power within households, they must realize that any policy, including a policy of doing nothing, will affect the intrahousehold allocation of resources. Policies targeting women are often accused of meddling in the private sphere of households. The discussions in this chapter, however, should make it clear that policies focused simply on the household head will also affect household decision-making. No policies can be neutral with regard to the distribution on bargaining power within households. Thus, it is important for policy makers to consider carefully the kinds of effects that proposed policies might have.

Let us briefly consider three examples of policies and the effects that they may have. First, a number of programs, especially in developing countries, are designed to increase the income of households living below the poverty line. Any program that increases the income of one individual relative to another within the household will affect the bargaining power in that household. This is true regardless of who receives the income.

A second example is of programs to restock animals that have been lost in a drought. In Africa, following droughts where many animals die, governments and NGOs work to help households restock their herds. The practice of simply providing animals to the household head will consolidate bargaining power within this one individual. This may have detrimental affects on other household members.

A final example where it is important to consider intrahousehold issues is with the introduction of new technologies. In Africa, new technologies are developed to improve agricultural production of smallholder farmers. These technologies will have differential impacts on the well being of individual household members and may or may not be adopted depending on which individuals receive and benefit from the technologies. For example, in the Gambia, rice was a crop grown by women on their own plots of land. The introduction of centralized pump irrigation, which was designed to benefit women, resulted in rice becoming a community crop under the authority of the male compound head. Thus, men consolidated their bargaining power within the household as a result of the program designed for women (Joachim von Braun and Patrick Webb 1989).

In all of these cases, ignoring the intrahousehold implications of policies would result in unintended consequences. Thus it is crucial for policy makers to consider the effects of their policies on the allocation of resources within households.

NOTES

1   The Nash model specifies that the equilibrium is the point on the utility possibilities frontier equidistant from both threat points.
2   Chapter 11 by Irene Powell in this volume presents a brief overview of how to interpret regression results.

REFERENCES

Doss, Cheryl R. 1996. "Testing Among Models of Intrahousehold Resource Allocation." *World Development* 24(10): 1597–609.

Hoddinott, John and Lawrence Haddad. 1995. "Does Female Income Share Influence Household Expenditures? Evidence from Cote D'Ivoire." *Oxford Bulletin of Economics and Statistics* 57(1): 77–96.

Horney, Mary Jean and Marjorie B. McElroy. 1988. "The Household Allocation Problem: Empirical Results from a Bargaining Model." *Research in Population Economics* 6: 15–38.

Lundberg S., R. A. Pollak and T. J. Wales. 1997. "Do Husbands and Wives Pool Their Resources? Evidence from the U.K. Child Benefit." *Journal of Human Resources* 32(3): 463–80.

Phipps, Shelley A. and Peter S. Burton. 1993. "What's Mine Is Yours?: The Influence of Male and Female Incomes on Patterns of Household Expenditure." *Economica* 65(260): 599–613.

Quisumbing, Agnes and John Maluccio. 2000. "Intrahousehold Allocation and Gender Relations: New Empirical Evidence from Four Developing Countries." IFPRI, Food Consumption and Nutrition Division discussion paper no. 84.

Schultz, T. Paul. 1990. "Testing the Neoclassical Model of Family Labor Supply and Fertility." *Journal of Human Resources* 25(4): 599–634.

Senauer, Benjamin, David Sahn, and Harold Alderman. 1986. "The Effect of the Value of Time on Food Consumption Patterns in Developing Countries: Evidence from Sri Lanka." *American Journal of Agricultural Economics* 68(4): 920–7.

Senauer, Benjamin, Marito Garcia and Elizabeth Jacinto. 1988. "Determinants of the Intrahousehold Allocation of Food in the Rural Philippines." *American Journal of Agricultural Economics* 70(1): 170–80.

Thomas, Duncan. 1993. "The Distribution of Income and Expenditure within the Household." *Annales d'Economie et de Statistique* 29: 109–36.

——. 1994. "Like Father, Like Son; Like Mother, Like Daughter: Parental Resources and Child Height." *Journal of Human Resources* 29(4): 950–88.

von Braun, Joachim and Patrick Webb. 1989. "The Impact of New Crop Technology on the Agricultural Division of Labor in a West African Setting." *Economic Development and Cultural Change* 37(3): 513–34.

The Division of Work in the Household

Gains from Trade and Specialization: The Division of Work in Married Couple Households

Leslie S. Stratton

This chapter explores how married couples allocate their time. Understanding the factors underlying married couples' time allocation decisions is important because two-thirds of the United States' population resides in such households. The standard of living and quality of life for those living in these households depends upon their intrahousehold allocation of goods and time. Of particular interest in this chapter is the household division of work and leisure, and how it differs by gender.

Definition and Measurement Issues

Before we can discuss the division of time between work and leisure, we must first define work and leisure. Labor economists studying the labor supply decision, the decision to seek employment, have struggled with this distinction for some time. The simplest approach is to define employment in the marketplace as "work" and all other activity as "leisure." This approach has yielded some important insights into the operation of the labor market.

On the other hand, is all time for which we are not paid truly leisure? What about time spent preparing for or commuting to work? What about activities that are essential for life, like eating and sleeping? What about activities that are important for good health, like exercising? Basic housework tasks like laundry and dishes and lawn care are considered leisure activities using the simple classification scheme discussed above. Would you consider them work or leisure? What about childcare activities? Distinguishing between work and leisure is not always an easy task.

Yet some definition must be chosen. For the remainder of this chapter, I distinguish between employment in the market (typically for pay), employment in the house on activities commonly known as housework, and "leisure" or everything else. Sleeping, therefore, falls under the classification of leisure. Child-related meal preparation, cleaning, and laundry fall under housework, while watching children and helping with homework is designated leisure. The latter classification makes some sense if we consider the decision to have a child a choice that brings happiness or utility to parents. Thus, activities with a child must constitute in part a consumption activity like leisure for the parent.

To analyze the division of labor, we must somehow measure work, housework, and leisure. Possible units of measure include: the quantity of goods, housework, and leisure produced; the value of goods, housework, and leisure produced; and the time spent on work, housework, and leisure. Ideally a quantity measure would be utilized because more is typically preferred to less and quantity provides an absolute scale that does not differ from location to location. Five apples are five apples. Quantity, however, is in this context difficult to measure, since there is no single measurable good produced. Each activity results in its own array of output: employment produces sales or widgets or haircuts; housework produces meals and clean clothes and clean rooms; leisure produces exercise and sleep and conversation. This is much the same problem encountered by macroeconomists who would like to measure the quantity of output produced within the economy as a whole.

The solution employed in macroeconomics is to substitute the value of all goods produced for the quantity of all goods produced. Thus, Gross Domestic Product or GDP measures the value of all final goods produced within an economy not the quantity. To calculate the value of an individual's output on the job is relatively easy, as the individual's wage or earnings provides a natural measure. The valuation of housework and of leisure, on the other hand, is substantially more difficult. Each time an individual chooses to engage in housework or leisure rather than paid employment, that individual signals that he/she values the output of home production or leisure more highly than the market values his/her employment. In this case, foregone earnings serve as a lower bound estimate of the value of these alternative activities. The existence of market alternatives to housework, like maid service, helps establish further bounds on its value. Each time an individual chooses to engage in housework him or herself rather than to purchase a market alternative such as maid service, that individual signals that he/she values the resulting home production less than the market charge for such services. In this case, the market charge serves as an upper bound estimate of the value of housework. Conversely, for those purchasing housework services, the market charge serves as another lower bound estimate of the value of housework. In general, however, the market valuation only reflects the valuation of the marginal individual, and, as it is not possible to purchase things like sleep on the market, no market valuation of leisure activities is even possible.

Given these difficulties, the unit of measure most commonly used to analyze the division of work and leisure in the household is that of time. Difficulties remain in actually measuring time spent,[1] but these are modest compared to the difficulties in measuring output or value. An additional advantage to using time measures is that time is uniform across individuals and across activities. One hour is one hour, whether spent by Linda vacuuming or by Tina sleeping. Another advantage is that because time is available in fixed and limited quantities, identifying time spent in two of three activities necessarily identifies time spent in the third. In part for this reason, the empirical analysis below focuses only on market and housework. Identifying time spent on these activities identifies time spent on leisure.

Theoretical Motivation

But how is the time allocation decision made? What motivates individuals to work for pay, do housework, engage in childcare and leisure activities? Economists typically model such choices by assuming that each economic agent acts to maximize his or her own utility or happiness. This does not mean that every action requires immediate gratification. Happiness or utility can be measured in a lifetime context, with individuals maximizing *expected lifetime utility* with every choice. Unfortunately for us, we face constraints that place restrictions on our flow of happiness. If goods and leisure increase utility, as is the case with the simplest models, then limited income/wealth constrains the purchase of goods and limited time constrains the consumption of leisure. Budget and time constraints are typically binding, with budget constraints binding over the lifetime and time constraints binding in each unit of time. We may not find work as a cashier or shelf stocker exciting, but it does provide the money necessary to pay for food, shelter, and leisure activities. We may want to get a little more sleep at night, but we have to be at work by nine a.m. in order to get paid. These constraints are real and the utility maximization paradigm helps to explain behavior.

Multiperson households, however, pose a problem. If economic theory posits that each economic agent acts to maximize utility, what is the "economic agent" in a multiperson household?[2] Does each individual remain his/her own economic agent, retaining his/her own utility function, albeit with some modification to recognize other household members? Does the household itself become an economic agent, with a new utility function representing the household as a whole? Do individuals make a binding contract at the time the household is formed that determines all future allocation decisions or is bargaining a never-ending process that changes the course of future outcomes over time?[3] In multiperson households, the exact identity of the economic agent is subject to some debate.

The exact utility function is also unknown. Utility is, after all, not truly measurable. Nor are the factors that influence utility clear in this multiperson, multiproduct context. Is utility a function of total household goods consumption or does it matter who in the household does the consuming? Leisure time probably needs to be measured separately for each individual, but might utility also be influenced by the ability to spend that leisure time with our spouse?[4] If cleanliness increases utility, how is it measured when information is limited to time spent on housework by each family member? One person may be more productive than another during any given hour spent on housework and even separate measures of housework time are not likely to fully capture such productivity differentials.

The theoretical and measurement problems associated with modeling decisions in married couple households are severe, particularly when the model is extended to include home production activities. Some of the discussion of housework time that follows is therefore focused not on utility comparisons but on determining the degree to which economies of scale arise and specialization takes place when two individuals form a joint household. Economic theory and common sense suggest that doing housework for two will take less than twice the time it takes to do housework for one, if nothing else changes. Preparing a meal for two takes little more time than preparing a meal for one. Small laundry loads can be combined into bigger laundry loads. Vacuuming need only be done once. Of course other changes often accompany marriage – many married couples purchase homes and have children. These factors need to be accounted for, but if there are economies of scale in housework, the formation of joint households could decrease the time both men and women spend doing housework.

Economic theory further suggests that if individuals specialize according to their comparative advantage, all parties can be made better off. Specialization within a multiperson household could take the form of one individual working in the market and the other working in the home, and/or of specialization by type of task within the home.[5] If there is specialization, then one individual may spend more time on housework and another less, following the establishment of a joint household. If there is both specialization and economies of scale, then (*ceteris paribus*) theory predicts that one individual will spend less time on housework while the other could spend more. This prediction can be tested.

Finally, while the emphasis within this volume is upon economics, any discussion of household behavior that focuses exclusively on economic motivations is at best incomplete. Other researchers, particularly sociologists and psychologists, have contributed valuable work in this area. The role of social norms and expectations is particularly relevant when modeling employment and housework choices, as gender appears to have significant predictive power even after controlling for economic factors.

Empirical Work

Despite the considerable problems encountered in addressing questions about the division of work and leisure in the household, the empirical literature in the area is substantial. The remainder of this chapter introduces this literature. Sections on the division of market work and the division of housework within married couple households are followed by a discussion of how these sectors and decisions interact. Throughout, the emphasis is on recent evidence from the United States.

Table 4.1 Labor force participation rates by sex, marital status, age, and presence of young children

Panel A: Women

Year	Single	Married	Age 25–34 and married	Children under 6 and married
1900	43.5	5.6		
1930	50.5	11.7		
1960	58.6	31.9	28.8	18.6
1970	56.8	40.5	38.8	30.3
1980	64.4	49.8	58.8	45.1
1990	66.7	58.4	69.6	58.9
2000	69.0	61.3	70.5	62.8

Panel B: Men

Year	Single	Married	Age 25–34 and married
1960	69.8	89.2	98.8
1970	65.5	86.1	98.0
1980	72.6	80.9	97.5
1990	74.8	78.6	96.9
2000	73.5	77.3	96.7

The 1900 and 1930 measures are not strictly comparable because they include married women whose husbands are not present, they exclude those working without pay for family businesses, and they include 15 year olds.

Source: All 1900 and 1930 data, and 1960 participation rate for women with children from U.S. Bureau of the Census 1975 *Historical Statistics of the United States*, Series D49–62 and D63–74. Remaining data from 2001 *Statistical Abstract of the United States*, Nos. 575 and 577.

Market work

The empirical research on gender differences in market work encompasses both differences in labor force participation rates and differences in hours worked. An individual is said to be participating in the labor market if he/she is either being paid for his/her labor, working 15 or more hours per week for a family business, or actively seeking employment and ready to begin work immediately. The labor force participation rate is defined as the fraction of the population over the age of 16 that is participating in the labor market.

Table 4.1 presents data on labor force participation rates in the United States. Panel A presents the statistics for women; panel B for men. These figures clearly demonstrate that women have a lower participation rate than men, that the gender differential is greater for married persons, and that it has fallen over time. In 1960, the labor force participation rate was 11 percentage points higher for single men than for single women. The gender differential was five times greater (57 percentage points) for married persons. While men continue to have higher labor force participation rates today, the gender differential has fallen to only 5 percentage points for single and 16 percentage points for married persons. The gender differential for married persons is less than 30 percent what it was 40 years ago, primarily because of a 29 percentage point increase, a doubling (from 31.9 to 61.2) in the participation rate for married women. Further evidence from 1900 and 1930 suggests that this phenomenal shift began decades earlier.

Restricting the analysis to those ages 25 to 34 provides some further indication of the trends at work. First, while married men as a whole experienced a rather significant decrease in labor force participation (from 89 percent in 1960 to 77 percent in 2000), the evidence among 25 to 34 year olds is that the decline was much smaller for prime aged men (from 99 percent to 97 percent). Much of the overall decline observed for men is in fact attributable to substantial decreases in the labor force participation rate of older men (over age 55) and to the ageing of the population. Second, the data suggest that the labor force participation rate of married women aged 25 to 34 has increased more rapidly than that for married women as a whole. As these data are reported at 10-year intervals for individuals in a 10-year age range, they represent distinct cohorts of women. Those ages 25 to 34 in 1960 were born before those ages 25 to 34 in 1970. Each such 10-year cohort shows a greater than 10 percentage point jump in labor force participation rates between 1960 and 1990, when the participation rate flattens out. Indeed there is substantial evidence that much of the increase in the labor force participation rate for married women is due to changes in each cohort of women to arrive in the labor market.

For those participating in the labor market, the number of hours worked provides another measure of labor supply. Gender differences in this employment outcome are most readily demonstrated by comparing the part-time employment rate by gender. Part-time employment is defined in the United States as employment that usually entails less than 35 hours per week. The part-time employment rate compares the number employed part-time with the total number employed. Measures of the part-time employment rate have been relatively constant since 1970, averaging around 23 percent for women and 7 percent for men. These figures suggest a gender difference in labor supply even for those working (U.S. Department of Labor, Bureau of Labor Statistics 1968–2000).

Employees, however, do not typically control their work hours. Most jobs come with fixed hours, and job applicants are faced with a take it or leave it offer. Claudia Goldin (1990) argues that part-time work as we know it did not arise until around 1950. The lack of part-time employment options prior to 1950 may have distorted the labor force participation rate of married women, if current part-time employment rates reflect individual preferences. On the other hand, the current part-time employment rate may overstate women's preference for part-time work if social norms dictate that women are more likely to be offered part-time jobs.

One method for gauging preferences for part-time work is to examine information on the fraction of all part-time workers who report preferring part-time hours. While this fraction has been falling over time for both men and women, it was still over 84 percent for women and over 79 percent for men aged 20 and above in 2000 (U.S. Department of Labor, Bureau of Labor Statistics January 2001: 175). Thus, most part-time workers appear to have voluntarily chosen such hours. Gender differences in employment hours are substantial and primarily reflect gender differences in choices.

How are such choices made? According to economic theory, individuals participate in the labor force if participation yields them more utility than their next best alternative use of time. Likewise, hours of market work are chosen such that the value of the next hour in the marketplace is just equal to the value of the next hour spent in the next best alternative use of time. The value of the next best alternative use of time is typically modeled as a function of the number and ages of the children present in the household. Generally speaking, children have a positive and marginally statistically significant impact on the labor supply decision for men and a significant and substantial negative impact on the labor supply decision for women (particularly for those with children under the age of six). Men with children are more likely to seek employment and to seek longer hours; women with children (particularly young children) are less likely to seek employment and, if employed, more likely to seek part-time employment. These findings suggest that gender differentials in childcare are an important determinant of gender differences in labor supply.

Gender differences in the responsiveness to children combined with smaller family sizes explains a portion of the dramatic convergence in the labor force participation rate of married persons. The birth rate fell from 23.7 per 1000 women in 1960 to 14.8 in 2000 and an increasing fraction of those births are to unmarried mothers, 33.1 percent in 2000 versus 22 percent in 1985 (1960 figure from Table 77 of U.S. Bureau of the Census *2000 Statistical Abstract of the United States*; 1985 measure from Table 99 of U.S. Bureau of the Census *1999 Statistical Abstract of the United States*; 2000 figures are from Joyce Martin et al. 2001). For married men, having fewer children means less pressure to work in the market: for married women, having fewer children means less reason not to work in the market.

Changing family composition alone, however, is not sufficient to explain the time trends. The final column of table 4.1, panel A demonstrates that married women with young children have been increasingly likely to participate in the labor market. In 1960, fewer than 20 percent of married women with children were working; by 2000 over 60 percent were. Empirical work (see Francine Blau 1998) suggests that women have become less sensitive to the presence of children. Thus, holding all else constant, women with young children are more likely to work today than they were 20 years ago.

Other factors motivating women to increase their labor force participation over time include increases in women's wages and in divorce rates. Whereas in the 1950s, women working full-time earned 60 cents to the dollar for men, by 1999 that ratio had risen to 76.5 percent (Francine Blau and Lawrence Kahn 2000). A higher valuation of market time makes participation more likely. Furthermore, evidence indicates that married women have become more sensitive to wages in making their labor supply decisions. Greater sensitivity pared with rising wages would certainly increase labor participation rates, though estimates suggest that wage factors alone account for no more than half and possibly only one quarter of the differential (Dora Costa 2000). Between 1960 and 1981, divorce rates rose from 2.2 to 5.3 per 1,000 people (Table 91, U.S. Bureau of the Census *1999 Statistical Abstract of the United States*). Generally speaking individuals who are not married need to be employed to be self-supporting. Rising divorce rates suggest less stable marriages and a greater need for the backup income provided by employment. No fault divorce laws and smaller divorce settlements have also served to encourage employment by married women. Since the mid 1980s, however, divorce rates have fallen to 4.2 – still twice the 1960 rate but considerably below their peak value (1998 provisional data from the National Center for Health Statistics 2001). The impact of the rising divorce rate on married women's labor force participation, while clearly significant, is probably less influential than their rising relative wages.

Analysis of the time series data is also hindered by a controversy similar to the chicken versus the egg debate – which came first? Just as there are researchers studying how the decrease in family size, the increase in women's relative wages, and the rising divorce rate might have contributed to the rising labor supply of married women, there are also researchers studying how increased employment among married women might have caused the decrease in family size, the increase in women's relative wages,[6] and the rising divorce rate. The question of causation is a serious one that makes empirical analysis of changes over time difficult.

Most researchers conclude that a significant fraction of the increase in women's employment is as yet unexplained. Some attribute the unexplained component to changing social norms and expectations. Married women were expected to stay at home in 1900: now the majority of married women work. Evidence that married women's labor supply decisions are now less sensitive to other household income and to the presence of young children in the household is suggestive of such a behavioral shift.

Housework

But not all work is paid. Time and energy are also spent on housework or home production activities. A well kept home, regular meals, and clean laundry all take effort. Even in the heavily industrialized United States, many goods are produced within the home. One estimate places the value of home production within the United States at about 30 percent of GDP (Robert Eisner 1988). While married men have historically specialized in market activities, married women have historically specialized in housework. An analysis of the household division of labor that ignores this sector of the economy clearly underestimates the role played by women.

As discussed in the introduction in this chapter, for lack of a better alternative, housework is measured in terms of time spent. Still unanswered, however, is time spent on what. Cooking, cleaning, laundry, home repair, and lawn service are among the first housework activities to come to mind. Many also consider bill paying, auto repair, pet care, shopping, and sewing, to be housework. Time use surveys that ask respondents to record their every activity for a certain period of time constitute the most accurate source of housework time data. Unfortunately, such data sets are relatively rare. The last large-scale panel study of time use in the United States was conducted in 1975–6. Much of the data in this field instead consist of respondents' retrospective reports of "usual time spent" on housework.

Historical data are particularly hard to come by. The best estimates available suggest that time spent on housework has changed little since 1900. Meal preparation and clean up times have decreased as technological advances have made these tasks easier; but time spent on childcare, shopping, doing laundry, and cleaning house has increased. The number of children in each home has declined, but the time spent with each child has increased. Shopping takes more time because more goods are purchased rather than made at home. Cleaning takes longer because homes are larger. Finally, overall expectations regarding home production have risen; the standard of cleanliness has changed. Individuals were once content to don on a clean shirt once a month or to clean house once a year. Many now wear fresh cloths every day and clean house once a week.[7]

The data set employed here to provide current measures of housework time is the National Survey of Families and Households, henceforth called the NSFH. This is a national sample of 13,008 households that were interviewed once in 1987–8 and again in 1992–4. This data set has particularly good retrospective data for a number of reasons. First, respondents provide measures of time spent on nine different household activities. Thus respondents are prompted to provide information that is likely more consistent and more inclusive than the many studies that ask for only a single measure of housework time and leave it up to the respondent to decide what constitutes housework and what does not. Second, the NSFH provides panel data that allow us to examine changes in reported housework activities over time. Third, both spouses reported their housework time, making intrahousehold analysis possible. These data provide interesting evidence on the division of labor within married couple households.

Column 1 of table 4.2, panel A relates total housework time for married men and women using population weighted measures from the first wave of the NSFH. Married men report spending an average of 18 hours per week while married women report spending an average of 35 hours per week on housework. As married men in this sample are employed for an average of 35 hours per week and married women for an average of only 20 hours per week, total time spent working in the market and at

Table 4.2   Total hours spent on housework per week

Panel A: Cross-section data
Housework time by marital status

	Married	Never married	Previously married	Differences by gender	Differences by marital status
Full sample					
Men	18.0	17.6	21.4	1, 2, 3	b, c
Women	35.5	21.9	29.5		a, b, c
Full-time workers					
Men	17.3	17.6	20.4	1, 2, 3	b, c
Women	30.2	20.4	27.9		a, b, c

The Differences columns test for statistical significance in the difference of the means at the 5% significance level:
1, 2, and 3 Indicate significant gender differences between married, never married, and previously married persons respectively.
a Indicates significant differences between never married and married persons.
b Indicates significant differences between never married and previously married persons.
c Indicates significant differences between married and previously married persons.

Panel B: Longitudinal data
The normalized change in housework time
for those changing marital status

	Begin marriage	End marriage
Full sample		
Men	−0.5	4.1**
Women	5.8**	−3.9**
Employment hours unchanged		
Men	0.2	4.3**
Women	3.4**	−1.0

* Indicates measure is significantly different from zero at the 5% level.
** Indicates measure is significantly different from zero at the 1% level.

Source: National Survey of Families and Households.

home appears to be remarkably similar by gender. The key difference appears to be in who specializes in what. Further examination of the data challenges this interpretation. When the sample is restricted to include only full-time workers, average housework time remains substantially different by gender, with married men contributing 17 hours and married women 30 hours per week. The gender difference in housework time remains large and statistically significant, even though time spent employed is approximately equal.

The fact that wives do more housework than husbands does not, however, prove that individuals specialize within married couple households. It may instead be the case that women do more housework than men, no matter what their marital status. Women may derive greater utility from housework or from a cleaner household than men. Evidence of such a general gender differential in housework time is in fact presented in panel A of table 4.2. Women spend significantly more time on housework than men, no matter what their marital status. Column 2 presents sample averages for individuals who have never married (primarily young persons) while column 3 presents sample averages for individuals who have been but are not now married (that is, for separated, divorced, and widowed persons). Restricting the data to include only full-time workers yields the same results.[8]

Preferences aside, marriage may still influence the time allocation decision. As discussed earlier, marriage is likely to yield economies of scale in home production as well as gains from specialization according to comparative advantage. Theory suggests that at least one spouse will spend less time on housework while the other could spend less (if the reduction from economies of scale outweighs the increase from specialization) or more (if the increase from specialization outweighs the reduction from economies of scale). The data in panel A of table 4.2 indicate that total time spent on housework is approximately the same for both married and never married men (18 hours per week) and substantially larger for married women than for never married women (35 versus 22 hours per week). Thus, while economic theory suggests that reported housework time should fall following marriage for at least one marriage partner, these data indicate that housework time is at best invariant to marital status.

Is this evidence that economic theory is wrong? Not quite. The theory suggests that individuals will change their time allocation when they marry. The data in panel A are cross-sectional in nature. They show reported housework time by marital status for respondents to the survey. Differences between those who were and were not married at the time of the survey may arise either because their marital status differs or because these are different people with different preferences regarding housework. It could be, for example, that men who spend more time on housework are more likely to get married. Once they do marry they reallocate their time just as economic theory would suggest but in the cross-sectional analysis we do not see what happened to their reported housework time because they are only observed married. To test this hypothesis we need not cross-section data, but panel data; we need to follow the same individuals over time and observe how they change their time allocation when they marry.

The NSFH is a panel data set: each respondent was asked the same housework questions twice over a period of about six years. Information on how reported housework time changed as marital status changed is reported in panel B of table 4.2. These figures control for individual specific effects by subtracting the time spent on housework at the time of the first survey from the time spent on housework at the time of the second survey. Thus any determinants of housework that are unchanged for the individual over time (like preferences) are subtracted out. Since some changes may be a function simply of the passage of time and the ageing of the population, the average reported change in housework time for those who do not change marital status is used to normalize all the results. These normalized measures of the change in reported housework time are presented for those who marry in column 1 and for those whose marriages end (whether by separation, divorce, or death of a spouse) in column 2.

These data, like the cross-sectional data, indicate that marriage increases the time women spend on housework. While the cross-sectional data show a mean difference in reported housework time of 13.6 hours between never married and married women, however, the longitudinal data in panel B indicate a normalized increase of only 5.8 hours with marriage. Women whose marriages end report spending 3.9 hours less time per week on housework versus 6 hours less in the cross-section analysis. Furthermore, much of this differential appears to be attributable to women who change labor force status when they change marital status. When the analysis is restricted to women whose employment status is unchanged – where employment status is measured simply as "not employed," "employed part-time," and "employed full-time" – women whose marriages end do not report a significant reduction in their housework time and women who marry report spending only 3.4 hours more. Thus, it appears that cross-sectional estimates overstate the impact of marriage on women's housework time.

There is no evidence of such a bias for men. The longitudinal results are virtually identical to the cross-sectional results. When a marriage begins, men on average report no significant change in housework time. When a marriage ends, men increase their reported housework time by an average of 4 hours per week.

Further analysis of the data (not shown here) suggests that changes in reported housework time are greatest for those entering their first marriage and for those whose marriages end with the death of a spouse. If housework requires learned skills, specialization is optimal only in a long-term relationship. Individuals who have experienced a marital failure may be less confident in the durability of any marriage and so less willing to specialize. Similarly, individuals who are having marital problems may be less willing to specialize. In general, simple differencing of longitudinal data provides only limited evidence supporting the economic theory of specialization.

Stronger evidence requires more detailed analysis of the data. While differencing panel data removes any individual specific components that are unchanged over time, other significant lifestyle changes often arise at about the same time individuals marry. Married persons are more likely to have children and to purchase their own homes. Both children and home ownership will likely increase housework time. Using regression analysis to examine changes in reported housework time as a function of changes in marital status, changes in the number and ages of children in the household, changes in employment, changes in home and car ownership, and changes in the composition of the rest of the household does suggest that men who marry spend less time on housework. Holding all these other factors constant, men who marry reduce time spent on housework by 5 hours per week while men whose marriages end increase their time spent on housework by about 6 hours per week. This time change is substantial given that on average men spend less than 20 hours a week on housework, and it is statistically significant. The comparable results for women indicate that time spent on housework increases 2 hours per week for those who marry and falls about 5 hours per week for those whose marriages end. In this case, however, only the effect of marital dissolution is statistically significant. The finding that men who marry spend less time and women who marry spend about the same amount of time on housework is consistent with economic theory regarding specialization and economies of scale.

More detailed breakdowns of housework time provide further evidence of specialization. As mentioned earlier, the NSFH contains information on nine different housework activities. These are summed to create the total housework measure discussed above, but data on all nine are available. These activities include: "meal preparation" (Meals), "washing dishes and cleaning up after meals" (Dishes), "house cleaning" (Cleaning), "washing, ironing and mending" (Laundry), "outdoor and other household maintenance tasks" (Outdoor and maintenance), "auto maintenance and repair" (Auto repair), "shopping for groceries and other household goods" (Shopping), "driving other household members to work, school, or other activities" (Driving others), and "paying bills and keeping other financial records" (Bills).[9]

Table 4.3 presents detailed information on housework time for those married households in which each spouse provided a complete report. The figures in columns 1 and 2 of table 4.3 show the average time reported on each activity for each spouse. Column 3 reports the fraction of total housework time on each activity that is contributed by the husband. These data suggest that there is specialization within households not only between market and housework, but also in the type of housework performed by each spouse. Sociologists have used similar figures to differentiate between housework done predominantly by women (meals, dishes, cleaning, laundry), housework done predominantly by men (Outdoor and maintenance, Auto repair), and neutral type housework (Shopping, Driving others, Bills). In fact specialization is even greater than the sample averages in column 3 suggest. The final column in table 4.3 reports the fraction of all households in which one spouse contributes at least 80 percent of the reported time in an activity. While on average husbands contribute about 45 percent of household time to paying bills and driving others, about 60 percent of households report rather extreme specialization in these activities. Husbands and wives do not split the time, rather husbands and wives are equally likely to specialize in these activities. Time is most nearly split in shopping where only 36 percent of households have one spouse contributing more than 80 percent of the time but in all likelihood spouses specialize by type of store.

Once again, the amount of time an individual spends on each activity may be affected not just by marital status but also by individual preferences. An analysis of the

Table 4.3   Detailed housework time per week

	Husband's housework time	Wife's housework time	% of household time contributed by husband	% of households in which 1 spouse contributes > 80% of the time
Total housework	19.03	33.75**	36.8	19.0
Meals	2.71	8.94**	24.7	57.4
Dishes	2.29	5.71**	29.9	45.7
Cleaning	2.01	7.17**	24.5	53.6
Laundry	0.85	4.03**	16.2	69.0
Outdoor and maintenance	5.17	1.88**	74.6	60.1
Auto repair	1.59	0.16**	90.2	88.8
Shopping	1.78	2.86**	34.9	35.9
Driving others	1.18	1.50**	47.3	59.8
Bills	1.45	1.51	44.7	59.7
Number of observations	3883			

** Indicates significant gender differences in average reported housework time at the 1% level.
* Indicates significant gender differences in average reported housework time at the 5% level.
Source: National Survey of Families and Households.

longitudinal changes in each of the nine types of housework (not shown here) suggests that men spend significantly less time preparing meals and doing laundry following marriage (more following the end of a marriage) and more time on outdoor and maintenance activities following marriage (less following the end of a marriage). Meanwhile, women spend significantly more time preparing meals, doing dishes, cleaning, doing laundry, and shopping following marriage (less following the end of a marriage) and somewhat less time doing auto repair following marriage (more following the end of a marriage). Individuals do apparently reallocate their time when they marry in a manner that suggests specialization.

Housework and market interactions: the housework time allocation

But how is that allocation decision made? A study by Joni Hersch and Leslie Stratton (1994) uses data on white, married, dual earner couples age 20–64 from the Panel Study of Income Dynamics (PSID) to address this question. Time spent on housework is recorded in the PSID as the answer to the question, "About how much time do (you or your spouse) spend on housework in an average week? I mean time spent cooking, cleaning, and doing other work around the house." Note that this question is rather vague and could be interpreted quite differently by different respondents. On average, reported housework time from the PSID is lower than that reported in the NSFH, particularly for men. Husbands report spending 7.4 while wives report spending 19.7 hours per week on housework. Activities such as yard work, bill paying, and auto repair that are more commonly performed by men may not have been considered "other work around the house" and hence may be underreported. While the division of housework time between married and employed spouses may be somewhat overstated within this sample, however, the differences are still worth exploring.

Hersch and Stratton (1994) use these data to identify what factors cause some husbands to contribute a greater amount of time and a greater share of housework time. Ideally these data could be used to distinguish between bargaining theory and human capital theory as explanations for the division of housework time. Unfortunately, these theories yield very similar predictions. It is, however, possible to test these theories against the alternative explanation that social norms, not economic factors, dictate who does housework.

The key variable in this analysis is earnings or relative earnings. Earnings are important if bargaining or human capital theory explains the intrahousehold time allocation, but not if social norms alone are key. Bargaining theory suggests that the bargaining power of each spouse is related to his or her own next-best alternative. This next-best alternative is often called the threat point. If not being married is the alternative to being married, then the earnings power of each spouse provides a measure of this threat point. The greater the share of earnings a spouse contributes, the more power that spouse has within the household. If housework is not a desired activity, the spouse with more power will contribute less housework and a lesser share of the housework. Thus, bargaining theory suggests that the greater the husband's share of labor income, the less time he will spend on housework and the lower will be his share of housework time. Human capital theory suggests that household utility will be greater if household members specialize according to their comparative advantage. Holding relative productivity in home production constant, relative productivity in the marketplace can be gauged by looking at relative earnings. The spouse with the higher earnings share is likely the spouse with the comparative advantage in the market. Thus human capital theory also predicts that the greater the husband's share of labor income, the less housework and the lower the share of housework he will contribute. The other variables in the model are included to control for household differences in the value of leisure time, in home productivity, and in the type of housework demanded.

The results reported by Hersch and Stratton (1994) are highly supportive of economic theory. The greater the husband's share of labor income, the lower his share of housework time, the less time he spends on housework, and the more time his wife spends on housework. A 10 percentage point increase in the husband's share of labor income reduces his share of housework by 2 percent, reduces his reported housework time by about 20 minutes per week, and increases his wife's reported housework time by almost 1 hour a week. Social norms alone do not dictate the allocation of housework time within the household; economics plays a role.[10]

Social norms and expectations do, however, have some explanatory power. Several researchers (Scott South and Glenna Spitze 1994; Theodore Greenstein 2000; Michael Bittman et al. 2000), have noted that in households where wives contribute more than half of family earnings, reported housework time tends to be higher for women and lower for men than in households where earnings are more equally divided. Sociologists have suggested that tasks may be allocated within such households in part to emphasize gender and identity. Thus, women with high paying jobs relative to their husbands may spend more time on traditionally female housework tasks in order to "do gender," in order to prove that they are women and to counteract somewhat the economic dependence of their husbands.

Housework and market interactions: wages

Taken alone, the finding that married women spend more time on housework in part because married men earn more is neither surprising nor of great concern. A number of researchers, however, have documented a negative relation between wages and housework, suggesting that more time spent on housework reduces wages! Empirically, a consistent negative effect has been found for women using at least five different data sets (see Stratton 2001 for a listing). Typically an additional 10 hours of housework time reduces hourly wages by about 2 percent. Evidence of an inverse relation for men exists but is both smaller and less statistically significant. This suggests that there may be a vicious cycle. Women spend more time on housework then men because their wages are lower, and the additional time they spend on housework lowers their wages further.[11]

Explanations for the negative relation as well as for the possible gender bias in this relation abound. Time spent on housework may proxy for market drive or ambition. Those individuals who are more interested in succeeding in the market may spend less time on housework and be more successful in the market. To test this hypothesis, Hersch and Stratton (1997) use longitudinal data from the PSID to examine how changes in reported housework time for married persons are correlated with changes in reported wages. This comparison removes any individual specific effects like ambition. They find a smaller but still significant negative correlation between housework time and wages for women. This suggests that part of the explanation may be unobserved individual specific productivity differences, but not all, at least not for women.

Alternatively, Gary Becker (1985) has suggested that it is not housework *per se* but the effort expended on housework that negatively influences wages. According to this theory, effort or energy is in limited supply. The more effort expended on housework, the less effort available for the job. If increased effort increases productivity it will increase wages, too. If time spent on housework is positively related to effort expended, then increased time on housework will lower wages. The effect may differ by gender because men report spending so much less time on housework and much of this time may be spent on weekend home repair; their energy level on the job may not be significantly altered. Women, on the other hand, who perform a greater share of daily housework tasks like cooking and cleaning, may experience more fatigue on the job. If time rather than effort is the constraining factor, then women with more workday household chores may seek out jobs with flexible hours that allow them to accommodate those chores. If firms offering flexible hours pay lower wages, women but not men may be willing to accept that tradeoff. Stratton (2001) tests both these hypotheses using data that include self-reported measures of effort and hours flexibility. While she finds that increased effort on the job is associated with significantly higher wages on the job, controlling for effort does not reduce the negative relation between housework and wages. Likewise, controlling for hours flexibility does not reduce the negative relation between housework and wages. Much work remains to explain the links between the market and home sectors.

Summary

In summary, there exists substantial evidence of gender differences in the allocation of time with married couple households. Married men have higher labor force participation rates and work more hours per week than do married women. Married women, on the other hand, spend substantially more time on housework than do married men. Research confirms that both preferences and economic factors contribute to these differences.

On average men supply more time to the labor market than do women. Some of this differential is due to men's higher relative wages and some to women's natural advantage in childbirth. But the gender differential in labor force participation among married couples has narrowed dramatically over time. Married women's labor supply has increased as their relative wages rose making employment more attractive, as household size dwindled making childbearing and childcare less critical, and as the divorce rate increased and women were encouraged to become more financially independent.

Much less data exist on the household sector. Women on average spend more time on housework than men, though marriage does appear to influence the allocation of housework time. Men who marry spend less time on housework as a whole but more on outdoor and maintenance activities. Women who marry spend some more time on housework, particularly cooking and cleaning, but less on auto repair. Within married households there is evidence that, at least up to a point, the greater the fraction of income earned by the wife, the less time she spends on housework.

While economic forces do influence time allocation decisions in married couple households, other forces are also at work. Much of the increase in married women's labor supply remains unexplained and though women may have a comparative advantage in certain household tasks like childbearing and infant care, it is not at all clear why they might have an advantage in cooking and cleaning and not in auto repair. There is also evidence that women who earn more than 50 percent of the household income actually increase their time on housework contrary to economic theory, but in line with sociological theories of "doing gender." Economic theory provides an important framework for the analysis of time allocation decisions, but can not alone explain the observed gender differences in that allocation.

NOTES

1   For example, while surveys designed to identify how people spend their time often recognize hundreds of distinct activities, even they are challenged to classify someone who is eating breakfast, reading the paper, and talking on the phone all in the same ten minutes.
2   This discussion applies equally well to married and cohabiting households.
3   Many of the issues raised in the part II Economics of Marriage chapters that appear earlier in this volume arise again when analyzing the household division of labor.
4   Researchers have only just begun to look at how market work is timed within married households. See Harriet Presser (1995) for one of the most recent contributions to this area.
5   While economies of scale can arise in all multiperson households, specialization may not. If changing activities is costly, specialization will be more likely in married couple households rather than cohabiting households, because marriages generally are of longer duration.
6   See chapter 9 by Irene Jacobsen's in this volume for an explanation of this relation.
7   See Juliet Schor (1991) and Stanley Lebergott (1993) for further discussion of the historical data.
8   Evidence of a gender difference in reported housework time is, in fact, virtually universal. Thomas Juster and Frank Stafford (1991) provide a variety of international estimates. They also report evidence that time spent on housework has risen for men and fallen for women between 1960 and 1990.
9   See Hersch and Stratton (2002) for a further description of these data and some of the peculiar problems encountered in the measurement of reported housework time.
10 There also exists evidence that economic forces influence such leisure activities as time spent sleeping. J. E. Biddle and Daniel Hamermesh (1990) find that women who earn higher wages sleep less than women who earn lower wages.
11 Since higher earnings reduce housework time, the inclusion of housework time in a wage equation could be subject to simultaneity bias. Several authors have controlled for this possibility and continue to observe the inverse relation between housework and wages.

REFERENCES

Becker, Gary S. 1985. "Human Capital, Effort, and the Sexual Division of Labor." *Journal of Labor Economics* 3: S33–S58.
Biddle, J. E. and Daniel S. Hamermesh. 1990. "Sleep and the Allocation of Time." *Journal of Political Economy* 98(5, pt. 1): 922–43.
Bittman, Michael, Paula England, Nancy Folbre, and George Matheson. 2000. "When Gender Trumps Money: Bargaining and Time in Household Work." Mimeo.
Blau, Francine D. 1998. "Trends in the Well-Being of American Women, 1970–1995." *Journal of Economic Literature* 36(1): 112–65.

Blau, Francine D. and Lawrence M. Kahn. 2000. "Gender Differences in Pay." *Journal of Economic Perspectives* 14(4): 75–100.

Costa, Dora L. 2000. "From Mill Town to Board Room: The Rise of Women's Paid Labor." *Journal of Economic Perspectives* 14(4): 101–22.

Eisner, Robert. 1988. "Extended Accounts for National Income and Product." *Journal of Economic Literature* 26(4): 1611–84.

Goldin, Claudia. 1990. *Understanding the Gender Gap.* New York: Oxford University Press.

Greenstein, Theodore N. 2000. "Economic Dependence, Gender, and the Division of Labor in the Home: A Replication and Extension." *Journal of Marriage and the Family* 62: 322–35.

Hersch, Joni and Leslie S. Stratton. 1994. "Housework, Wages, and the Division of Housework Time for Employed Spouses." *American Economic Review Papers and Proceedings* 84(2): 120–5.

——. 1997. "Housework, Fixed Effects, and Wages of Married Workers." *Journal of Human Resources* 32(2): 285–307.

——. 2002. "Housework and Wages." *Journal of Human Resources* 37(1): 217–29.

Juster, F. Thomas and Frank P. Stafford. 1991. "The Allocation of Time: Empirical Findings, Behavioral Models, and Problems of Measurement." *Journal of Economic Literature* 29(2): 471–522.

Lebergott, Stanley. 1993. *Pursuing Happiness.* Princeton, New Jersey: Princeton University Press.

Martin, Joyce A., Brady E. Hamilton, and Stephanie J. Ventura. 2001. "Births: Preliminary Data for 2000." *National Vital Statistics Reports* 49(5).

National Center for Health Statistics. 2001. On-line. Available http://www.edc.gov/nchs/fastats/divorce.htm (September 2001).

Presser, Harriet B. 1995. "Job, Family, and Gender: Determinants of Nonstandard Work Schedules Among Employed Americans in 1991." *Demography* 32: 577–98.

Schor, Juliet B. 1991. *The Overworked American: The Unexpected Decline of Leisure.* New York: Harper Collins, Basic Books.

South, Scott J. and Glenna Spitze. 1994. "Housework in Marital and Nonmarital Households." *American Sociological Review* 59(3): 327–47.

Stratton, Leslie S. 2001. "Why Does More Housework Lower Women's Wages?: Testing Hypotheses Involving Job Effort and Hours Flexibility." *Social Science Quarterly* 82 (1): 67–76.

U.S. Bureau of the Census. 1975. *Historical Statistics of the United States: Colonial Times to 1970.* Washington, DC: U.S. Government Printing Office.

U.S. Bureau of the Census. 1999–2001. *Statistical Abstract of the United States,* 119th edition. Washington, DC: U.S. Government Printing Office.

U.S. Bureau of the Census. 2000. *Statistical Abstract of the United States,* 120th edition. Washington, DC: U.S. Government Printing Office.

U.S. Bureau of the Census. 2001. *Statistical Abstract of the United States,* 121st edition. Washington, DC: U.S. Government Printing Office.

U.S. Department of Labor, Bureau of Labor Statistics. 1968–2001. *Employment and Earnings* 14–48(1). Washington, DC: U.S. Government Printing Office.

Chapter 5

But ... Who Mows the Lawn?: The Division of Labor in Same-sex Households

Lisa Giddings

Picture a white middle-class Omaha neighborhood *circa* 1981: mother, father, two children, one dog. I grew up in that neighborhood, and when the house next door to my childhood home went up for sale, we assumed another nuclear family would move in, retaining the status quo. Instead, two women signed the mortgage. The neighbors immediately congregated on the sidewalk, speculating on the nature of their relationship: sisters, friends, ex-nuns, lesbians? My ageing dad did not wonder about them for long. While unsuccessfully attempting to wake his Lawn-Boy from its winter hibernation, one of the "girls next door" came to his rescue. From then on, he affectionately distinguished them as "the outdoor one" and "the indoor one." In Dad's day, gender roles were immutable and it made sense to him to apply them to the couple next door. It was clear to him that one person should clean the house and take care of the kids while the other pay the bills and mow the lawn. Once he got passed the initial shock of having a lesbian couple next door, the roles applied just the same.

Households allocate two distinct categories of labor among their members: non-wage labor within the household and for-wage labor in the market. Until recently, the majority of households in the United States followed a strict division of labor in which women performed the domestic tasks within the household, while men worked for wages in the labor market. In determining the origins of this traditional pattern of labor allocation, economic theories assign causal roles to comparative advantages, bargaining power, institutional constraints, and gender roles. Comparative advantages are differences in preferences and skills that give an individual a relative advantage in a particular task. The argument maintains that biological differences as well as social institutions and gender roles give women a comparative advantage in household labor. In contrast, bargaining power theorists contend that men tend to work in the private sector because they earn a higher income and effectively "bargain" out of performing household chores. Arguments that rely on institutional constraints and gender roles focus less on rational decisions made by household members and more on habits of behavior that lead to the traditional division of labor.

These economic theories have mainly been applied to the sexual division of labor within the context of heterosexual couples. If there are no biological differences that could contribute to the division, questions arise concerning the relative importance of these factors. Do lesbian and gay families exhibit different household divisions of labor than heterosexual families, and if so, then who mows the lawn? This chapter explores the division of labor in gay and lesbian households, that is, how gay and lesbian couples assign domestic tasks within the household, how they allocate their labor time between the paid market and the home, and possible explanations as to why they choose certain divisions of labor. The essay concludes by advocating for the passage of a federal employment non-discrimination act, legal civil unions and other federally guaranteed rights in an effort to level the institutional playing field and expand the range of possibilities that same-sex couples face in terms of making choices regarding the division of labor.

Within the context of the economic theories of the household, both inherent and institutional differences suggest that gay and lesbian couples would exhibit a different pattern of labor allocation than heterosexual couples. Lesbian and gay couples have no biological or genetic differentiation that would lead to comparative advantages in the household. Lesbian and gay families cannot bear their own biological children, leading neither partner to an automatic advantage in caring for the child. Same-sex couples are more likely than heterosexual couples to earn similar incomes[1] resulting in no bargaining advantage for either partner. Lastly, without differences in socialized gender roles, same-sex couples are unlikely to rely on such institutions to guide their decisions and are, therefore, less likely to develop a traditional division of labor in the household.

Additionally, lesbian and gay families are differently constrained than heterosexual households by many institutional factors, including laws banning gay marriage/civil unions, inheritance laws, adoption laws, tax benefits, domestic partner benefits, and hospital rights. Some informal institutions are beginning to be adopted by same-sex couples, such as legal agreements that substitute for marriage or domestic part-nership benefits offered by companies. These *ad hoc* benefits, however, are associated with high transactions costs and, as such, have yet to be implemented in a widespread manner. Without readily available legal parameters, gay and lesbian couples may be less stable than their heterosexual counterparts, and a strict division of labor in which one partner works only within the household while the other earns a wage in the labor market may be considered too risky. Without a legal marriage contract, for example, one partner may not have legal recourse if the partnership were to dissolve, and alimony and child support are not in the homosexual vernacular.[2] In this way, the institutional context may inhibit certain patterns of labor allocation within same-sex households.

Such differences have political ramifications. Family policies are theoretically designed to enhance efficiency in reaching social goals. If lesbian and gay families are qualitatively different than heterosexual families and face different constraints that affect their allocation of labor within the household, then policies must be designed that account for such differences. Recent attempts to equalize the institutional context faced by lesbian and gay families include the introduction of the Employment Non Discrimination Act (HR2355 and S1276), employment protection at the state and firm level, and attempts by several states to pass legal civil unions for homosexual couples (of which only Vermont has seen success).[3] Additionally, the passage of domestic partnership benefits in some states and within some corporations has also served to limit constraints felt by lesbian and gay families. These changes may increase the range of options available to same-sex couples in terms of their labor allocation choices.

This chapter begins by introducing the economic theories of the household and how they have treated lesbian and gay couples. This section is followed by empirical findings on the division of labor in lesbian and gay households. The next section of the chapter presents political implications including a description of recent developments in employment discrimination acts, domestic partnership benefits, and civil unions for gay and lesbian couples. The chapter concludes with Conclusions and suggestions for further research.

Theoretical Treatment of Households in Economics

Gary Becker (1981) uses the notion of comparative advantage to explain the sexual division of labor between men and women. The theory assumes that women, because they biologically bear children, will choose to specialize in household labor while men, with greater earning power, will specialize in the paid labor market. Specialization leads to the development of comparative advantages with women producing goods and services in the private sphere (home) and men in the public sphere (market). Thus, preferences and comparative advantages (based on both biological differences and socialized gender roles) lead to a sexual division of labor between the men and women.

When attempting to explain the division of labor in lesbian and gay households, Becker points to both the inherent biological differences between heterosexual and homosexual couples and some of the institutional constraints faced by gay and lesbian couples. Becker (1981) concludes that the model of comparative advantage is inapplicable because gay and lesbian couples have similar abilities and thus, cannot exploit the "inherently" balanced comparative advantages existing between men and women. He assumes that because gay and lesbian couples cannot bear children, that they will invest less (emotion, effort, and money) in marriage-specific capital. As a result, the partners in "homosexual unions" will be less stable (Becker 1981: 330).

In terms of institutional constraints, Becker points to both the lack of a legal marriage contract and discrimination faced by lesbian and gay couples as further evidence that they would have a less extensive division of labor than heterosexual couples. He questions the sustainability of gay and lesbian relationships because there is no legal contract involved. "[H]omosexual unions, like trial marriages, can dissolve without legal adversary proceedings, alimony, or child support payments" (Becker 1981: 330). Additionally, "the opprobrium attached to homosexuality has raised the cost of search to homosexuals and thereby has reduced the information available to them" (Becker 1981: 330). These factors lead him to conclude that lesbian and gay couples exhibit a less extensive division of labor than heterosexual marriages.

Critiques of Becker's theory emphasize the role of culturally constructed norms and social institutions that shape the behaviors and activities of economic agents. Institutions structure long-term relationships in a manner that minimizes the transaction costs associated with the relationship (Robert Pollack 1985). The institution of marriage, for example, is a type of map consisting of informal gender roles and traditions, as well as formal social and legal agreements, that spell out the rules of the ongoing relationship and the rights of each member, should the relationship dissolve (Francine Blau et al. 1998). As such, institutions can serve as stabilizing devices. Heterosexual couples, for example, may unconsciously adopt a traditional division of labor rather than making a decision based on preferences or abilities.

Bargaining models of the household in which families negotiate with each other in order to reach an agreement were developed as a critique of Becker's neoclassical model (Marilyn Manser and Murray Brown 1980; Paula England and George Farkas 1986; England and Barbara Kilbourne 1990). Returns from the marriage contract are commensurate with each member's "bargaining power" or negotiating strength. Historically, men have had more education, experience and higher incomes, which led to greater bargaining power in the home and an unequal division of labor with women performing the majority of housework. Within same-sex couples, however, large differences in income are less likely than among heterosexual couples. It stands to reason that neither partner would garner any bargaining power leading to a more egalitarian division of labor.[4]

Nancy Folbre's (1994) "structures of constraint" tie together several aspects of these economic models of the household in order to broaden our understanding of the sexual division of labor. She defines structures of constraint as "sets of asset distributions, rules, norms, and preferences that empower a given social group" (Folbre 1994: 51). The fact that women, worldwide, perform the majority of the domestic responsibilities in families may be due to some combination of these constraints. Traditions and implicit social roles may affect women's preferences and their choices about education and career – ultimately shaping their opportunities. Furthermore, access to fewer assets, and explicit legal institutions may limit women's choices outside of marriage. As was the case with the biological argument, a lack of gender differentiation within same-sex couples would lead to less of a difference between the partner's gender socialization, preferences, and ultimately the legal institutions each partner faces. Again, this would lead to a more egalitarian division of labor in gay and lesbian households as opposed to the strict public/private pattern exhibited within heterosexual households.

Empirical Findings in Lesbian and Gay Households

It is possible that the division of labor in lesbian and gay households tends to be egalitarian, but the determinants of this division are more complicated than Becker theorized and require further explanation. Several empirical studies have shown that lesbian couples in particular tend to distribute their household labor more equally than their heterosexual counterparts (Alan Bell and Martin Weinberg 1978; D. Merilee Clunis and G. Dorsey Green 1988; Letitia Peplau and S. D. Cochran 1990; S. Desaulniers 1991; H. F. Peace 1993; Charlotte Patterson 1998; Gillian Dunne 1998a, 1998b). The factors influencing this result vary from Becker's comparative advantage thesis. Egalitarian norms, a lack of gender differentiation, and social and legal institutions may encourage lesbian and gay households to adopt a more equal division of labor.

Several studies indicate that both lesbians and gay men reject the notion of gender differentiation. Philip Blumstein and Pepper Schwartz (1983) and Lawrence Kurdek (1993, 1995) argue that lesbian couples actively defy existing gender roles and are careful to divide tasks equally. They speculate that lesbian couples avoid task specialization because of the low status traditionally associated with women who perform housework. Further, lesbians refuse to take on the "provider role" as women do not expect to support their partner financially (Blumstein and Schwartz 1983: 130). Peace (1993: 30) finds that lesbian couples do not specialize in tasks along any stereotypically gendered lines such as outdoor versus indoor tasks. Kath Weston (1991) found that even in cases where gender differences existed, such as within couples who exhibited "butch/fem" identities, it was seldom the case that one partner would work outside of the house while the other performed only domestic labor.

With regard to gay men, Blumstein and Schwartz (1983) find that work was an integral part of their self-esteem. Furthermore, unlike heterosexual men, gay men did not feel an obligation to provide financially for their partner (Blumstein and Schwartz 1983). Gay men preferred that their partner work rather than for either partner to assume the role of full-time homemaker. "Otherwise, one partner may feel he is relinquishing some of his maleness, and that is not an appealing prospect for most gay men" (Blumstein and Schwartz 1983: 129).

M. V. Lee Badgett (1995a, 2001) questions Becker's failure to separate out the effects of comparative advantage and the effects of institutions on the division of labor in the household. She claims that "gendered patterns of specialization would be much rarer among lesbian and gay households" because homosexual couples do not have access to the legal and social institutions supporting heterosexual couples and enforcing gender norms (Badgett 1995a: 131), rather than due to comparative advantages. For example, institutions that keep same-sex partners from adopting may discourage lesbian couples from having children. Same-sex couples might perceive investment in marital capital and specialization to be too large a risk without the legal frameworks defining the beginning and ending of relationships.

Although the division of labor within lesbian and gay couples tends to be equal relative to heterosexual couples, not all lesbian or gay couples divide household labor equally, and it is not entirely clear that conditions for specialization do not exist for some same-sex couples. Partners may exhibit different preferences for household tasks. It is reasonable to assume that heterosexual and homosexual couples alike would develop relative advantages for domestic tasks within the house based on preferences and abilities. Household tasks are many and varied – cleaning, cooking, shopping, childcare, finances, repairs, and so on. Differences in preferences for performing the tasks could lead to differences in ability, and ultimately a division of labor within the household that may or may not be equal. Several studies have shown that lesbian couples do, in fact, use preferences and comparative advantages to guide their division of labor (Desaulniers 1991; Peace 1993). Weston (1991) found that both individuals in lesbian couples generally worked in the labor market for money and individuals either rotated household tasks, or performed those that they did best or enjoyed most.

The presence of children within the same-sex household may alter the division of labor and encourage specialization in different activities. Many authors have noted a recent increase in childbearing among lesbians[5] (V. Mitchell 1996; Patterson 1992, 1994, 1995; Patterson et al. forthcoming; Nancy Polikoff 1990; C. Riley 1988; F. Tasker and Susan Golombok 1991; Weston 1991). Raymond W. Chan et al. (1998) find that although lesbian couples with children maintain a fairly equal division of labor, the non-biological mother tends to work more hours in the labor force and perform less childcare than the biological mother.

Blumstein and Schwartz (1983) argue that the division of labor in gay and lesbian households is the result of an absence of traditional gender relations. They claim that within a same-sex partnership,

> [t]here is no assumption about the primacy of one partner's career, and if a conflict arises, it is negotiated between them. Neither job is automatically considered of secondary or of auxiliary importance. Fights may flare up over career issues, but rarely over who should work… The same-sex couples profit in this instance by being guided by neither institution nor gender. (Blumstein and Schwartz 1983: 153)

In contrast, preliminary empirical and theoretical work suggests that gender roles may still play a role. Sarah Oerton (1998) asserts that though gender differences in lesbian households may be less obvious, the absence of a heterosexual man in a household does not "erase all the processes and practices associated with gendering" (Oerton 1998: 76). Lisa Giddings (1998) argues that lesbian couples may either purposefully or subconsciously emulate the traditional roles and traditions found in heterosexual marriages in their allocation of domestic tasks within the household. Were we to understand gender as a category that is not fixed, we may find more subtle examples of gendered patterns of behavior. For example, in their study of lesbians in the 1940s and 50s, Elizabeth Lapovsky Kennedy and Madeline D. Davis (1993), find that partners become more or less masculine in a given context and relative to a particular partner, performing the household tasks associated with that role.

Bargaining models may also be applied to explain divisions of labor in lesbian and gay households. Differences in the standard determinants of threat points such as education, experience, wealth, income, or the probability of finding another partner, may exist within the lesbian or gay household. The belief within same-sex couples that both partners should work in the market can change if they have incomes large enough to make two wage earners unnecessary (Blumstein and Schwartz 1983: 130). These differences could lead to power asymmetries and, ultimately, an unequal division of labor. It is also conceivable that increased risks associated with the lack of formal legal contracts in lesbian and gay relationships could exaggerate power differences in times of crisis.

With regard to institutional constraints faced by same-sex couples, official contracts and legal agreements may proxy some of the rights homosexual couples cannot access. Gay and lesbian couples are increasingly turning to wills, power-of-attorney agreements, health-care proxies and contracts to protect their relationships (Steven James and Bianca Murphy 1998: 108; Hayden Curry and Dennis Clifford 1992). As gay and lesbian couples substitute formal and informal agreements for legal ones, they may be more willing to specialize and create divisions of labor within the household.

Political Implications

Gay and lesbian families are different than heterosexual families in that they face greater biological and institutional structures that constrain their ability to make choices about their allocation of labor within the household. Recent policies have been proposed in an attempt to limit the constraints faced by lesbian and gay families in the United States and around the world. The policies address discrimination of sexual minorities in employment, housing, access to services, and other areas of public life. In addition to discrimination of various sorts, policies also appeal to registered partnerships, marriage or civil unions at both the federal and state levels. With access to civil rights that are analogous to heterosexual couples, gay and lesbian partners can enjoy a greater array of choices with regard to their division of labor within and outside of the household.

Critics of the traditional division of labor between men and women argue that immense risks exist for the individual specializing at home. Barbara Bergmann (1981) identifies several economic risks associated with being a "housewife."[6] The most obvious economic risk is that working in the private sector for one's family is not compensated with a wage or salary[7] and, as such, receives no current or future benefits (health and dental care, paid leave or retirement to name a few). A "housewife" has little job mobility within the same "occupation" and if the job ends (either at her own or at her husband's discretion) the human capital generated from performing housework leads only to other low-pay, low-status jobs. Furthermore, without wages or a salary, housewives may be unable to generate savings that could be relied upon during a job search or were he/she to exit the relationship. Lastly, the occupation of housewife is unique in that precisely as his/her partner's value in the private sector is increasing, the value of a "housewife's" labor devalues over time as children grow up and move out of the household (Ferber and Bonnie Birnbaum 1977).

In this light, one may wonder why it would be good for gay and lesbian couples to move toward the more traditional division of labor. I am arguing here that it is important for gay and lesbian partners to have the *choice*, and that in order to enable this choice, greater protections for the home-specializing partner (in either heterosexual or homosexual relationships) is necessary. It is conceivable that the availability of such a choice – while not for an entire lifetime – would be beneficial to couples at various life stages, such as after childbirth or adoption. Because institutional constraints appear to be a motivating factor in determining the allocation of labor, their expansion (or removal) would afford gay and lesbian couples the range of choices available to heterosexual couples.

Discrimination in the labor market

Being gay, the last time I thought about it, seemed to have nothing to do with the ability to read a balance book, fix a broken bone or change a spark plug. (President William Jefferson Clinton 1997)

Workers that identify as being gay or lesbian combat issues in the workplace that are not related to the productivity of their time or labor. Prejudice against gays and lesbians manifests itself in the workplace through discrimination in both hiring and firing, harassment, promotion, and compensation, as well as in more subtle ways. "These forces present significant challenges for employees deciding whether to reveal their sexual orientation and for managers trying to create a climate that promotes understanding and productivity" (Human Rights Campaign 2000).

Fears of discrimination on behalf of gay, lesbian, bisexual and trans-gendered (GLBT) individuals are not unfounded. A 1992 survey found that between 16 and 44 percent of GLBT people reported incidences of anti-gay discrimination in the workplace (Badgett et al. 1992). Between a fourth and two-thirds of lesbian, gay, and bisexual people report having lost a job or a promotion as a result of their sexual orientation (Badgett 1997a: 1).[8] Evidence of similar cases of discrimination exists even in "tolerant" professions such as law, medicine and academia. Heterosexual witnesses corroborate this evidence. The results from two surveys targeting heterosexual employees found that between 15 and 25 percent had witnessed anti-gay discrimination (Badgett 1997a: 2). Furthermore, contrary to popular myth, gays and lesbians do not earn more than heterosexuals. In fact, one study suggests that similarly qualified gay workers may earn less than their heterosexual counterparts (Badgett 1995b, 1997b; Marieka Klawitter and Victor Flatt 1998).

Actual or perceived employment discrimination against gay and lesbian workers serves to constrain individual behavior. Discrimination in the workplace can create salary inequities, impede promotions, and accentuate job loss. Within a heightened climate of discrimination, gay and lesbian couples may be less inclined to adopt traditional divisions of labor due to the uncertainties surrounding potential losses associated with discrimination in the workplace.

This environment of workplace uncertainty has been removed for certain Americans with the passage of three federal laws. Title VII of the Civil Rights Act of 1964 prohibits employment discrimination on the basis of race, color, religion, sex or national origin. The Age Discrimination in Employment Act of 1967 prohibits employment discrimination on the basis of age and the Americans with Disabilities Act of 1990 prohibits employment discrimination on the basis of disability. At the time of writing, however, no federal law protects lesbian, gay, bisexual or transgendered individuals from discrimination in the workplace on the basis of their sexual orientation.

A series of state and local laws do protect LGBT individuals to some extent. At the time of writing, 11 states, 116 cities and counties, and the District of Columbia have laws protecting gay men and lesbians against discrimination in the private sector. The states include: California, Connecticut, Hawaii, Massachusetts, Minnesota, Nevada, New Hampshire, New Jersey, Rhode Island, Vermont and Wisconsin.[9] At the time of writing, 257 Fortune 500 companies, 931 private sector employers, 319 colleges and universities, 235 state and local governments, and 37 federal government department agencies include sexual orientation in their non-discrimination policies (Human Rights Campaign 2001).[10]

> The closer a company is to the top of the Fortune 500 list, the more likely it is to include sexual orientation in its non-discrimination policy, suggesting that the most successful companies in America are those that embrace diversity and work toward providing an inclusive work environment for lesbian and gay employees (Human Rights Campaign 2000: 8).

If passed, the Employment Non Discrimination Act, or ENDA, (HR2355 and S1276) would prohibit discrimination in the workplace on the basis of sexual orientation at the federal level. First introduced in Congress on June 23, 1994, the federal bill bars employers from basing hiring, firing, promotion or compensation decisions on an individual's sexual orientation. The bill would apply to businesses with more than 15 employees and would not require any affirmative action, quotas, or preferential treatment on behalf of employers. Contrary to popular myth, the bill does not create "special rights" for gay and lesbian people in the workplace. It simply ensures equal protection under the law. The bill came within one vote of passing the Senate on September 10, 1996 and was reintroduced in the summer of 2001 co-sponsored by Senators Edward M. Kennedy, Arlen Specter, Joseph Lieberman, and James Jeffords, and by House Representatives Christopher Shays, Mark Foley, Barney Frank, and Ellen Tauscher.

Patchworks of social policies protect GLBT individuals against discrimination inconsistently around the world. While the Universal Declaration of Human Rights (UDHR) 1948, does not explicitly address sexual orientation, a 1994 case decided by the United Nations Human Rights Committee, Nicholas Toonen v. Australia, held that the term "sex" found in the list of protected categories in the International Covenant on Civil and Political Rights (analogous to Article 2 of the UDHR) should be understood to include "sexual orientation." As of April 1999, 21 countries had enacted some kind of anti-discrimination act protecting LGBT people from discrimination in work, education, the provision of goods, services and facilities, and accommodations. The countries include: Australia (Anti-Discrimination Act of 1991; various state acts), Canada (Canadian Charter of Rights and Freedoms Section 15(1), 1982; Human Rights Act, 1996), Columbia, Costa Rica (Law No. 7771, Art. 48), Denmark (Penal Code, 1987; Act 459, 1996), Ecuador (Constitution, Article 23, 1998), Fiji (Constitution, Section 38(2) of the Bill of Rights, 1998), Finland (Constitution, Section 5, 1998; Penal Code, Section 9, 1995), France (penal Code, 1985 and Code of Labor, 1986, 1990), Iceland (Penal Code, 1996), Ireland (Prohibition of Incitement to Hatred Act, 1989; The Unfair Dismissals Act, 1993; The Health Insurance Act, 1994), Israel (Equal Opportunities in Employment Act, 1992), Luxembourg (Penal Code, Article 454–457, 1997), The Netherlands (Constitution, Article 1 DC, 1983; Penal Code, 1992; The General Equal Treatment Act, 1994), New Zealand (Human Rights Act, Section 21, 1993), Norway (Penal Code, Paragraph 135a, 1981; Work Environment Law, 1998), Slovenia (Penal Code, Article 141, 1996; Law About Work Relations, Article 6, 1998), South Africa (Constitution, 1996), Spain (Penal Code, 1995), Sweden (Penal Code, 1987), United States (Equal Employment Opportunity in the Federal Government, 1998).[11]

Domestic partnership benefits

Employers offer fringe benefits to their employees as a way to both compensate their workers, attain a competitive advantage, and to attract (and retain) highly skilled workers. These benefits include medical and dental insurance, disability and life insurance, pensions benefits, family and bereavement leave, tuition assistance, relocation and travel expenses, and profit sharing. These benefits have historically been offered to employees' spouses and legal dependents; however, extending them to domestic partners of unmarried employees (including gay and lesbian employees) is only a recent trend.

In 1982, the Village Voice became the first employer to offer domestic partner benefits to its gay and lesbian employees (Human Rights Campaign 2000). "By 1990, there were fewer than two dozen U.S. employers that offered 'spousal equivalent' benefits to their gay employees' partners" (Human Rights Campaign 2000).[12] At that time no Fortune 500 Company offered domestic partner benefits. By 2000, 20 percent of Fortune 500 companies did so (Badgett 2000: 1). According to the Human Rights Campaign, there are currently 3,647 employers that offer domestic partner health benefits, 116 Fortune 500 companies, 602 other private companies, non-profits or unions, 129 colleges and universities, and 98 state and local governments (Human Rights Campaign 2000).[13] Additionally, three cities including San Francisco, Los Angeles and Seattle have established "equal benefits ordinances" which require companies with whom they do business to provide domestic partner benefits (Human Rights Campaign 2000: 19).[14] Furthermore, six states (California, Connecticut, New York, Oregon, Vermont, and Washington) cover the partners of their employees.

Employers can benefit from offering domestic partnership benefits to gay and lesbian couples. During periods of low unemployment, for example, benefits can provide firms with a competitive advantage in recruitment and retention. By creating a social safety net for employees and their dependents, domestic partnership benefits can also improve employee productivity. Lastly, offering benefits signals that the firm values diversity in the workplace.

As with non-discrimination acts, domestic partnership benefits can also expand the range of choices available to gay and lesbian couples with regard to their allocation of labor. Without access to insurance and health care, for example, it could be impossible for one partner to stay at home and focus on domestic labor. This is particularly pertinent for lesbian and gay couples with children. The decision concerning who will bear a child, for example, may be predicated on who has access to the most comprehensive benefits to protect the child, rather than on other factors such as health of the mother or even preference.

Gay marriage/civil unions

The rights associated with marriage convey economic, social, and civil benefits that vary widely across countries and cultures. The rights provided by marriage may include the right to joint custody of children to adoption, inheritance, spousal immigration rights (and extending one's citizenship to one's spouse and children), rights to power of attorney, property, the execution of living wills, medical decision-making power, and insurance and pension benefits. These benefits are limited to heterosexual couples only by political decision, not by logic or efficiency reasons. M. V. Lee

Badgett and Josh Goldfoot (1996) argue that marriage provides a sort of social safety net creating "property, spousal inheritance, and social security survivor benefit rights in the event of divorce or death, all of which enhance the economic security of the family" (Badgett and Goldfoot 1996: 2). If extended to gay and lesbian couples, such benefits would provide security to those partnerships as well.

Although gay and lesbian couples cannot currently marry through the same institutions and mechanisms as heterosexual couples anywhere in the world, four forms of "gay marriage" have been legislated throughout the world in an attempt to equalize the institutional setting for gays and lesbians. These forms of marriage include "Civil Unions" in Vermont, "Reciprocal Beneficiaries" in Hawaii, "Registered Partnerships" in Denmark, Greenland, Iceland, Norway, and Sweden, and "Statutory Cohabitation Contracts" in Belgium.

A law establishing the institution of civil unions for gay and lesbian couples went into effect on July 1, 2000 in the state of Vermont. The first of its kind, this law gives gay and lesbian couples all of the rights and privileges afforded to married couples. Under the law, gay and lesbian couples are eligible to receive spousal benefits afforded to married couples by their employers. It also requires insurance carriers to cover gay and lesbian couples in civil unions.

According to the Human Rights Campaign (2000) two states (Hawaii and California) and 53 cities and counties have established domestic partnership registries in the United States. While not equivalent to marriage, these laws give gay and lesbian couples certain rights and benefits including hospital and jail visitation rights. They do not, however, require employers to provide domestic partnership benefits.

Several states have recently introduced civil union bills. California Assembly Bill No. 1338 would allow gay and lesbian couples to obtain a civil union license and assume the same rights and obligations provided by marriage. The Connecticut House Bill No. 6032 would provide legal recognition to same-sex couples. The Maine Domestic Partnership Bill (Maine House Legislative Document No. 1703) requires insurers and HMOs to offer domestic partnership coverage to people living together including both heterosexual and gay/lesbian couples. The state is also considering two domestic partnership bills that would exclude same-sex couples from such coverage. Additionally, legislatures in Rhode Island, Hawaii and Washington have held hearings on proposals modeled after Vermont's law.

Thirty-six states have passed laws that prohibit the recognition of civil unions or marriages between same-sex couples. President Clinton signed the Defense of Marriage Act (DOMA) on September 21, 1996, allowing a state to choose to not recognize same-sex marriages performed in another state. The Act further seeks to create a legal definition of marriage as a "union between a man and a woman." DOMA was introduced by Reps. Bob Barr and Steve Largent, and passed the House of Representatives by a vote of 342 to 67 on July 12, 1996.

The United States lags behind other countries in accepting some variation of same-sex unions, such as domestic partner registries and gay marriages, particularly Northern

European countries.[15] Denmark enacted a same-sex partnership registry that took effect on October 1, 1989, making it the first country in the world to grant gay and lesbian couples the civil benefits accorded to heterosexual couples. With the exception of the recognition of weddings performed in churches, access to adoption, and the use of national socialized medicine for artificial insemination, the law is equivalent to marriage under Danish law. Greenland, a dependency of Denmark, adopted the law in 1994. Norway passed a law mirroring Denmark's partnership law in 1993, and Sweden followed suit by legally recognizing same-sex couples in 1995.

In 1995, the Constitutional Court in Hungary ruled that common law marriages can be applied to same-sex couples. The court said that a law limiting common-law marriages to "those formed between adult men and women" was unconstitutional. This ruling provides same-sex couples the same basic civil benefits as an unmarried heterosexual couple (same as marriage except adoption of children).

The Netherlands' Second Chamber of parliament approved a same-sex partnership law with benefits mirroring the Danish model in 1996. By January 1, 1998, gay and lesbian Dutch couples had access to all of the benefits except adoption. In 2001 the country passed a new law giving gay couples equal rights with other married couples under civil law. Under the new law, same-sex couples are able to apply for court approval to adopt children after living together for 3 years, and the law eliminates legal ambiguities on inheritance, pension rights, taxes and divorce.

In 1996, Iceland approved a same-sex domestic partnership law. In Canada same-sex partnerships must be given the same legal benefits given to heterosexual couples who can legally be married. Finland legalized homosexual "unions" giving gay and lesbian couples many of the same rights and responsibilities as married couples, but not the same status. Same-sex couples are also not allowed to adopt children.

Germany passed a same-sex partnership law in the summer of 2001 giving couples access to inheritance and health insurance rights. The law does not give gay partnerships the same tax privileges as heterosexual marriages. In France registered partnerships are available, including tax benefits, public insurance and pension benefits, inheritance and lease protections. Additionally, property acquired together is considered to be jointly owned and partners can demand concurrent vacation schedules. Within Italy, Pisa and Florence allow same-sex couples to register as domestic partners, and within Great Britain, London established the London Partnerships Register for unmarried couples in 2001. The Spanish parliament passed a domestic partner-ship law in 1997 that was similar to the Danish model. In addition to existing laws, many of these countries have signed treaties that recognize each other's registered partnership laws.

Many other countries are considering legislation that would offer some nation-wide protection including Australia, Luxembourg, Portugal, the Czech Republic, Slovenia, and Switzerland. Furthermore, Israel has not yet legalized gay partnerships, however legal decisions appear to be leaning toward such a law including decisions concerning the inheritance rights of the surviving gay partner to the late partner's pension.

South Africa, while not yet providing legal same-sex marriage rights, contains language in its new constitution that bans discrimination on sexual orientation. The Belgium parliament is debating a bill that would legalize gay and lesbian marriages, granting same-sex couples nearly the same legal status as heterosexual couples. Same-sex couples would not be allowed to adopt children. It is expected that the bill will become law in early 2002.

As was the case with employment non-discrimination and domestic partnership benefits, the implementation of "gay marriages" or civil unions extends the social safety net to gay and lesbian couples and establishes a greater level of institutional support for these families. The more extensive civil union legislation requires employers to extend domestic partnership benefits, which, as we have seen, can extend the range of choices available to gay and lesbian couples in terms of their allocation of labor. Civil unions do more than simply create and extend available benefits. They also provide gay and lesbian couples with a legal contract that binds couples together and provides a mechanism for resolution were the partnership to dissolve. With a contract, the couple may be more willing to take risks in terms of their labor allocation and adopt a more traditional division.

Conclusions

Same-sex households tend to allocate their labor in a manner that is more egalitarian than their heterosexual counterparts. In other words, it is much more rare for gay and lesbian couples to exhibit a pattern in which one household member performs for-wage labor in the market, while the other performs non-wage labor in the home. Economists have theorized that this is due to the fact that same-sex couples do not develop comparative advantages based on biological differences, or differences in social norms that lead heterosexual couples to adopt the traditional division of labor. Same-sex couples, for example, are less likely to bear their own children, and are thus, unlikely to support the mother at home caring for her child.

Empirical evidence suggests that while it may be true that same-sex couples do exhibit more egalitarian divisions, that this may be the result not of comparative advantage issues but of institutional constraints. Without access to employment protection, domestic partnership benefits, or legal marriage, same-sex couples might find the risks associated with a traditional division of labor too great. In response, proxy contracts and legal benefits are increasingly being adopted to ensure legal protection for their families. The current changes in the institutional environment faced by gay and lesbian couples (including the increase in employer provision of domestic partnership benefits, civil unions and domestic partner registries) could decrease these constraints. Future research is necessary to examine the long-term effects of informal contracts as well as the changing institutional environment, and their effects on the division of labor in same-sex households.

NOTES

1 Due to the existing wage gap between men and women (Blau and Kahn 1994), hetero-sexual couples are more likely than same-sex couples to have differences in their earnings. Thus, although members of same-sex couples may have differences in their income due, for example, to human capital discrepancies, they will not *necessarily* have differences in their incomes on average.

2 The term "galimony," however, is. Galimony is a descriptive term for what is owed to the "divorced" partner of a rich/famous lesbian, coined after Marilyn Barnett sued Billy Jean King upon the dissolution of their relationship. Martina Navratilova was also sued by her former partner, Judi Nelson upon their break up.

3 ENDA was reintroduced into both the Senate and the House during the summer of 2001. This and other relevant policies will be discussed in greater detail in the section Political Implications.

4 Of course, large differences in income between same-sex partners are possible and may lead to one member gaining bargaining power over the other.

5 This has been coined the "lesbian baby boom."

6 I will follow Bergmann here in using the term "housewife" to refer to either women or men who work at home without wages.

7 Rolande Cuvillier (1979) points out that housewives do, in fact, receive a return on their work in non-cash benefits including room, board, clothing allowances, etc. She character-izes the housewife as an "unjustified financial burden on the community" because he/she receives non-cash benefits that go untaxed.

8 Please see the following Human Rights Campaign report for a detailed description of more than 130 cases of discrimination among gay and lesbian workers in the United States: *Documenting Discrimination* at http://www.hrc.org published 2001.

9 In 1982 Wisconsin became the first state to enact anti-gay employment discrimination. Minneapolis became the first municipality to do the same in 1974.

10 In 1975, AT&T was the first employer to add sexual orientation to its non-discrimination policy. See www.hrc.org/worknet for a complete list of employers.

11 See the International Gay and Lesbian Human Rights Commission at http://www.iglhrc.org for updates on anti-discrimination legislation around the world.

12 In 1992, Lotus Development Corporation became the first publicly traded company to offer such benefits. See www.hrc.org/worknet for a complete list of employers offering at least full medical coverage to domestic partners.

13 The Human Rights Campaign tracks employers with domestic partner benefits through surveys, partnerships with other organizations, news articles and through other informal methods.

14 As a result of the San Francisco Equal Benefits Ordinance 2,707 employers have instituted domestic partner benefits. More information about the specific requirements of the ordinance can be obtained from the San Francisco Human Rights Commission at http://www.ci.sf.ca.us/sfhumanrights/ (Human Rights Campaign 2000: 19). See also http://cityofseattle.net/contract/equalbenefits/, regarding the city of Seattle.

15 For an interesting discussion on the history of lesbian and gay marriages see "Lesbian and Gay Marriage through History and Culture" by Paul Halsall, http://www.bway.net/~halsall/lgbh/lgbh-marriage.html.

REFERENCES

Badgett, M. V. Lee. 1995a. "Gender, Sexuality, and Sexual Orientation: All In the Feminist Family?" *Feminist Economics* 1(1): 121–39.

——. 1995b. "The Wage Effects of Sexual Orientation Discrimination." *Industrial and Labor Relations Review* 48(4): 726–39.

——. 1997a. "Vulnerability in the Workplace: Evidence of Anti-Gay Discrimination." *Angles: The Policy Journal of the Institute for Gay and Lesbian Strategic Studies* 2(1). On-line. Available http://www.iglss.org (August 2001).

——. 1997b. "Beyond Biased Samples: Challenging the Myths on the Economic Status of Lesbians and Gay Men," in Amy Gluckman and Betsy Reed (eds.) *Homo Economics: Capitalism, Community, and Lesbian and Gay Life*. London: Routledge.

——. 2000. "Calculating Costs with Credibility: Health Care Benefits for Domestic Partners." *Angles: The Policy Journal of the Institute for Gay and Lesbian Strategic Studies* 5(1). On-line. Available http://www.iglss.org (August 2001).

——. 2001. *Money, Myths, and Change: The Economic Lives of Lesbians and Gay Men*. Chicago and London: The University of Chicago Press.

Badgett, M. V. Lee, Colleen Donnelly, and Jennifer Kibbe. 1992. *Pervasive Patterns of Discrimination Against Lesbians and Gay Men: Evidence from Surveys Across the United States*. National Gay and Lesbian Task Force Policy Institute. New York.

Badgett, M. V. Lee and Josh Goldfoot. 1996. "For Richer, for Poorer; The Freedom to Marry Debate." *Angles: The Policy Journal of the Institute for Gay and Lesbian Strategic Studies* 1(2). On-line. Available http://www.iglss.org (August 2001).

Becker, Gary. 1981. *A Treatise on the Family*. Cambridge: Harvard University Press.

Bell, Alan P. and Martin S. Weinberg. 1978. *Homosexualities: A study of diversity among men and women*. New York: Simon & Schuster.

Bergmann, Barbara. 1981. "The Economic Risks of Being a Housewife." *American Economic Review* May: 81–6.

Blau, D. Francine and Lawrence Kahn. 1994. "Rising Wage Inequality and the US Gender Gap." *American Economic Review* 84(2): 23–8.

Blau, Francine D., Marianne A. Ferber, and Anne E. Winkler. 1998. *The Economics of Women, Men and Work* (3rd edition). Upper Saddle River, NJ: Prentice Hall.

Blumstein, Phillip and Pepper Schwartz. 1983. *American Couples: Money, Work and Sex*. New York: William Morrow.

Chan, Raymond W., Risa C. Brooks, Barbara Raboy, and Charlotte J. Patterson. 1998. "Division of Labor Among Lesbian and Heterosexual Parents: Associations With Children's Adjustment." *Journal of Family Psychology* 12(3): 402–19.

Clinton, President William J. 1997. Speech to First National Dinner, the Human Rights Campaign November 8.

Clunis, D. Merilee and G. Dorsey Green. 1988. *Lesbian Couples*. Seattle: Seal Press.

Cuvillier, Rolande. 1979. "The Housewife – An Unjustified Financial Burden on the Community." *Journal of Social Policy* 8: 1–26.

Curry, Hayden and Dennis Clifford. 1992. *A Legal Guide For Lesbian and Gay Couples*. Berkeley, Berkeley: Nolo Press.

Desaulniers, S. 1991. "The Organization of Housework in Lesbian Households," paper presented at the Canadian Women's Studies Association Learned Societies, Queen's University, Kingston.

Dunne, Gillian A. 1998a. "Pioneers Behind Our Own Front Doors: New Models for the Organization of Work in Partnerships." *The Journal of Work Employment and Society* 12(2).

——. 1998b. "A Passion for 'Sameness': Sexuality and Gender Accountability," in E. Silva and C. Smart (eds.) *The 'New' Family?* London: Sage.

England, Paula and George Farkas. 1986. *Households, Employment, and Gender: A Social, Economic and Demographic View*. New York: Aldine De Gruyter.

England, Paula and Barbara Stanek Kilbourne. 1990. "Markets, Marriages, and Other Mates: The Problem of Power," in Roger Friedland and A. F. Robertson (eds.) *Beyond the Marketplace*. New York: Aldine de Gruyter.

Ferber, Marianne A. and Bonnie G. Birnbaum. 1977. "The 'New Home Economics': Retrospects and Prospects." *Journal of Consumer Research* 4(1): 19–28.

Folbre, Nancy. 1994. *Who Pays for the Kids?: Gender and the Structures of Constraint*. New York and London: Routledge.

Giddings, Lisa A. 1998. "Political Economy and the Construction of Gender: The Example of Housework Within Same-Sex Households." *Feminist Economics* 4(2): 97–106.

Human Rights Campaign (HRC). 2001. On-line. Available http://www.hrc.org (August 2001).

Human Rights Campaign (HRC). 2000. *The State of the Workplace for Lesbian, Gay, Bisexual, and Transgendered Americans*. Washington, DC. On-line. Available http://www.hrc.org (August 2001).

James, Steven E. and Bianca Cody Murphy. 1998. "Gay and Lesbian Relationships in a Changing Social Context," in Charlotte J. Patterson and Anthony R. D'Augelli (eds.) *Lesbian, Gay, and Bisexual Identities in Families: Psychological Perspectives*. Oxford, New York: Oxford University Press.

Kennedy, Elizabeth Lapovsky and Madeline D. Davis. 1993. *Boots of Leather, Slippers of Gold: The History of a Lesbian Community*. New York: Routlege.

Klawitter, Marieka and Victor Flatt. 1998. "The Effects of State and Local Antidiscrimination Policies for Sexual Discrimination." *Journal of Policy Analysis and Management* 17 (Fall): 658–86.

Kurdek, Lawrence. 1993. "The Allocation of Household Labor in Gay, Lesbian and Heterosexual Married Couples." *Journal of Social Issues* 49(3): 127–39.

——. 1995. "Lesbian and Gay Couples," in Anthony R. D'Augelli and Charlotte J. Patterson (eds.) *Lesbian, Gay, and Bisexual Identities Over the Lifespan: Psychological Perspectives*. Oxford, New York: Oxford University Press.

Manser, Marilyn and Murray Brown. 1980. "Marriage and Household Decision-Making: A Bargaining Analysis." *International Economic Review* 21(1): 31–44.

Mitchell, V. 1996. "Two Moms: Contribution of the Planned Lesbian Family to the Deconstruction of Gendered Parenting," in J. Laird and R. J. Green (eds.) *Lesbians and Gays in Couples and Families: A Handbook for Therapists*. San Francisco: Jossey-Bass.

Oerton, Sarah. 1998. "Reclaiming the 'Housewife'?: Lesbians and Household Work." *Journal of Lesbian Studies* 2(4): 69–83.

Patterson, Charlotte J. 1992. "Children of Lesbian and Gay Parents." *Child Development* 63: 1025–42.

——. 1994. "Children of the Lesbian Baby Boom: Behavioral Adjustment, Self-concepts, and Sex Role Identity," in B. Greene and G. M. Herek (eds.) *Lesbian and Gay Psychology: Theory, Research, and Clinical Applications.* Newbury Park, CA: Sage Publications.

——. 1995. "Families of the Lesbian Baby Boom: Parents' Division of Labor and Children's Adjustment." *Developmental Psychology* 31: 115–23.

——. 1998. "The Family Lives of Children Born to Lesbian Mothers," in Charlotte J. Patterson and Anthony R. D'Augelli (eds.) *Lesbian, Gay, and Bisexual Identities in Families: Psychological Perspectives.* Oxford, New York: Oxford University Press.

Patterson, Charlotte J., Susan Hurt and Chandra Mason. Forthcoming. "Families of the Lesbian Baby Boom: Children's Contacts with Grandparents and other Adults." *American Journal of Orthopsychiatry* (invited paper for special issue on sexual orientation and families).

Peace, H. F. 1993. "The Pretended Family – A Study of the Division of Domestic Labour in Lesbian Families." Leicester University Discussion Papers in Sociology, No. S93/3.

Peplau, Letitia A. and S. D. Cochran. 1990. "A Relationship Perspective in Homosexuality," in David P. McWhirter, Stephanie A. Sanders, and June M. Reinisch (eds.) *Homosexuality/ Heterosexuality: Concepts of Sexuality.* New York: Oxford University Press.

Polikoff, Nancy D. 1990. "This child does have two mothers: Redefining Parenthood to Meet the Needs of Children in Lesbian Mother and Other Nontraditional Families." *Georgetown Law Review* 78: 459–575.

Pollak, Robert A. 1985. "A Transaction Approach to Families and Households." *Journal of Economic Literature* 29(2): 581–608.

Riley, C. 1988. "American Kinship: A Lesbian Account." *Feminist Issues* 8: 75–94.

Tasker, F. L. and Susan Golombok. 1991. "Children Raised by Lesbian Mothers: The Empirical Evidence." *Family Law* 21: 184–7.

Weston, Kath. 1991. *Families We Choose: Lesbians, Gays, Kinship.* New York: Columbia University Press.

Part IV

The Economics of Childbearing and Childcaring

Chapter 6

Economic Theories of Fertility
Diane Macunovich

In the early stages of economic development, in most countries women averaged six to seven births during their reproductive years, but in country after country as development progresses, this number falls to two or even fewer births per woman.[1] What causes this decline? Although many initially assumed that births would remain low after this "fertility transition," most western nations experienced a "baby boom" after World War II that took the average number of births up to four or more, followed by a baby bust with birth rates well below the "replacement level" of 2.1 births per woman.[2] Can we expect more baby booms, or will fertility rates continue to fall, eventually leading to declining world population – and what role does economics play in bringing about these changes?

Table 6.1 describes measures that are usually used to describe fertility, and figure 6.1 illustrates the general pattern of fertility in the western industrialized nations over the past 150 years, using as examples the experience in England and Wales and the United States. Depicted in figure 6.1 is the Total Fertility Rate (TFR): a synthetic measure representing the number of children a woman would have in a lifetime spent at current age-specific fertility rates. All of the western nations first experienced a fertility transition – the long decline in fertility that culminated in the extremely low rates observed in the 1930s – and then some type of baby boom in the post World War II period.

Analysts very often treat these two aspects of fertility change – the fertility transition and the baby boom – as separate phenomena, assuming that different factors are responsible for each. We examine that assumption in this chapter and in the process try to isolate the effects of economic and non-economic factors.

What are some of the non-economic factors? Most of them can be subsumed under the heading of "changing values": for example, the growth of individualism, declining

Table 6.1 Definitions of various measures and phrases used in discussing fertility

Measure or Phrase	Numerator	Denominator
Crude Birth Rate (CBR)	Total births in a given year	Total population in the same year
General Fertility Rate (GFR)	Total births in a given year	Total number of women aged 15–49
Age specific birth rates	Total births in a given year to women of a specific age	Total number of women in that specific age group
Total Fertility Rate (TFR)	Calculated by summing all *age specific birth rates* in a given year, from 15 through 49	
Replacement level fertility	TFR = 2.1	
Fecundability	A woman's physical capacity to conceive and bear children, given that she is having sexual intercourse.	
Fertility transition	The decline from very high to replacement or very low levels of fertility that occurs along with each country's economic development. All nations are believed to have entered or completed this transition as of the beginning of the twenty-first century.	
Demographic transition[3]	The fertility transition in combination with a "mortality transition" in which mortality rates decline from very high to very low levels, especially at younger ages. In nearly every country's experience the mortality transition has preceded the fertility transition.	
Population momentum	The population increases represented by a large birth cohort when it enters its own reproductive phase, even at a reduced fertility rate.	
The Great Population Spike[4]	The one period in human history when it is hypothesized that the human race will experience any significant growth, roughly from 1775 to 2075.	

religious values and marriage rates, increasing materialism in a consumer society (arguably an economic factor), improved contraceptives, environmental concerns, and the increasing desire for "quality" over "quantity" in children.[5] This point of view can be seen, in the US, at least as far back as 1893:

> In the struggle for what is deemed a desirable mode of existence at the present day, marriage is being held less desirable, and its bonds less sacred, than they were forty years ago. Young women are gradually being imbued with the idea that marriage and motherhood are not to be their chief objects in life, or the sole methods of obtaining subsistence; that they should aim at being independent of possible or actual husbands, and should fit themselves to earn their own living...[and] that housekeeping is a sort of domestic slavery... (John Billings 1893: 281–2).

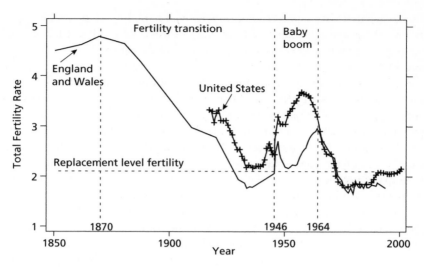

Figure 6.1   Patterns of fertility

Many of these factors are susceptible to changes in economic conditions, and it is usually by including economic fluctuations that the baby boom is explained as a component of the longer-term trend. That is, fertility rose in response to postwar euphoria combined with a booming economy and incentives like the GI Bill. It is harder to explain the baby bust in those same terms, however, since fertility rates began to decline in the late 1950s, long before the economic slump of the 1970s.

Another factor often cited as the reason for the sharp decline in Western fertility in the 1960s and 1970s is the modern contraceptive pill. Fertility, however, began to decline in the late 1950s, long before the Pill became widely available. And although the Pill made fertility control easier, we know that women have been capable of controlling their fertility – when they choose to – since at least the 1930s, when US fertility rates were about as low as they are now (and many European rates were even lower), and even as early as the nineteenth century.

> The availability of modern coitus-independent means of fertility control played no role in producing below-replacement fertility in the United States in the late nineteenth century. Such means of fertility control were not available in the late nineteenth century. Even without these modern methods, ever-married urban white women of native parentage born in 1846–55 and living in the Northeast in 1900 had an average of 3.0 live births over their reproductive span. (Warren Sanderson 1987: 307)

There are costs associated both with having children, and with preventing pregnancy (whether psychic or monetary or simply those associated with the inconvenience of using various contraceptive methods). The Pill simply reduced the latter costs, but if the costs associated with children (net of perceived benefits) are perceived to be sufficiently low, the relatively small cost reduction afforded by the Pill will not play a significant role in fertility and labor force participation decisions.

Many non-economists find it difficult to accept the idea that fertility decisions might be "explained" using economic models – but economists have long accepted that such models are appropriate, and have devoted considerable effort to their development. While they generally agree on the relevance of such an approach, there is considerable disagreement about the form the model should take. One of the most perplexing problems for economists has been the appearance of a decline in fertility as income rises, implying that children are an "inferior" good, in an economic sense – which to many people is an unpalatable assumption. After all, it does not bode well for the human race if children are an inferior good as incomes keep rising!

Economists have developed two primary models to explain how fertility might respond to economic factors. Both are based on the common assumption of an underlying positive relationship between income and fertility, and both attempt to put forward explanations for the negative relationship, which has often been observed in modern experience. Both in turn attempt to explain the postwar baby boom and bust. They differ fundamentally, however, in their identification of the driving force behind these movements, as indicated by the labels used to describe them: the "price of time" model and the Easterlin or "relative income" model. In this chapter, I consider these two models in both the industrialized and developing country contexts, as well as racial differences in fertility and the "problem" of teen pregnancy.

Economic models tend to treat the decision to have children as similar to the choice to purchase "consumer durables" like cars or refrigerators. Many non-economists have objected to this approach, pointing out that while one can trade in a car if it's unsatisfactory the same isn't true for children. But it is important to bear in mind that an economic approach does not preclude considerations of things like love between partners and by them for their children, pride taken in children's accomplishments, and the importance of family ties. It simply abstracts from these other factors (which are usually thought of as components of individuals' preferences for children), and tries to estimate the effects of changes in economic conditions holding all of these other factors constant.

Female Labor Force Participation and the Need for an Exogenous Wage

Before we turn to the two primary models, it is important to address the relationship between fertility and female labor force participation. You will often encounter the claim that low birth rates have resulted from women's increased labor force participation, but you are equally likely to hear that it is the other way around: fertility declined, and therefore women were "freed up" to enter the labor force. This turns out to be like explaining the upward motion of a pendulum by saying that it was caused by the preceding downward motion. This is a "chicken or egg" problem, and if we want to develop a truly causal model we must delve more deeply; that is, by identifying the factor(s) that initiated one or the other – or both.

Most often people assume that changes in the female wage were the causal factor: women's wages rose, attracting women into the labor force and at the same time causing them to reduce their fertility through mechanisms discussed in the next section on the "price of time" model. But a problem arises here because the wage is not exogenous; that is, changes in the wage are likely caused by changes in the women's own behavior. If wage increases were caused by women themselves (by increasing their level of education, for example, or by amassing more experience in the labor market, on average) then we are left with another "chicken or egg" problem: we have to explain *why* women decided to change their behavior *when they did*.

Perhaps an example will help here. Imagine that there are only three types of jobs available in the labor market, depending on level of education, and women were offered, on average, $5 per hour if they had less than a high school education, $10 per hour for high school graduates and $15 per hour for college graduates. Suppose there are currently an equal number of women in each type of job, so the average "observed" female wage is $10 per hour. Suddenly, the number of women in the labor market is doubled by a group of younger women just entering who are more highly educated: half are high school graduates and half are college graduates, so the average wage among new market entrants is $12.50, and the average observed wage among all women in the labor market becomes $11.25.

The typical media report on a development like this would point to the increase in average wages from $10 to $11.25 – and particularly the increase among new market entrants (wow! a 25 percent increase!) – suggesting that it had caused the change in women's behavior. But the actual wage paid for any given job had not changed, so it cannot explain either the desire by younger women to achieve a higher level of education at that point in time, or their desire to participate in the labor market in greater proportions. This is the situation that occurred in the US after about 1973: although real wages had risen markedly during the 1960s, there was little if any increase, for a given job, after that period. Yet, because women's average level of education and average years of experience increased, the observed wage rose quite dramatically.

The "Price of Time" Model

Economists have long been aware that there are two effects when income rises: an "income effect" that causes us to purchase more of all "normal" goods, and a "price effect" as rising hourly wages raise the "opportunity cost" of any activities requiring an expenditure of our time. The opportunity cost of any activity is the value to us of the "next best" thing we might have done with our time; thus the opportunity cost of time spent with children might be thought of as the wage that is foregone by not working outside the home. In this context, women's time – its value and whether or not it's spent in labor market activities – is crucial in determining levels of fertility.

Gary Becker – a Nobel prize laureate – and his colleague Jacob Mincer applied these concepts (of "income" and "price" effects of one's wage) in the context of "production" within the home, pointing out that households produce utility for their members using inputs of purchased goods in combination with the time of the household's members.[6] That is, a pair of skis gives utility only if we spend the time to use them, thus the cost of obtaining utility from them includes not just the price of the skis (together with things like lift tickets), but also the price – the opportunity cost – of our time spent skiing. In this sense, all goods that we purchase and use involve an expenditure of our time. Becker and Mincer pointed out that children are *more time intensive* than other goods: that is, the opportunity cost of children represents a higher proportion of their total cost, than does the opportunity cost of most other goods. As a result, as our incomes rise the cost of children rises more rapidly than the cost of other goods and services. This was initially expected to "explain" the fact that the demand for children falls as incomes rise: the price effect might outweigh the income effect of increasing income.

The price of time model assumes that since childcare has traditionally been predominately a woman's responsibility, men's earnings should have almost exclusively an "income effect" on fertility – that is, a positive effect – while women's earnings should have a "price," or negative, effect. This effect might be significant both during the fertility transition in the early stages of economic development, as well as during baby booms and busts in industrialized nations. In poorer economies, for example, women's status and level of education generally increase with development (both in absolute terms as well as relative to men), causing the opportunity cost of children to rise as well. This increase in cost might outstrip the rate of growth of incomes more generally, leading fertility to decline even as income rises in developing countries.

During the postwar 1940s and 1950s in more developed economies, proponents of the price of time model suggest, women's wages likely had little effect on fertility. Women were displaced by men returning from the military, and female labor force participation was low. Thus women's wages did not rise as rapidly as men's.[7] Conversely, it is assumed that women's wages rose more rapidly than men's in the 1960s and 1970s, and in addition the strong increase in women's labor force participation dramatically increased the relative importance of women's wages, producing a net negative effect on fertility in those decades.[8]

Studies over the years indicate that the price of time effect is not enough to explain all of the changes in fertility that have occurred over time. Critics have pointed out other shortcomings, most notably the fact that mothers often do not provide all of their children's care: fathers provide an increasingly significant share, and as women's

Table 6.2   Terminology used to refer to various types of income

Wage	Hourly pay
Earnings	Annual pay (wage × hours worked in a year)
Non-earned income	Income received from sources other than paid labor, such as rent, interest and dividends. The term is also used to refer to an individual's "share" of his/her spouse's income.
Income	Money received by an individual from all sources, both earned and non-earned.

incomes rise they find themselves able to purchase replacements for their own services in the home: nursery school, cooks, housekeepers, and so on. In this sense, then, rising women's wages make it more rather than less likely that they will combine motherhood and a career: their wages would have a stronger income effect, and a weaker price effect, on the demand for children.

Thus, Becker and Nigel Tomes (1976) augments the price of time model with a "quantity : quality" argument: potential parents can tradeoff quantity for quality. Parents have a demand for quality as well as quantity of children, and then as income rises the demand for quality rises more rapidly than the demand for quantity. Critics of this hypothesis maintain that parents are not free to choose any level of quality – for example, to choose six "low quality" children rather than three "high quality" children. Instead, they are constrained by their own education and standard of living to a given level, or at least range, of quality.

The Concept of "Relative Income"

Researchers have repeatedly demonstrated that people evaluate their income in *relative* as well as in absolute terms. For example, one recent study found that, given a choice between a world in which survey respondents have more of a good than everyone else, and one in which everyone (including the respondent) has more but the respondent has less than everyone else, half of respondents preferred to have *50 percent less real income*, but high relative income (Sara Solnick and David Hemenway 1998). Similarly, other researchers have found that subjects in experiments are willing to pay out of their own winnings in order to reduce the winnings of others, and that this decision to "burn" others is relatively insensitive to the "price" of burning.

"Relative income" in Richard Easterlin's model refers to young adults' earnings relative to their material aspirations – their desired standard of living.[9] He focuses specifically on preference formation among young adults: those just making initial and often formative decisions regarding labor force entry, household formation, marriage and fertility.[10] What criteria do they apply when evaluating their own earning potential in terms of its ability to support their desired lifestyle? To what standard of living do they aspire? Although a multitude of influences probably impinge on preferences at this stage in life – those associated with siblings, personal and occupational peers, geographical area and socio-economic reference groups, to name a few – Easterlin drew on the literature in sociology and psychology to suggest that an obvious one, and one probably highly significant and fairly easy to quantify, must be the standard of living enjoyed in their parents' home.

In general, Easterlin postulated a systematic shift in preferences resulting from each successive generation, under economic development, experiencing a successively higher parental standard of living. "In effect, a . . . 'subsistence level' constraint is added to the analysis of [fertility behavior] along with the budget line and production constraints"[11] (Easterlin 1978: 115). In other words, an individual's sense of wellbeing associated with a real annual income of, say, $20,000 will be different if that individual is living in the year 2000, rather than in 1920 – because the individual's expected standard of living would be different in the two periods. Because of this "subsistence level" constraint, economic or demographic fluctuations could cause periodic reversals in the secular downtrend in fertility, such as that observed in the developed countries in the postwar period.

In the historical context young men's earnings have been viewed by a young couple as the primary component of their own total income, the basic determinant of their own standard of living. Thus Easterlin focuses primarily on *male* relative income, defined as young *men's* earnings relative to the material aspirations of young adults. Male relative income in the United States is characterized by a sharp decline from 1970 to 1985 followed by a brief increase and another decline, with some improvement occurring again after 1995. During this period young white men in the United States experienced, on average, a 40 percent decline in their relative income, while young African Americans experienced a *60 percent decline*.[12]

Effects of Relative Cohort Size on Relative Income

The word cohort originally denoted a type of Roman military unit, like a platoon, but is now used to refer to a group of people who have banded together in a common cause, or who share some common statistical characteristic. Easterlin's model focuses on "birth cohorts": individuals who were born in the same year or period and who will thus experience all of the various stages of the life cycle at about the same time. A crucial aspect is the size of a given cohort relative to that of its parents' cohort – hence "relative cohort size."

Although relative cohort size may have significant effects at many points in the life cycle, the focus in Easterlin's model is at the point of labor market entry, when members of a given cohort are in their late teens and early twenties, just emerging from high school or college. In the United States over the past 50 years relative cohort size at this point of labor market entry has been halved (during the 1950s), then doubled (in the 1970s), and then halved again (in the 1990s). Currently – looking at the cohort just entering the labor market in the beginning of the twenty-first century – relative cohort size is about 1 : 2. Relative cohort size is a direct function of fertility rates at any given time : high (low) fertility produces large (small) relative cohort size.

Studies have demonstrated that the primary effect of relative birth cohort size is on male relative income, acting through changes in the ratio of young men's earnings relative to their fathers' earnings (Welch 1979; Smith and Welch 1981; and Macunovich 1999). This effect occurs largely because young, less experienced workers are not perfect substitutes in the labor market for older, more experienced workers, and the "production function" is sensitive to the balance of these two types of workers.

If there is an oversupply of one type of worker relative to the other (think of it as an oversupply of assembly-line workers relative to management) the wages of the oversupplied group will tend to go down relative to the wages of the undersupplied group. This will occur even in a period of strong economic growth: in that case the wages of both groups might rise, but on average the wages of the oversupplied group will not rise as rapidly as those of the undersupplied group. In addition, the age group in greater relative supply will experience increased levels of unemployment and part-time employment, leading – through the "discouraged worker effect" – to reduced labor force participation rates among those in the oversupplied group.

How Fertility is Hypothesized to Adjust to Changes in Relative Income

What happens in a society when these relative earnings decline sharply – as they did from the 1960s through the 1980s in the United States, and possibly in the West as a whole? In general male relative income in the United States declined by close to 50 percent – 60 percent for African-Americans. Among young African-American men relative income fell by 50 percent for college graduates and nearly *85 percent* for high school dropouts.

We assume that individuals are ultimately concerned with *per capita disposable income*, relative to their desired standard of living. An individual evaluates his/her earning potential as dictated by the market: how much s/he can earn by and for him or herself. Given this level of personal earnings, an individual then decides how many people can be supported on that income: self only? self plus spouse? self and spouse with children? Per capita disposable income is what is available to the individual and his/her dependents after making these demographic choices.

In the relative income model, individuals focus on this per capita disposable income and make the necessary adjustments to keep it on a par with material aspirations. In an attempt to close the gap between income and aspirations, members of relatively large cohorts will tend to make a number of adjustments including increased female labor force participation and delayed/reduced marriage – and along with this they will choose to have fewer children in order to spread their income over fewer heads. This model replaces the common assumption that declining fertility and marriage rates resulted from changes in female labor force participation – or vice versa – with the assumption that all three behavioral shifts were at least in part a response to changes in relative income. In addition, considerations covered by the price of time model's "quantity:quality" trade-off are addressed in the relative income model by the fact that the quality of child desired by a young couple will be a function of their rising material aspirations.

Easterlin hypothesized that young adults in the 1950s, who were born and raised in the Depression and war years, set a lower threshold on average than young adults in the 1960s and 1970s, who were raised in the affluent postwar years (Easterlin 1987). Compounding this effect of changing tastes, young adults in the 1950s were members of a very small birth cohort (product of the 1930s baby bust) relative to the size of the rest of the labor force, so that their wages were driven up relative to those of older workers in their parents' generation.[13] The result was higher wages relative to their own (already low) material aspirations, making children appear very affordable. Thus young couples in the 1950s entered enthusiastically into marriage and family formation, causing the postwar baby boom. The bust, according to the relative income model, occurred when those baby boomers flooded the labor market 20 years later, depressing their own wages relative to those of their parents – and thus relative to their own expectations.

In addition to its application to the baby boom and bust, the relative income model sheds light on the problem of out-of-wedlock fertility among teens and young adults. When a pressured generation chooses to delay/forego marriage, more young women will be at risk of non-marital pregnancy. This factor, together with delayed/reduced fertility within marriage – also a function of relative income – means that an increased proportion of all births will be outside of marriage. This would explain to a great extent the rash of out-of-wedlock fertility that has occurred in the US since the 1970s, as well as its marked decline in the 1990s.

But Haven't Gender Roles Changed?

Objections have been raised to what some have interpreted as the portrayal of young women as able to achieve fulfillment only through marriage and childbearing, the depiction of marital bonds as dependent on children, and the emphasis on *male* relative incomes. It is felt that this characterization is no longer relevant to the young women of today: they will no longer treat affluence merely as an opportunity to marry and have children.

But has society today really moved so far from traditional gender roles? A 1995 Gallup Poll of adults in 22 countries indicated a surprising tenacity among Americans, in terms of traditional gender roles: it reported that "nearly half of the

Americans surveyed said the ideal family structure was one in which only the father earned the living and the mother stayed home with the children" (T. Lewin 1994: A1). A more recent study concluded

> Our findings suggest that only the male partner's economic resources affect the transition [from cohabitation] to marriage, with positive economic situations accelerating marriage and deterring separation. Our results imply that despite trends toward egalitarian gender-role attitudes and increasing income provision among women, cohabiting men's economic circumstances carry far more weight than women's in marriage formation. (Pamela Smock and Wendy Manning 1997: 331).

It could be argued however, that despite the tendency among the population generally, young people's attitudes have become more progressive in the last few decades. Several surveys of Williams College students between 1990 and 1995 seem to suggest otherwise. The results have been remarkably consistent over this period:[14]

1. The average desired number of children consistently falls between 2.3 and 2.5 among both women and men, and whereas Easterlin (1987: 11) reports that in a "recent survey on young adults...three out of every four single women aged eighteen to twenty-one expected to have at least two children," among Williams College students this figure reaches over 85 percent for women, and 89 percent for men.

2. Ninety-six percent of men and 91 percent of women expect to marry, with average intended age at marriage 26.7 years for both sexes. These proportions are considerably higher than the 75 percent reported for American high school seniors in the 1970s and 1980s (Eileen Crimmins et al. 1991).

3. Average expected age at birth of the first child is 28.7 for men and 28.8 for women: on average these young women do *not* expect to delay childbearing until after they have established themselves in a career. A surprising 85 percent expect to have their first child by age 30 – 96 percent by age 33. Perhaps even more surprisingly, the corresponding figures for the men are 81 percent and 96 percent.

4. Respondents were asked to rank the following possible career arrangements for parents in the presence of young children:
   (a)   both parents work full-time outside the home
   (b)   both parents work part-time
   (c)   wife full-time and husband part-time
   (d)   husband full-time and wife part-time
   (e)   husband full-time and wife at home
   (f)   wife full-time and husband at home
Men ranked (d) and (e) highest and (a) lowest, while women ranked (b) highest, (d) second highest and (a) lowest.

5. Young women indicated that they would on average work about 43 hours per week before having children, but then intended to cut back on average to about 22 hours per week when children were under three years old. Young men on average

shared these expectations for their wives, although they had a much higher tendency than the women to expect wives to drop out of the labor force altogether, or work 20 hours per week or less when children were young.

6.   Among young men, there was a statistically significant difference between those whose fathers had stayed at home full-time for some portion of their childhood, and those with full-time career dads, in intentions regarding their own participation in childcare. Those with stay-at-home fathers (7 percent of the sample) intended to cut back from 44 hours per week outside the home, to 30 hours per week, while those with career dads intended to cut back only to 40 hours per week on average when children are under three.

These survey results paint a picture of fairly traditional family aspirations among Williams College students in 1995, with the only concession to women's career aspirations being a somewhat later age at the birth of the first child, and the mutual acceptance of mothers' part-time work outside the home when children are young.

Improving on These Models: The Importance of the Female Wage

Fertility failed to increase in the 1980s as Easterlin's relative income model had projected, and some suggest his model errs by ignoring effects of the female wage. Similarly, significant problems have been identified in assumptions used to estimate women's wages in the primary studies testing the price of time model. Women's wages did not increase as assumed, after controlling for changing levels of education and experience (Diane Macunovich 1995). In addition, even using its original wage series the price of time model failed to predict the actual course of fertility after the mid-1970s, suggesting that it should continue falling into the 1980s. As it turned out, fertility rates in the United States at that time simply stabilized, and have not changed greatly until very recently.

More recent work brings together the price of time and relative income models, testing for effects of both relative income and women's wages on young women's age-specific fertility rates – particularly that of women in their twenties, because as explained earlier the relative income theory is expected to be most relevant at younger ages.[15] This work not only includes the female wage (controlling for education and experience), it also allows for changes in its net effect over time. In theory, the female wage is expected to exert both a positive (income) and a negative (price of time) effect on fertility. In practice, however, proponents of the price of time model expect that any positive effect would be greatly outweighed by its negative effect. In addition, they have tended to ignore that theory dictates an increasingly dominant income (positive) effect with rising wages and hours worked. The effect of an hourly wage increase is magnified, in terms of additional income produced, as hours of work increase (since income = wage × hours) – and at the same time, the marginal utility of non-work hours/activities rises as individuals work longer hours. An individual in these circumstances has more income to spend, and one of the most important things to spend it on will tend to be time for non-work activities.

In addition to the standard theoretical explanation underlying an increasingly positive effect of the female wage on fertility over the last century, it is possible to imagine at least two others. The first has to do with a declining negative – price of time – effect of the wage. This negative price effect depends on the assumption that a woman is the primary provider of childcare: every hour she spends in childcare will "cost" her the foregone wage. To the extent that alternative (purchased) methods of childcare are both available and socially acceptable, this negative price effect will be diminished: a woman can work the extra hour and pay for a replacement for her time in the home. We have certainly observed the development of such conditions over the past 30 years.[16]

Secondly, the positive income effect of the female wage tends to be higher, all other things equal, the higher the woman's material aspirations. Why? Because the perceived value of her non-labor income (income from sources other than her own wages) appears diminished relative to those higher material aspirations, and her participation in the labor force is thus higher, all other factors equal. As mentioned above, the income effect of an individual's wage strengthens with increased time in the labor force. In addition, to the extent that marriage is delayed/foregone in a period of low male relative income, fewer women will have husbands as a source of non-labor income. In that event, even the absolute value of women's non-earned income will decline, on average – resulting, again, in higher female labor force participation rates, all other things equal. Women's greater number of hours in the labor force in both cases will tend to increase the income effect of a wage increase, since income equals the hourly wage times number of hours worked.

The combined "relative income and price of time" model explains the observed pattern of fertility in the second half of the twentieth century in the United States, and estimates a strongly positive effect of male relative income and a strong underlying negative price effect of the female wage. Interaction terms in the model show that the price effect of the female wage has been declining over time, while its income effect has been increasing with declining male relative income (Macunovich 1996, 1998b).

The combined model also provides an explanation for differences between African-American and white fertility and marriage patterns during this time. The relative income of African-American males was more than one-third *higher* than that of whites in the late 1960s and early 1970s. Young African-American males would have felt themselves to be in a better position than whites relative to their own material aspirations during that period. This could have been an important factor in establishing the notable differences between African-Americans and whites in terms of age at first birth and age at marriage. The decline in African-American male relative income in the 1970s was much more pronounced than that of whites – and was then followed by a much stronger recovery in the late 1980s. (This was also true for young men at lower levels of education.) In addition, both men and women in the African-American community enjoyed a pronounced economic recovery after 1985 – at the same time that African-American women's fertility rose more sharply than white women's.

The Fertility Transition

This chapter has largely focused on fertility fluctuations in a more developed country context. Are these concepts relevant at earlier stages of economic development? Economists think that they are. Many studies have found a significant price effect of rising women's wages in these contexts – although in the absence of reliable data on women's hourly wages (these did not even become available in the United States until 1976!) researchers often use education levels to estimate a woman's earning potential. Some attempts have also been made to include indicators of women's status, the idea being that as women gain more status in the home, through an increased ability to work outside the home and contribute to household income, they will have more say in family planning decisions – and perhaps even more importantly will no longer have to rely on their reproductive capacity to justify their own existence.

Education is seen as a significant factor in its own right, as well. Researchers tend to find a U-shaped effect of education on fertility: both low and high levels of education produce relatively high fertility, while middle levels (such as the completion of grade school) result in the lowest levels of fertility. Although this may seem counterintuitive, the explanation given is that the first few years of education contribute to women's basic knowledge of nutrition, the causes of disease, and the functioning of their own bodies, and as a result produce a healthier population in which mortality and morbidity levels are reduced and women's fecundability rises. Middle levels of education then provide the "price effect" as women's potential earnings rise – and also enable women to understand and accept a wider array of contraceptive methods. And at the highest levels of education it is possible that the "income effect" of women's wages – which gives them the ability to purchase low-cost replacements for their own time with children – might become more significant.

Researchers have also established that other factors peculiar to the institutional context in developing countries are probably also very significant in triggering the fertility transition.[17] The most important of these is probably the rapid reduction in infant mortality that occurs with development: couples find that they need fewer births in order to achieve a given number of surviving children, and women's education plays a significant role in bringing about such reductions in infant mortality.

In rural areas prior to economic development, children are often seen as a source of income, over and above any costs the parents might incur. They can help out in agriculture and in the home, and in the absence of governmental programs for old age security (social security or pension plans, for example) children provide parents with a source of support at older ages. This situation changes dramatically with development, however, as the population urbanizes and children are required to attend school: suddenly children become a net burden rather than a benefit, in economic terms. Thus as development proceeds the "demand" for surviving children declines and the number of births needed to fill that demand falls.

The issue of "population explosion" that we so often associate with developing countries is thought to be an integral part of this process. Prior to economic development couples' "demand" for children is actually higher than their ability to "supply," given infertility due to malnutrition and illness, and high rates of infant mortality. Thus the number of surviving children tends to increase in the early stages of development until the rising net cost of children begins to reduce the demand for them, in economic parlance. That initial larger birth cohort then provides what is termed "population momentum," in the sense that even if its members exhibit lower birth rates themselves they will still produce another large cohort. This initial burst of fertility has been the cause of most of the significant population increase that the human race has ever experienced – in the currently developed nations as well as in the less developed ones. One writer has coined the phrase "the Great Population Spike" to describe the fact that overall rates of population increase on earth were negligible before about 1776, and are expected to be so again after about 2076, but in between those dates the growth rate soars as each country goes through its "demographic transition" (Walt Rostow 1998).

While researchers have established a number of factors that seem to be important in the process of fertility transition, they have not been able to discern what triggers the initiation of the transition in the first place. Countries began the transition over a wide range of infant mortality rates, levels of income, degrees of female emancipation, and levels of urbanization: there does not seem to be any pattern, nor does there seem to be any pattern to the rate of decline once it has begun.

The cost of fertility regulation, in relation to the perceived cost of an "excess supply" of children, might be important.[18] In this sense, the cost of fertility regulation includes not just the monetary cost, but also such factors as the ease of access to fertility clinics, the psychological stress involved in contravening any social and religious norms, and the physical inconvenience associated with implementation. In many countries, prior to the initiation of fertility decline there is little or no individual control of fertility; rather, any control that occurs takes the form of "social sanctions" – for example, with regard to the "appropriate" age of marriage. Easterlin (1978: 123) suggests:

> It is possible that the emergence of a pressure for fertility limitation is one of the first forms in which modernization comes to impinge directly on the mass of the population. The appearance of a problem that had not previously existed – that of limiting family size – and

thereby the need for decision making of an entirely new sort, creates a pressure for attitudinal changes in a fundamental and immensely personal area of human experience. From this viewpoint the "population problem" may have positive consequences, by contributing to modernized attitudes that may more generally favor economic and social development.

In this sense another promising lead comes in the form of the "relative income" model. Data on over 150 countries in the period from 1950 to 2000 suggest that the fertility transition begins when and if relative cohort size begins to increase among young labor market entrants. The popular image of developing countries tends to be one of ever-increasing relative cohort size, given high fertility rates. High mortality rates among children and young people imply relative cohort size does not begin to increase until well after the start of decline in infant mortality. Once it begins to increase, however, in country after country the fertility transition has also begun (Macunovich 2000).

The mechanism might be similar to that documented in the US and other industrialized nations. An excess supply of young relative to prime-age males depresses the relative wages of the young men, to the extent that they are poor substitutes for older more experienced men. Alternatively, in less sophisticated economies the relative decline in earning potential for younger workers may occur in the form of reduced size of land holdings passed on from parent to child, when parents are forced to split land among a larger number of surviving offsprings. However it occurs, it is important to note that this need only be a *relative* decline. That is, concurrent economic development might raise absolute wages at all age levels; but if the wages of younger workers progress more slowly than those of older workers, as they will for large cohorts, those younger workers will still tend to feel some level of relative deprivation.

The effects of this labor market crowding may be exacerbated by crowding in the family, given increasing child survival rates, and in schools to the extent that they are available. The earning potential of young men will be reduced relative to their material aspirations as shaped in their parental households. They will feel less able to support themselves at an (age adjusted) standard commensurate with that experienced in their parents' homes. The resultant decline in relative income would lead young couples to wish to delay or forego marriage and/or reduce fertility in an attempt to maintain a higher level of per capita disposable income.

In this way, a society with little or no individual control of fertility will begin to experience a strong motivation for such control. Large cohorts are known for their disruptive effects on social norms (as, for example, in the United States in the 1960s and 1970s, and in Iran today). In this case, a large cohort's need for fertility control may mark a turning point in the society's attitudes with regard to contraception, and with regard to the individual's – as opposed to society's – right to control fertility. Thus it would appear that the "price of time" and "relative income" models *are* relevant in developing countries as well, but within a very different institutional context.

NOTES

1   It's important to note, though, that despite these high fertility rates there was little if any population growth because mortality rates were also very high. Women tended to have large numbers of births in the hope of having at least a few surviving children.

2   The replacement level of 2.1 births per woman is the level needed for a generation to replace itself exactly in the next generation.

3   The original description of the demographic transition was presented in Kingsley Davis (1945) and Notestein (1945), and the current "state of the art" is described in John Caldwell (1997) and in John Caldwell and Pat Caldwell (1997).

4   This is terminology developed and explained in Walt Rostow (1998).

5   Some of these factors are set out in Frank Bean (1983), Davis et al. (1986), Ron Lestaeghe and Johan Surkyn (1988), and Robert Pollak and Susan Watkins (1993).

6   For a full description of the models of the "new household economics" developed by Gary Becker, see Becker (1981). Alternatively, he provides very readable summaries of his models in Becker (1988, 1993).

7   It is necessary to speculate about women's wages because we do not have any detailed information on them during the 1950s and early 1960s, and for the entire period up to 1976 it is difficult to identify an hourly wage, which is needed to estimate "price of time" effects.

8   The most well-known version of this model is described and tested in William Butz and Michael Ward (1979).

9   For a full description of the Easterlin relative income model, see Easterlin (1987). For critical reviews of tests of his hypothesis, see Macunovich (1998a), Fred Pampel (1993), and Pampel and H. Elizabeth Peters (1995).

10   A woman's highest fecundability (her ability to conceive) occurs around age 24, and it is well established that births delayed in the early years are never fully replaced in later years, since fecundability declines fairly markedly in the later twenties and especially after age 30. Thus decisions at young ages have a direct effect on a woman's "completed fertility" (the total number of births in her lifetime) and are therefore very important to model.

11   This concept is developed further in Dennis Ahlburg (1984).

12   All estimates of male relative income and relative cohort size reported in this section of the chapter are taken from calculations reported in Macunovich (2002).

13   These developments in the youth labor market are documented in James Smith and Finis Welch (1981), Welch (1979), and Macunovich (1999).

14   The figures reported here are taken from a survey of 228 first year students (116 male and 112 female) in November 1995, as reported in Macunovich (2002).

15   For a full description of this combined model, see Macunovich (1996) and for the model with racial differences, see Macunovich (1998b).

16   Availability of affordable childcare has been demonstrated in numerous studies to be an important factor in determining the labor force participation rates of mothers with young children: see, for example, Mark Berger and Dan Black (1992) and Harriet Presser (1989). Although most of the analyses look at the effect of childcare on labor force participation, we might assume that there would be a corresponding effect on fertility. There is no consensus on this point, however. But it is generally recognized that social acceptability is an important

factor in the use of paid childcare to permit young career-oriented women to become mothers, as discussed by Samuel Preston (1986) and Norman Ryder (1990).

17 See Pampel (2001) for an excellent discussion of institutional factors affecting fertility decisions.

18 The full model describing the "demand for" and "supply of" children, and the potential effect of the cost of fertility regulation, is set out in Easterlin and Crimmins (1985).

REFERENCES

Ahlburg, Dennis A. 1984. "Commodity Aspirations in Easterlin's Relative Income Theory of Fertility." *Social Biology* 31(3/4): 201–7.

Bean, Frank D. 1983. "The Baby Boom and Its Explanations." *The Sociological Quarterly* 24(3): 353–65.

Becker, Gary S. 1981. *A Treatise on the Family*. Cambridge: Harvard University Press.

——. 1988. "Family Economics and Macro Behavior." *American Economic Review* 78(1): 1–13.

——. 1993. "Nobel Lecture: The Economic Way of Looking at Behavior." *Journal of Political Economy* 101(3): 385–409.

Becker, Gary S. and Nigel Tomes. 1976. "Child Endowments and the Quantity and Quality of Children." *Journal of Political Economy* 84(4, Part 2): "Essays in Labor Economics in Honor of H. Gregg Lewis": S143–S162, Special Supplement.

Berger, Mark C. and Dan A. Black. 1992. "Child Care Subsidies, Quality of Care, and the Labor Supply of Low-Income, Single Mothers." *The Review of Economics and Statistics* 74(4): 635–42.

Billings, John S. 1893. "The Diminished Birth-rate in the United States," as reproduced in "An 1893 View of the American Fertility Decline." *Population and Development Review*, 1976 2(2): 279–82.

Butz, William P. and Michael P. Ward. 1979. "The Emergence of Countercyclical U.S. Fertility." *American Economic Review* 69(3): 318–28.

Caldwell, John C. 1997. "The Global Fertility Transition: The Need for a Unifying Theory." *Population and Development Review* 23(4): 803–12.

Caldwell, John C. and Pat Caldwell. 1997. "What Do We Now Know About Fertility Transition?" in Gavin W. Jones, R. M. Douglas, John C. Caldwell and Rennie M. D'Souza (eds.) *The Continuing Demographic Transition*, pp. 15–25. Clarendon Press: Oxford.

Crimmins, Eileen, Richard Easterlin, and Yasuhiko Saito. 1991. "Preference Changes Among American Youth: Family, Work, and Goods Aspirations, 1976–86." *Population and Development Review* 17(1): 115–33.

Davis, Kingsley. 1945. "The World Demographic Transition." *Annals of the American Academy of Political and Social Science* 237: 1–11.

Davis, Kingsley, Mikhail S. Bernstam, and Rita Ricardo-Cambell. 1986. "Below-Replacement Fertility in Industrial Societies." *Population and Development Review*, Supplement to Volume 12.

Easterlin, Richard A. 1978. "The Economics and Sociology of Fertility: A Synthesis," in Charles Tilly (ed.) *Historical Studies of Changing Fertility*. Princeton, NJ: Princeton University Press.

——. 1987. *Birth and Fortune, second edition.* New York: Basic Books (first published without Chapter 10 in 1980).

Easterlin, Richard A. and Eileen M. Crimmins. 1985. *The Fertility Revolution: A Supply–Demand Analysis.* Chicago: University of Chicago Press.

Lestaeghe, Ron and Johan Surkyn. 1988. "Cultural Dynamics and Economic Theories of Fertility Change." *Population and Development Review* 14(1): 1–45.

Lewin, T. (1994). "Men Whose Wives Work Earn Less, Studies Show" *New York Times,* October 12, 1994.

Macunovich, Diane J. 1995. "The Butz-Ward Fertility Model in the Light of More Recent Data." *Journal of Human Resource,* 30(2): 229–55.

——. 1996. "Relative Income and Price of Time: Exploring Their Effects on U.S. Fertility and Female Labor Force Participation," in *Fertility in the United States: New Patterns, New Theories, Population and Development Review,* Supplement to Volume 22: 223–57.

——. 1998a. "Fertility and the Easterlin Hypothesis: An Assessment of the Literature." *Journal of Population Economics* 11: 1–59.

——. 1998b. "Race and Relative Income/Price of Time Effects on U.S. Fertility." *Journal of Socio-Economics* 27(3): 365–400.

——. 1999. "The Fortunes of One's Birth: Relative Cohort Size and the Youth Labor Market in the U.S." *Journal of Population Economics* 12: 215–72.

——. 2000. "Relative Cohort Size: Source of a Unifying Theory of Global Fertility Transition?" *Population and Development Review* 26(2): 235–61.

——. 2002. *Birth Quake: the Baby Boom and Its Aftershocks.* Chicago: University of Chicago Press.

Mincer, Jacob. 1962. "Labor Force Participation of Married Women," in Gregg Lewis (ed.) *Aspects of Labour Economics,* pp. 63–105. Princeton, NJ: Princeton University Press.

Notestein, Frank W. 1945. "Population – The Long View" in Theodore W. Schultz (ed.) *Food for the World.* Chicago: University of Chicago Press.

Pampel, Fred C. 1993. "Relative Cohort Size and Fertility: The Socio-Political Context of the Easterlin Effect." *American Sociological Review* 58: 496–514.

——. 2001. *The Institutional Context of Population Change: Patterns of Fertility and Mortality Across High-Income Nations.* Chicago: University of Chicago Press.

Pampel, Fred C. and H. Elizabeth Peters. 1995. "The Easterlin Effect." *Annual Review of Sociology* 21: 163.

Pollak, Robert A. and Susan Cotts Watkins. 1993. "Cultural and Economic Approaches to Fertility: Proper Marriage or Mesalliance?" *Population and Development Review* 19(3): 467–96.

Presser, Harriet B. 1989. "Can We Make Time for Children? The Economy, Work Schedules, and Child Care." *Demography* 26(4): 523–43.

Preston, Samuel H. 1986. "Changing Values and Falling Birth Rates," in *Below-Replacement Fertility in Industrial Societies, Population and Development Review,* Supplement to Volume 12: 176–95.

Rostow, Walt W. 1998. *The Great Population Spike and After: Reflections on the 21st Century.* Oxford: Oxford University Press.

Ryder, Norman B. 1990. "What is Going to Happen to American Fertility?" *Population and Development Review* 16(3): 433–54.

Sanderson, Warren. 1987. "Below-Replacement Fertility in Nineteenth Century America." *Population and Development Review* 13(2): 305–13.

Smith, James P. and Finis Welch. 1981. "No Time to be Young: The Economic Prospects for Large Cohorts in the United States." *Population and Development Review* 7(1): 71–83.

Smock, Pamela J. and Wendy D. Manning. 1997. "Cohabiting Partners' Economic Circumstances and Marriage." *Demography* 34(3): 331–41.

Solnick, Sara J. and David Hemenway. 1998. "Is More Always better? A survey on positional concerns." *Journal of Economic Organization and Behavior* 37: 373–83.

Welch, Finis. 1979. "Effects of Cohort Size on Earnings: the Baby Boom Babies' Financial Bust." *Journal of Political Economy* 87(5, Part 2): S65–S97.

Chapter 7

The Childcare Economics Conundrum: Quality versus Affordability

Julie A. Nelson

Introduction

According to the most recently published comprehensive survey, in the United States, nearly 60 percent of all children under age 6 are in some form of non-parental care, regardless of their parent's work status. For children under age 1, the figure is 45 percent (National Center for Education Statistics 1996). Childcare quality, the affordability of childcare services, and the compensation of childcare staff are the crucial issues in the economics of childcare.

Parents are concerned about the quality of care their children receive. The good news is that the sort of research on "maternal deprivation" that, decades ago, caused worry and guilt among many working parents, has now been discredited. Such research had been done in long-term residential orphanages that bear little resemblance to contemporary childcare centers, family day-care homes, and in-home childcare arrangements. Current research tends to show no overall negative effects of maternal employment on cognitive or social development of children (Francine Blau and Adam Grossberg 1992; Elizabeth Harvey 1999). Child development research indicates that high quality childcare can, in fact, significantly enhance children's wellbeing and readiness to learn, particularly for children from less rich home environments (National Center for Early Development and Learning 1999; Janet Currie 2001; Deborah Lowe Vandell and Barbara Wolfe 2000). Most professionals in the field of child development prefer the phrase "early education and care" to simply "childcare," to emphasize the attention given to children's emotional and cognitive needs in high quality programs.

The bad news is that many children today do not get high quality care. A recent nationwide study of cost and quality in randomly selected childcare centers rated only

24 percent of preschool centers (usually serving children ages 3 to 5) as good to excellent. Worse, only 8 percent of infant care centers (for age 2 and under) and 3 percent of unregulated family day-care homes (serving a variety of ages, with no license) were rated as good to excellent. Most centers were rated as minimal to mediocre. Some 40 percent of infant care centers were rated even lower, giving care of such inadequate quality that children's safety was potentially jeopardized (Cost, Quality, and Child Outcomes Study Team 1995).

In high quality childcare centers and family day-care homes, the providers are attentive and caring, knowledgeable about child development, and skilled in managing groups and communicating with parents. In low quality environments, the staff is more often stretched thin, watches too many children, and is hired under the philosophy that possession of a warm, adult body is qualification enough for childcare work. Since labor costs are a major component of childcare costs (two-thirds of total costs, according to John Morris 1999), quality issues are also cost issues. Averaging $4,000 to $6,000 per year, the cost of care for a 4 year old can rise to $10,000 or more for the top centers, according to a recent survey (Karen Shulman 2000). The average annual cost for a 4 year old in an urban area is more than the average annual cost of public college tuition, in nearly all states (Shulman 2000). Care for infants is even more expensive, and if a family has more than one child in care the costs multiply accordingly. Current limited tax credits and under-funded programs for low-income parents do little to reduce the overall quality/affordability dilemma.

The high costs are not due to childcare workers being highly paid. Quite the contrary, childcare work and childcare management are some of the lowest paid occupations in the country. In the United States, childcare workers – who are overwhelmingly female – on average, make $6.61 per hour. If they have the educational and experience background to be classified as preschool teachers, the wage rises to an average of $8.32 per hour. According to a 1998 government survey, only 17 occupations (out of 774 surveyed) have lower average wages than childcare workers. The occupations paying more include parking lot attendants and food servers (Center for the Child Care Workforce 2000). Not surprisingly, given these low wages, national statistics indicate annual job turnover rates of between 30 and 40 percent among childcare workers (Center for the Child Care Workforce 2000). Since emotional and cognitive development of young children requires attachment to trusted adults, quality directly suffers when turnover is this high.

Low quality, lack of affordability, low wages – is there any way out of this vicious cycle? This chapter could go on and on presenting grim statistics, or follow the standard "economics of..." model by presenting, for example, indifference curve models of parental childcare choices, or regression models illustrating the cost structure of the childcare industry.[1] While such work has its usefulness, the rest of this chapter takes an approach that should be more relevant for you, the economics student.

Focusing on the issue of wage levels in childcare, let us ask what the standard economic model you have learned tells us about such wages. To what extent does this model help us analyze the quality-affordability-wages dilemma? To what extent does the issue of childcare wages itself pose challenges to "the economic way of thinking"?

Can Care be Studied by Standard Methods?

Autonomy, self-interest, and rationality: the assumptions of neoclassical economics

The basics of neoclassical economic theory are taught in all the standard economics textbooks. I discovered in my 12 years of teaching economics, however, that the assumptions are sometimes memorized, rather than really understood. When they are not contrasted to alternative assumptions, and their implications are not drawn out, they may simply be uncritically accepted.

The core assumptions of the model are that people are autonomous (that is, independent of each other) and self-interested (as opposed to interested in other's well-being). People are assumed to make rational choices about their purchasing, investment, and work situations in such a way as to maximize their utility (that is, satisfaction). Hence, explanations of behavior based in notions of, say, impulsivity, socialization, group solidarity, habit, or influences like peer pressure, concern for others, family loyalty, emotional connection, or advertising, are considered tangential, if not completely ignored, in mainstream economic analysis. The focus is on the individual in the moment of choice.

While non-economists often tend to assume that prices and wages should reflect some idea of the real "value" or "worth" intrinsically contained in a commodity or type of labor, the neoclassical story is different. According to neoclassical economics prices and wages are set entirely by neutral market forces of supply and demand. If there is an excess supply of something (for example, unsold inventory on store shelves, or unemployed workers in a particular sector), the associated price or wage will fall. If there is an excess demand, the price or wage will rise. When the quantity supplied equals the quantity demanded, the equilibrium price is determined. Economics textbooks typically illustrate the idea that price is determined by relative scarcity, rather than intrinsic value to human life, by pointing to the example of water versus diamonds. Water is indispensable for life, but free or cheap, while diamonds, a mere luxury, are extremely expensive.

What this means, for analysis for the market for caring labor, is the following. If markets work according to the neoclassical theory of perfect competition, *a wage level cannot be systematically "too low."* After all, it is reasoned, if childcare workers *choose* to work at a wage lower than what they could make elsewhere, in an office or store or factory, then that must be their utility-maximizing *choice*. If childcare workers complain that their work is "undervalued," this can be dismissed as mere grumbling and politicking. Who would not want to be paid more for what they do, after all? If such a worker is really dissatisfied, she or he is free to choose another line of work – just as, in the case of you and your peers, someone who does not want to live on the wages of a social worker or English major is free to choose to study computer science or economics. The idea that childcare (or social work, or literature) has a high intrinsic "value" is quickly dismissed as irrelevant to the question of wages, within neoclassical thought, along the lines of the water/diamond example given above. Childcare work may, like water, be very valuable in preserving life, but according to the neoclassical analysis this is irrelevant for the question of wage determination. If childcare markets are characterized by low wages and low quality care, well, that simply reflects the choices of workers and parents.

Are the assumptions that agents are autonomous, rational, and self-interested as ethically neutral as the textbooks portray?

Relationship, concern, and warmth: the norms of child development

> Child development research indicates that preschool teachers who are warm, responsive, and engage in one-to-one relationships have positive effects on children's learning. For the preschool child, the "subjects" are all combined and integrated into a whole and learned simultaneously. Brain development research suggests that the strongest element for successful teaching at any level is the ability to form relationships and the ability to be responsive. (Center for Career Development in Early Care and Education 2000: 25)

Relationships and the valuing of the child are at the core of developmentally appropriate childcare. This is not due to some kind of mushy sentimentality, but is well backed up by a large quantity of research on the development of cognitive, emotional, and social skills. Since much of brain development takes place in the first five years of life, developing the *ability* to learn at these ages sets the groundwork for all later learning. The young child learns by being in the company of trusted adults who give appropriate feedback to the child's actions in the world. As the Code of Ethical Conduct of the National Association for the Education of Young Children states, programs should be committed to "helping children and adults achieve their full potential in the context of relationships that are based on trust, respect, and positive regard" and to "appreciating childhood as a unique and valuable stage of the human life cycle" (National Association for the Education of Young Children 1997). Note that this frame of reference is in some ways diametrically opposed to neoclassical thought. Instead of emphasizing individual autonomy, it emphasizes human connections. Instead of elevating self-interest, it emphasizes altruism and care. It assumes that what is important about being human is our ability to give and receive, to connect with others in their personhood rather than instrumentally. It entertains the possibility that childcare organization might not be as interested in maximizing profits as in satisfying authentic human needs. We generally find little trace of this point of view within most economics departments, but it may sometimes be found in areas of sociology and the humanities, and often predominates within other cultural institutions such as families and religions.

Regarding wages for childcare, child development advocates argue that these are a sign of a societal *undervaluing* of this kind of work (National Association for the Education of Young Children 1995). Childcare workers are seen as personally "subsidizing" the sector by being willing to do work they know is important for low wages – at least until they burn out (Center for Career Development in Early Care and Education 2000). Low wages and low quality are seen as serious problems.

Economics, children, and care

Thinking back to neoclassical economics textbooks for a moment, have you ever wondered where the children went? Children do not fit the model of independent, rational actors. If you search the neoclassical literature, you will find that children are included mainly as "goods" to their parents. They may be consumption goods (on a par with ice cream), or investment goods (like insurance policies for old age support). Also, in discussions of the formation of productivity-enhancing skills, children may be considered as future workers. Most discussions of "human capital" in labor economics textbooks, however, still skip childhood completely and start with the decision whether or not to attend college. The child, as a child, is rarely present. Within neoclassical economics the phrase "economics of childcare" is something of an oxymoron (a contradiction in terms, like "personal computer"), since neither *children* nor *care* fit within the models and norms considered "economic."

Do you think that we have to make a choice, between choosing to follow one set of norms, or choosing to emphasize the other? Let us continue to explore the contrast between them by looking at specific theories that purport to explain why wages for childcare are low, and then finish by seeing if we can discover a more adequate model of care and work.

Why are Wages for Childcare so Low?

The model of individual, self-interested, rational choice behavior offers three explanations of why wages are low: *human capital* (the work is unskilled), *compensating wage differentials* (the work is fun), and *crowding* (too many workers in the field). From another angle, the *protection* explanation argues that childcare should be low paying in order assure that motivations are *not* self-interested. Lastly, the explanation according to *affordability* is based on a comparison of childcare costs to mother's wages.

Human capital theory

Maybe childcare just is not that hard to do. The neoclassical concept of "human capital" is based on a metaphor with physical capital, like machinery. Just as firms may purchase machinery now in order to produce more in the future, people are seen as investing in education and training in order to increase their skills and hence their future productivity. When people are skilled and productive in ways that the market values, they receive high wages. Hence, one explanation for *low* wages in any sector would be if the sorts of skills required correspond only to *low* levels of human capital investment. Certainly, in the realm of childcare, there tends to be a popular perception that anyone – or at least any woman – can do it. Women have raised babies and small children, without any special training, for generations, right? It must be a "natural" thing, inborn and instinctive – or so the perception goes. With no perceived need for investment in education, training, and skill development, there is no reason to expect that this field will pay a high wage.

One fact that may raise some suspicion about this argument is that even *among* people with *similar* levels of investment in education, caring work is paid disadvantageously. A study in the 1980s found that the annual wages of teaching staff in childcare centers were less than 50 percent of the average wages for similarly-educated women, and less than a third of the average wages of similarly-educated men (Marcy Whitebook et al. 1989). More generally, an *Education Week* study indicates that teaching, in general, seems to require that the workers subsidize the product: people with MA degrees in teaching make an average wage of $43,313, while those in all other fields make an average of $75,824 (Center for Career Development in Early Care and Education 2000: 11).

Evidence, in fact, suggests that work requiring nurturing tasks of any kind may be systematically paid less. One regression study looked at the effect on wages of being in an occupation that involves "providing a service to an individual or a small group with whom the worker has a face-to-face relationship." It found that, even after controlling for factors like education, the percentage of jobs in an occupation held by women, and other skills required by the job, such "nurturance" *reduced* wages for women by between 22 and 44 cents per hour, and for men between $1.25 and $1.71 per hour (Paula England 1992). In the corporate world, the managers of human resources and public relations departments tend to be paid less than managers of areas like finance and purchasing (U.S. Department of Labor 1996). Far from being recognized and rewarded, it seems that current cultural and market norms actually may *penalize* activities that reflect human contact, warmth, relationship, and care. Is it coincidence that these are aspects of life that are the same aspects of life systematically missing from "economic" analysis?

When looking at childcare work, some see only physical tasks like lifting and diaper-changing, and perhaps "educational" work in teaching songs and the alphabet. Without a grasp of the unique intricacies and significance of early childhood physical, emotional, and cognitive development, and the importance of real, caring, strong, individualized and warm human relationships for developing human beings, childcare appears to be either passive baby-sitting or watered-down school teaching. But child development research indicates that good childcare requires many skills. Knowledge about the capacities and growth stages of the particular ages of children in our care, and the ability to find and use the teachable moment, are skills that require both education and experience on the part of the caregiver. Skills in active management of groups, including attention to the children's own social dynamics and the provision of appropriate behavioral feedback, is not a "natural" skill, but rather one gained through learning and experience, perhaps with a teacher-mentor. Good care also requires emotional warmth, kindness, and patience, necessary to foster the child's sense of her or himself as a valuable being. While some people find it easier than others to manifest these emotional skills (even if all had similar education and work experience), these traits cannot be dismissed as "instinctual" and therefore free. Some people find it easier to shoot baskets or pitch baseballs than others do, and we don't call *that* instinct. We call that talent, and reward those superstars with multimillion dollar contracts. The knowledge, skills and talents required for really good childcare work are real; they are only largely invisible when childhood is thought to be uninteresting, and the ability to be responsive and form warm relationships is not valued.

Compensating wage differentials theory

Maybe childcare is just fun. Some people believe that economists assume that people are only interested in money, and try to maximize their income, but this is not true. Neoclassical labor economics includes a theory that says that people also care about their working conditions. The theory of "compensating wage differentials" states that all else equal, jobs with worse conditions will tend to pay more, and those with better conditions will tend to pay less. For example, since most people would rather not work nights, a night shift in a factory will often be rewarded with a wage premium, even though the tasks done are exactly the same as during the day. Applied to childcare, it is often argued that taking care of children is fun and rewarding. Those who choose this occupation are therefore seen as "taking part of their pay" in good feelings. According to this argument, the occupation will pay less in monetary income than other jobs, because it also generates "psychic income."

Usually, however, this model is presented as though a particular job characteristic is either universally liked, or universally disliked, when in fact for many characteristics people are likely to be split. Some people like working with children and some do not, just as some people prefer to work outdoors and others do not. Figure 7.1 illustrates the labor market for some particular occupation with such a characteristic. Suppose the wage elsewhere in the economy for people with the skills for this job is W'. Those potential employees represented by the supply curve to the left of L' are those whose preferences are such that they would accept a wage *cut* in order to take this job, in order to enjoy the appealing characteristic. Those who are represented by the supply curve to the right of L' would need to be offered a wage *premium* to enter this occupation, because, given their preferences, this characteristic is something they would only endure if given a pay incentive.

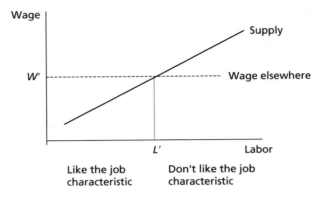

Figure 7.1   Compensating wage differentials

Childcare may be fun in some ways, but long hours, lack of breaks, isolation from other adults, exposure to feces and viral infection, stressful interactions with less cooperative children (and less cooperative parents), are also working conditions faced by many childcare workers. And, of course, for some people simply being with children is itself a drawback. Far from finding children fun and entertaining, many adults consider them to be largely noisy and boring, or feel that they as adults are "not cut out for" such work and would experience fear, stress, failure, frustration or other discomforts if put in charge of a group of children.

The fact that, on balance, childcare work cannot be considered to be universally desirable should give one pause in too quickly applying a compensating wage differential argument. And what about other characteristics that some people find desirable, in jobs that pay *well?* Suppose you plan to become a stock broker or financial analyst, not only because of the money, but also because you enjoy the excitement of fast-paced deal-making or the detail work of mathematical evaluation. Should *you* expect a lowering of your monetary wage, just because you will enjoy your work?

Figure 7.2 is an extension of figure 7.1, now with demand curves added. Again, think of the supply curve *S* as representing the number of workers who would choose a line of work at a given wage, when the wage available elsewhere (for work of equivalent skill, etc.) is W'. Those to left of L' enjoy the special characteristic of this job, while those to the right of L' would prefer to work elsewhere unless given a wage premium. We might think of the current childcare market as being characterized by demand curve D_{care}, so that the actual wage, W_{care}, is less than in other jobs. The marginal worker sets the actual level of the wage. If demand is so low that the last worker hired is willing to take a negative compensating wage differential, all workers will have negative differentials. Because the willingness to pay is low, people who would enjoy caring for children are faced with a choice *between* job enjoyment (working in this market for W_{care}) or merely normal pay (working elsewhere for W').

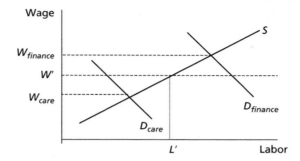

Figure 7.2   Compensating wage differentials and demand

The market for financial analysts, on the other hand, might be more characterized by demand curve $D_{finance}$, so that a higher wage than in comparable jobs, $W_{finance}$, is being paid.[2] The position of the demand curve is determined by people's (consumers, employers, and/or government) willingness to pay for the work. Because people are willing to pay a lot for financial services, demand is high, the marginal worker demands a positive differential, and all workers get this higher wage. Many financial analysts (those represented by the part of the supply curve to the left of L') get to have their cake and eat it too – they get job enjoyment *and* high pay. Those to the right of L' (who might find the work tedious) at least get high pay. Those lucky workers who find that what they like to do is highly valued by the market collect "economic rents." There is nothing intrinsically low-paying about childcare: if people's willingness to pay were higher – if the demand curve in figure 7.2 shifted to the right – childcare wages could be as high as wages elsewhere or even higher.

Crowding theory

Perhaps women are moving out of the childcare sector too slowly. The theory of crowding offers an explanation for why wages in traditionally female-dominated occupations (like childcare) tended to be low historically. If women were historically excluded from most professions and trades, then the fact that they were crowded into relatively few occupations would tend to drive the supply curve to the female occupations to the right, causing the wages to fall. This is shown by supply curve S_2 in figure 7.3, where the market illustrated is one of a limited number that employ women.

This explanation for low wages for childcare has some plausibility, especially since slow changes in gender norms create (at least for the time being, and for certain families) a competing sector of very low paid or completely unpriced childcare (of widely varying quality) provided by out-of-the-labor-force grandmothers, aunts, female neighbors, and so on.

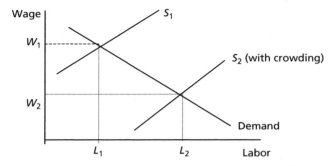

Figure 7.3   Crowding

The explanation cannot be the whole story, however, because the economist's solution to the problem of low wages in the case of crowding goes against the knowledge of the childcare market gained by those actually involved in it. Rather than raise wages directly, the economist's policy prescription in this case is to reduce discrimination elsewhere in the economy, so that more workers will *leave off* doing childcare, shifting the supply curve back towards S_1. Unfortunately, the idea that there are "too many" people doing paid childcare is directly counter to the current reality experienced by childcare directors, who are plagued with staff shortages.[3]

Protection theory

Arguments for low wages can also come from the other side of the spectrum. Maybe childcare *should* be low paid, to guarantee that children are cared for with genuine concern, and not by people doing it "just for the money." What I call the *protection* argument comes from a perspective that in some ways is quite opposed to economists' emphasis on self-interest, yet in important ways it shares some of the same assumptions.

Suppose that markets work more or less according the neoclassical assumptions given above, yet there is also an important, separate realm of human connection and care. Workers in their identity as wage-earners, for example, along with for-profit corporations, could be assumed to be materialistic and self-interested, just as neoclassical theory says. People in their identity as caregivers, on the other hand, and in non-profit and voluntary organizations, could be assumed to be social and altruistic. Furthermore, if the forces of economic self-interest are perceived as being very powerful, then it follows that actions must be taken to *protect* the social sphere from the incursion of market-oriented values.

Paying low wages is seen as an action that protects real care. Consider the following discussion of proposals to raise rates for foster care (that is, temporary, round-the-clock childcare in private homes) that appeared in a recent *Boston Globe* column:

> Other proposals [for raising foster care rates] have often run aground on the argument that paying more would attract parents who were simply in it for the money. "You don't

want a cottage industry of professional foster parents for pay," Jeffrey Locke, the interim [Massachusetts Department of Social Services] commissioner, said yesterday. (Adrian Walker 2000: B1)

From the protection point of view, real caregivers give out of love, not for money. Taking only an income other people would find unacceptably low, is seen to prove one's altruistic motivations, thus assuring that children are being cared for in a genuine way. Compensation similar to that received by other workers, professionals, and business people, on the other hand, would presumably bring in people motivated by market values. Presumably these profit-motivated people would put on only a show of superficial caring sufficient to keep the money coming. A caregiver who might request (much less demand) a higher wage, may be perceived as demonstrating by this very action that she or he is self-interested, selfish and therefore not a "real" caregiver. Putting this in terms of a supply curve for caring labor, the protection argument assumes that those at the low end are motivated by care, and those at the high end by money.

Moving away from neoclassical notions of why people work for money ("self-interest"), however, we might note that reality is more complicated, and that there is no necessary correlation between wages and genuineness of care. People *need* money – for rent, for clothes, for the needs of their own families and children. Real people have real responsibilities. In a modern economy, people need to participate in the money economy in order to provide for themselves and others. And people – whole people, not the single-dimensional actors of the neoclassical economic model – do not necessarily check their larger human values and their loving feelings at the door, when they enter into a market transaction. The protection argument correctly points out potential problems of selfishness and greed, but makes an unwarranted assumption that selfishness and greed will predominate whenever money is on the table. In the presence of real responsibilities of rent, groceries and other bills (like paying back college loans), the supply curve for caring labor may include at its high end many people who would make excellent caregivers, but who literally "cannot afford" to take the job if it pays too little.

Likewise, a low wage is no guarantee, as it is sometimes thought, that a worker will act "altruistically." A job that offers a low wage will attract not only committed workers willing to make a personal sacrifice (at least until they burn out), but also those workers with few alternatives – those with few skills for other lines of work – who may not care at all about children. You will recognize this as a question of "opportunity costs," that is, about what is given up (say, employment opportunities elsewhere) when any choice (say, employment in childcare) is made. Low wages will tend to attract employees with low opportunity costs. The more educated, skilled and talented a childcare worker is, in general, the more dissatisfied they will be when they compare a low childcare wage to what they could make elsewhere. In one study, more than half the childcare workers and directors interviewed expressed the sentiment, "I love my job but I'm about to leave it" (Kathy Modigliani 1993: 22).

A high wage will not necessarily disproportionately attract people in it "just for the money." A high wage will also make it possible for the best caring (where caring is understood as a feeling) people to care (that is, engage in care, understood as an activity). A high wage would also have important positive effects on the morale of childcare workers. Psychological research suggests that workers are motivated by both factors from outside themselves, like high wages, and factors inside themselves, like love of the work. These need not be either/or, or in contradiction. If the high wages are perceived to be acknowledging and supportive of the worker's own goals and desires, then they reinforce and magnify the worker's interior motivations and satisfaction. As put by a foster mother in a recent *Boston Globe* column, increased compensation of foster parents "would make people realize the state is behind them" (Walker 2000: B1). This morale argument gives a result exactly opposite to that of the protection argument: higher wages make people feel more valued themselves, leading them to be able, in turn, to provide more "real" care. This can be turned into an argument in neoclassical terms, to some extent, by trading the vocabulary of motivation, morale and retention to one of employers needing to pay *efficiency wages* in order to ensure worker loyalty.[4]

Affordability theory

Maybe it is the need to keep childcare costs down that makes wages inevitably low. Parents, it is argued, are responsible for paying for the care of their children, and will only be able to buy childcare that is *affordable*. Proposals to raise wages are considered to be impractical pipe dreams, in this view. Higher wages would cause the market for childcare to nearly disappear, since only the highest-earning women would then be able to afford to buy childcare.

While neoclassical economics does not generally emphasize this argument – the notion of "affordability" is much too slippery a concept, for a view committed to avoiding the vocabulary of needs – we can see that it yet has elements in common with the highly individualistic neoclassical view of the world. In this view, parents, and mothers in particular, are the "consumers" of childcare services. Childcare is seen as a service provided *to the mothers* to allow them to participate in other activities. (That fathers also have "childcare responsibilities" is rarely discussed.) Children are not seen as benefiting from childcare in their own right. Society is not seen as responsible in any way for children's situations. Nor is society seen as benefiting from well-cared-for children. Furthermore, society is not perceived as benefiting from the participation of mothers in economic, social, and political life. It is only in casting childcare issues in terms of individual family budgets alone, that the apparent impasse of affordability arises.

Yet childcare also has important social repercussions. Once again, we might use notions of "market imperfection" to, in a limited way, expand neoclassical arguments to argue that childcare quality is under-demanded. The relevant concepts are those of *externalities* (or *public goods*), *information failures*, and *liquidity constraints* (see, for example, Currie 2001; Vandell and Wolfe 2000). Good early childcare has documented benefits to society at large, beyond those for the parents and children themselves, in terms of greater economic productivity, reduced special education expenditures, lowered crime, and a better workforce to make the goods and services needed by even childless persons in their retirement (England and Nancy Folbre 1999; Currie 2001). Quality may be neglected because parents find quality hard to observe, in the absence of education about quality and enforcement of standards of quality care. Socially efficient investments in quality might not be made, if left entirely in the hands of parents who are likely to be at a relatively low-earning stage of their working lives. Good economic reasoning, then, indicates that parental payments alone will lead to a less than optimal quality of childcare, and that an efficient solution requires public intervention to raise demand. While such arguments still tend to ignore the actual, present well-being of children themselves, they are steps in the right direction.

Once it is recognized that the level of funding for any sort of childcare is, in fact, a political issue, and a matter of social and economic priorities, the impasse of costs versus budgets starts to loosen up. What would spending look like, in a society that put a high priority on guaranteeing healthy early childhood care and education to all its youngest members? Why do we think of budget constraints in childcare as a brick wall, when – economists would be the first to remind us – resource allocation is a matter of choosing the most desired from among alternative uses? Social responsibility for the next generation need not require a heavy-handed, communistic, approach to childrearing, as some critics will always immediately suggest. While some countries and localities that take a more active role in childcare provision have chosen the route of government-run centers, other methods, like childcare subsidies combined with parental leaves, education, information, and regulation, can also be effective routes to improved quality of care.[5]

Where would the funds for good childcare wages come from? One estimate puts the cost for a subsidy plan including quality incentives that would allow for better pay at approximately $39 billion per year in the United States (Barbara Bergmann 1999). This will seem outrageously expensive to those whose point of comparison is "free" childcare provided invisibly, by unpaid and underpaid women. Yet the question is one of priorities. Numbers in the high millions and into the billions are commonly bandied about at the local and federal levels when the topic of discussion is a highway project (federal spending on transportation totaled $47 billion in 2000), a new sports stadium, the military equipment (the Department of Defense discretionary budget was $278 billion in 2000), or a system of export subsidies for businesses (Executive Office of the President of the United States 2001). Public K-12 education, college loan programs, Social Security ($403 billion in 2000), Unemployment Insurance, and worker's compensation are big, decades-old programs inspired by the recognition of human development and human need, that have (despite problems) contributed substantially to national wellbeing.

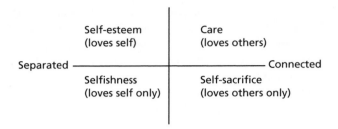

Figure 7.4   A broader view of interests

Toward a More Adequate Analysis of Care

Low wages and problems in the childcare sector fundamentally result from the fact that children, care, and connection are fundamentally *invisible* within the dominant, economistic worldview. Yet this view is so powerful that reactions against it – like the protection argument described above – still in some ways work within the same assumptions. Money and markets are on one side. Care and concern are on the other – or so it seems.

Consider an alternative. What if, instead, we started out by granting that every person is both unique, and interconnected – and in fact formed – within a web of relationships. What if we suppose that people could be respectful of *both* their more immediate self-interests *and* the joys and obligations of their interdependence, and act as such whole people wherever they might be. What if people could care for themselves while caring for others as well? What if people brought their deepest interests and values with them, when participating in the social realm we call "the economy"? What if we consider children to be people, too, and ones who need active care and guidance, within a whole web of important connections, to develop their own uniqueness and their own healthy attachments? While this image can be described rather simply, it is a radical departure from the culturally dominant ways of thinking of what a person is, and how a person acts. Instead of one set of values for the market (greed) and another for care (sacrifice), we would see value put on responsible interest in the good of the whole, which includes the good of oneself (Folbre and Julie Nelson 2000).

Consider figure 7.4, which visually broadens out the usual self-interest versus altruism dichotomy into four possibilities. The left side of the diagram contains aspects of human selfhood associated with an individualistic view of the human nature. The right side contains the elements, which arise from a connected view. The top part of the diagram includes positively valued attributes that work in tandem: in this case, self-esteem combined with care for others. The lower part of the diagram indicates what happens to each of these values if pursued alone. Self-esteem, without care, degenerates into selfishness. Care for others, without self-esteem, degenerates into loss of self. The dominant habit of thinking of the economic world as only self-interested, and the world of caregiving as one of self-sacrifice, recognizes only the lower part of the diagram. The purpose of figure 7.4 is to remind us that these are not the only options. If we believe that each child deserves self-respect in the home, center, or classroom, then equally so does each childcare *worker* in the society and economy.

Conclusion

The point of this chapter is not that all tools of standard economic analysis are wrong. Indeed, concepts such as opportunity costs and supply curves have been called on extensively to help make sense of the issues involved in the providing and financing high quality childcare. Standard concepts of market imperfection can be used to bolster the argument that the demand curve is currently in the wrong place, and should be shifted outwards. What must be dropped, however, for an analysis of childcare to make any sense at all, is blind allegiance to the definition of "economics" as being only about the choice behavior of rational, autonomous, self-interested agents. The wellbeing of future generations depends on it.

NOTES

1   Students interested in such subjects are invited to search under the topic of "childcare" in a database like *EconLit*.
2   It is not necessary to think of the alternative wages for financial analysts and careworkers as being exactly the same; it is shown this way on the graph for expositional simplicity.
3   Two other possible explanations neoclassical economists might give for low wages deserve brief mention. The neoclassical model does grant that wages can be systematically "too low" in the case of what is called *monopsony*. Instead of many employers competing for workers, in a monopsonistic labor market there is only one employer, who will use market power to suppress wages. While the graph for this is in all labor economics textbooks, it is not by and large applicable to markets like childcare where, in most cities and regions, there are many potential employers as well as opportunities for self-employment. The neoclassical policy prescription in the case of monopsony is to increase the number of employers in the labor market. Another possible explanation, used frequently to explain low wages in other sectors of the economy, is the factor of *global competition*. The wages of US textile workers are said to be low, for example, because these workers are competing for jobs with even lower-wage workers in other (mostly poor) countries. Like the monopsony model, this explanation has very limited applicability to childcare work. Few childcare centers could relocate over a border and still keep their clientele! In a broader sense, however, the availability of immigrant nannies and housekeepers could serve to increase somewhat the supply of childcare labor, thus lowering wages relative to where they might be in the absence of immigration.
4   Economists, however, tend to apply this theory only to jobs where training or monitoring the worker is expensive. Due to reasons already discussed, however, they are presently unlikely to see training, quality of work, or retention as major issues in childcare.

5   Neoclassical economists may bring up the usual arguments that social subsidization of child-care will "distort" the "prices" facing individuals (parents), leading to bad consequences such as parents having more than the optimal number of children. One need only to point to the very low birth rates in some of the European countries with the most substantial public support for childcare, to show that this argument seems to lack empirical verification.

REFERENCES

Bergmann, Barbara. 1999. "Making Child Care 'Affordable' in the United States," in Suzanne W. Helburn (ed.) *The Annals of the American Academy of Political and Social Science* Special Issue on *The Silent Crisis in U.S. Child Care* 563: 208–19.

Blau, Francine D. and Adam J. Grossberg. 1992. "Maternal Labor Supply and Children's Cognitive Development." *Review of Economics and Statistics* 74(3): 474–81.

Center for Career Development in Early Care and Education. 2000. *Briefing Booklet: Advance Reading for Sept. 14, 2000.* Boston MA: Wheelock College.

Center for the Child Care Workforce. 2000. *Current Data on Child Care Salaries and Benefits in the United States.* Washington DC Center for the Child Care Workforce.

Cost, Quality, and Child Outcomes Study Team. 1995. "Cost, Quality and Child Outcomes in Child Care Centers: Key Findings and Recommendations, Young Children," 40–4. Cited in Stanford Newman et al., *America's Child Care Crisis: A Crime Prevention Strategy*, 2000, Washington DC: Fight Crime: Invest in Kids, 10. http://www.fightcrime.org/pdf/childcare-report.pdf (February 18, 2001).

Currie, Janet. 2001. "Early Childhood Education Programs." *Journal of Economic Perspectives* 15(2): 213–38.

England, Paula. 1992. *Comparable Worth: Theories and Evidence.* New York: Aldine de Gruyter.

England, Paula and Nancy Folbre. 1999. "Who Should Pay for the Kids?" in Suzanne W. Helburn (ed.) *The Annals of the American Academy of Political and Social Science* Special Issue on *The Silent Crisis in U.S. Child Care* 563: 194–217.

Executive Office of the President of the United States. 2001. *A Citizen's Guide to the Federal Budget, Fiscal Year 2001.* http://w3.access.gpo.gov/usbudget/fy2001/pdf/guide.pdf (December 22, 2000).

Folbre, Nancy and Julie A. Nelson. 2000. "For Love or Money – Or Both?" *Journal of Economic Perspectives* 14(4): 123–40.

Harvey, Elizabeth. 1999. "Short-term and Long-term effects of Early Parental Employment on Children of the National Longitudinal Survey of Youth." *Developmental Psychology* 35: 2.

Modigliani, Kathy. 1993. *Child Care as an Occupation in a Culture of Indifference.* PhD dissertation, Wheelock College.

Morris, John R. 1999. "Market Constraints on Child Care Quality," in Suzanne W. Helburn (ed.) *The Annals of the American Academy of Political and Social Science* Special Issue on *The Silent Crisis in U.S. Child Care.* 563: 130–45.

National Association for the Education of Young Children. 1995. "Quality, Compensation, and Affordability." Position paper. Washington DC. http://www.naeyc.org/resources/position_statements/psqca98.htm (February 18, 2001).

National Association for the Education of Young Children. 1997. "Developmentally Appropriate Practice in Early Childhood Programs Serving Children from Birth through

Age 8." Position paper. Washington, DC. http://www.naeyc.org/resources/position_statements/dap1.htm (February 18, 2001).

National Center for Early Development and Learning. 1999. "The Children of the Cost, Quality and Outcomes Study Go to School: Executive Summary." University of North Carolina, Chapel Hill. http://www.fpg.unc.edu/~NCEDL/PAGES/cqes.htm (February 16, 2001).

National Center for Education Statistics. 1996. *Child Care and Early Child Education Program Participation of Infants, Toddlers, and Preschoolers* (NCES 95–824). Washington DC: U.S. Department of Education. Cited in Children's Defense Fund, *Overview of Child Care, Early Education, and School Age Care*, http://www.childrensdefense.org/childcare/99_overview.pdf. (February 19, 2001).

Shulman, Karen. 2000. "The High Cost of Child Care Puts Quality Care Out of Reach for Many Families." Washington DC: Children's Defense Fund. http://www.childrensdefense-fund.org/pdf/highcost.pdf (February 18, 2001).

U.S. Department of Labor (DOL), Bureau of Labor Statistics. 1996. *Employment and Earnings* 43(1): Table 39.

Vandell, Deborah Lowe and Barbara Wolfe. 2000. "Child Care Quality: Does It Matter and Does it Need to be Improved?" Washington, DC: Office of the Assistant Secretary for Planning and Evaluation, U.S. Department of Health and Human Services. Available at http://aspe.hhs.gov/hsp/ccquality00/index.htm.Accessed 7/22/01.

Walker, Adrian. 2000. Column in *Boston Globe*, March 20.

Whitebook, Marcy, Candace Howes, and Deborah Phillips. 1989. *Who Cares? Child Care Teachers and the Quality of Care in America*. Executive Summary of the National Child Care Staffing Study. Oakland, CA: Child Care Employee Project. Cited in The National Association for the Education of Young Children, "Guidelines for Compensation of Early Childhood Professionals," 1990 (1993), http://www.naeyc.org/resources/position_state-ments/pscomp98.pdf (February 18, 2001).

Chapter 8

The Childcare Problem for Low-income Working Families

Jean Kimmel

What are the childcare concerns facing low-income working families? I summarize these concerns as ones of affordability, availability, and quality, although the three are related. To get at the underpinnings of these concerns, it is helpful to start with a brief overview of the economic circumstances facing low-income working families and a description of their current childcare utilization patterns. Then I turn to a discussion of the relationship between childcare and employment, presenting first a theoretical derivation and then some empirical evidence. Next, I discuss the justification for governmental intervention in the childcare market, the types of intervention in existence today, and the possible consequences of such intervention. Finally, I suggest a set of proposals designed to alleviate some of the childcare problems facing low-income families today.

But first, what has brought our society to facing this discussion? During the latter part of the twentieth century, there were three driving forces behind the rising demand for (and subsequent concerns about) childcare: the rise in single parent families, the increase in the percentage of mothers with young children working, and more recently, evolving attitudes towards welfare recipients. The percentage of families with children under the age of 18 that are headed by a single parent has increased from 7.4 percent in 1950 to 27.3 percent in 1998. As shown in figure 8.1, female labor force participation (LFP) rates grew throughout the second half of the twentieth century, from 32.7 percent in 1948 to 60.2 percent in 2000. Both single and married women have experienced this upward trend in LFP rates, with singles increasing from 50.8 percent in 1955 to 68.7 percent in 1999, and married women increasing from 28.5 percent to 61.2 percent in the same time frame. While single mothers continue to work at higher rates, the gap has closed considerably in the past 45 years. Alongside the upward trend in female LFP rates has been an

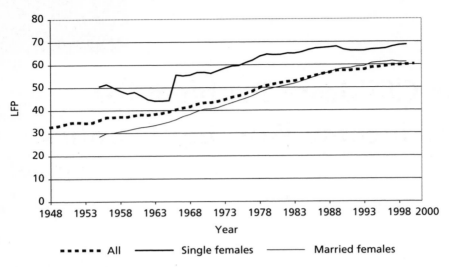

Figure 8.1   Female labor force participation over time
Sources: Handbook of Labor Statistics, U.S./DOL/BLS, June 1985, Bulletin 2217 and U.S. Census Bureau, *Statistical Abstract of the United States: 2000* (Table 645).

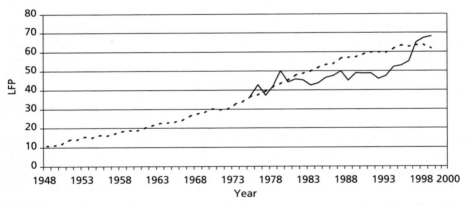

Figure 8.2   Labor force participation of mothers with children under the age of 6
Sources: Labor Force Participation Statistics derived from the Current Population Survey, 1948–87; US/DOL/BLS, August 1988, Bulletin 2307; and the 1993, 1997, and 2000 *U.S. Statistical Abstract of the United States.*

increase in the LFP rates of mothers with preschool-aged children (shown in figure 8.2), and mothers who work full-time. As seen in figure 8.3, in the year 2000, 76.6 percent of mothers with school-aged children worked full-time, compared to 68.3 percent in 1975. The percentage of working full-time mothers with preschool children barely budged over this time frame, increasing just 1.3 percentage points, from

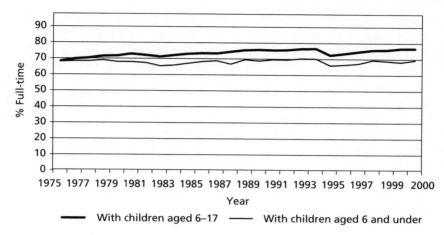

Figure 8.3   Employed females: percentage full-time, by age of children
Source: Bureau of Labor Statistics, Current Population Survey, March supplement, 1975 through 2000.

68.0 percent to 69.3 percent. Still, with the overall increase in female employment rates, the absolute number of children with working mothers has increased, and even the absolute number of mothers working full-time has increased as well. With the recent federal reform of welfare, the percentages of single parents participating in paid employment, and even working full-time is expected to increase even further.[1] All these demographic and political trends point to an increased demand for non-maternal childcare.

Low-income Working Families

According to Gregory Acs et al. (2000), one out of every six non-elderly Americans who work at least part-time still live with incomes that place them at or below twice the federal poverty level of income. This basic fact contradicts the common media representation of the poor as somehow deserving, either due to failure to work or due to single-parenthood. In fact, in these working poor families, nearly 70 percent are headed by a married couple. Evaluating data from the newly available National Survey of America's Families (NSAF), Acs et al. examine low-income working families in detail.[2] They define working as having had worked at least half-time for the year 1996. Working low-income families make up over 50 percent of the total low-income population in the United States; that is, more poor individuals live in working families than in non-working families.

Low-income families have family heads who are five years younger on average than higher-income family heads, with 63 percent of those heads male (versus 73 percent of the higher-income heads). Far more have low education levels: 22 percent of heads of low-income working families have less than a high school education versus 4 percent of the higher-income family heads. These characteristics serve as job market disadvantages. One outcome of this overall disadvantage is that the median hourly wage for these lower-income workers is $7.55, which is less than half of the $16.67 per hour wage earned by the primary earner in higher-income working families. Further, significantly fewer primary earners in low-income working families have employer-provided health insurance coverage, 54 percent versus 85 percent.

Finally, family composition varies by income level as well. Lower-income families are more likely to include children, partly because their family heads are younger, and are more likely to include more children on average than higher-income families. Also, the children tend to be younger in low-income families. Therefore, lower-income families are most likely to face costly childcare expenditures.

Childcare Expenses and Utilization Patterns

Linda Giannarelli and James Barsimantov (2000) use the 1999 National Survey of America's Families to describe childcare utilization patterns nationwide and for 12 key states. Their estimates are based on childcare usage for spring or fall of 1997, and provide information on the paid childcare usage for working families with children under age 13. Forty-eight percent of their sample of all working families pays for care. For these families who pay for care, the average payment per month is $286, and on average, these families pay 9 percent of their total earnings for this care. As the authors point out, these averages mask great variation across different family types in childcare expenses. For low-income families (which includes 36 percent of all working families with pre-teen children), 40 percent reported paying for care, compared with 53 percent of higher-earning families. On average, low-income families report paying $217 a month for care while their higher-earning families counterpart reported paying $317.[3] These expenditures reflect 16 percent of total family earnings for lower-income families but only six percent of earnings for higher earning families. In fact, 27 percent of lower earning families that pay for care report paying over one-fifth of earnings for care. As the authors report, there is still great variability within these figures for lower-earning families. Expenditures vary across families depending on the number and ages of the children in paid care, and whether the family is a single-parent or two-parent family. Because childcare is most expensive for the youngest children, low-income families with very young children pay the highest amounts for childcare and devote the largest percentages of their incomes to childcare.

Of parents who use non-maternal care, single parent low-income families are more likely to pay for care than two-parent low-income families, 50 percent versus 29 percent. Part of this difference might arise from the availability of subsidies for single-parent families, which typically support formal market types of care. Across income levels, single parents have less access to relatives who might be willing to provide care for free or at low cost. Of these two family types that pay for care, single parent families pay 19 percent of their incomes for childcare, versus 11 percent of two-parent families' incomes. So, while single-parent families are not all low-income as well, the two groups overlap greatly and share many of the same childcare problems.[4]

Jennifer Ehrle, Gina Adams, and Kathryn Tout (2001) also use the NSAF data to examine the childcare utilization patterns for very young children. Breaking down patterns of care by family income, they find that there are differences in the types of care used for these infants and toddlers. For example, younger children of lower-income families are more likely to be cared for by relatives while the same-aged children in higher-income families are more likely to be cared for in center-based care. When breaking down these differences based on the mother's work status (full-time versus part-time), however, the patterns become more complicated.

School-aged children still require adult supervision during the before and after school hours that their parents work. For these older children (in either single-parent or two-parent families), the care is often focused on structured activities or educational programs. Looking at after-school childcare arrangements for children ages 5 to 14 with an employed mother regardless of income level, 19 percent are cared for in their own home not by a parent, 19 percent in another home, 8 percent in an organized day-care facility, 21 percent by their father, 5 percent by their mother while she works, and 12 percent care for themselves (Committee on Ways and Means, Green Book Table 9-6: 581). Focusing on low-income families, children in low-income families are less likely to care for themselves (given a greater availability of non-working relatives and teenaged siblings), and also are less likely to participate in enrichment activities like lessons or sports after school.

Racial Differences in Childcare Utilization Patterns

Previous research has shown that racial background plays a role in childcare utilization patterns. (See, for example, Bruce Fuller et al. 1996.) It can be difficult to draw conclusions as to the reasons for observed racial differences because racial groups also differ in their rates of single-parenthood, income levels, and education levels. The NSAF data report cited earlier (Ehrle, Adams and Tout 2001) focuses on three groups: white non-Hispanic (referred to as white), African-American/non-Hispanic (referred to as African-American), and Hispanic. Other racial and ethnic groups are too small in available national surveys to permit this sort of stratification.

Hispanic children are much less likely to be placed in center care (10 percent) compared to white (24 percent) or African-American children (30 percent). White children are more likely to be cared for by nannies or babysitters than African-American children (8 versus 3 percent), and Hispanic children are most likely to be cared for by relatives (39 percent), compared with 27 percent of African-American children and

25 percent of white children. One mode choice that does not differ by race is the total number of non-parental arrangements used per child. Approximately 33 percent of young children are in more than one arrangement, regardless of race. A final observation concerning young children relates to the number of hours in non-parental care. Fifty-eight percent of African-American children of employed mothers are in full-time non-parental childcare, compared to just 36 percent of white children and 34 percent of Hispanic children. Obviously, this difference arises in large part from racial differences in mothers' probability of working full-time.

For school-aged children less than 10 years old, 27 percent of African-American children with working mothers rely on wrap-around care (that is, care before and after school) compared to 16 percent of Hispanic children. For older school-aged children (ages 10 through 12), 30 percent of white children use self-care as the primary mode of care, compared to 15 percent of Hispanic children and 11 percent of African-American children.

Availability and Quality of Care

Issues of the availability of childcare and the quality of that care are also issues of concern for low-income working families. While the research literature on the effects of childcare quality on child development and child wellbeing is somewhat contradictory, the bulk of studies are in agreement as to the particular importance of high quality care for disadvantaged children. These children (defined as disadvantaged due to low family income or low levels of parental education) are helped the most by high quality care and harmed the most by poor quality care (Deborah Vandell and Barbara Wolfe 2000). By most measures of quality, most available care in the United States is of mediocre or poor quality.

The most acute shortages of regulated suppliers are found in low-income neighborhoods. Also, there continue to be supply shortages in off-hours care, as required by those who work a non-standard work schedule. Finally, shortages also persist in infant care. All of these shortages are most felt by low-income workers (Ann Collins et al. 2000). Despite state and local efforts to increase supply in the 1990s, these shortages persist both due to the rising demand that resulted from welfare reform and the decline in the supply of childcare workers that resulted from the strong economy that provides better economic opportunities for those workers.

Childcare Costs and Employment Behavior

The relationship between childcare decisions and employment decisions can be modeled formally using behavioral models often employed by economists. Typically, these models assume utility-maximizing behavior on the part of individuals or families, and rely on choice constraints (such as confining budgets and time constraints) to yield model outcomes. One example of such a model that incorporates childcare costs into the employment decision is shown using graphical analysis in the Appendix at the end of this chapter. As shown in those figures, childcare costs enter into the theoretical model of individual labor supply both through a purely variable hourly cost that in effect lowers the worker's hourly wage rate (making the budget line flatter), and as a quasi-fixed costs of work that shifts the budget line downward. In this formulation, the theoretical model predicts that the effect of childcare costs on labor force participation depends on the relative preferences for income and leisure, as well as the hours of employment before childcare costs are considered.

There is a growing literature on the empirical relationship between childcare costs and employment behavior.[5] The bulk of this literature relies on estimates of the childcare price elasticity of employment, that is, the relative responsiveness of employment to changes in the price of childcare.[6] Jean Kimmel (1995) examines a group of low-income single mothers and estimates that the childcare price elasticity of employment is −0.35, which implies that a 1 percent increase in the hourly price of childcare will cause a 0.35 percent decline in the probability of employment. Estimates differ by marital status because married mothers are more likely to have more good substitutes for paid market care in their husbands as well their husbands' families.

An example of the complexity inherent in these studies is seen in the work of Rachel Connelly and Jean Kimmel (2001). They examine the importance of work status in estimates of these price elasticities. That is, they argue that the choice for part-time work is fundamentally different than the choice for full-time work (due to substantive differences in job opportunities, wage and benefit structures, and hourly childcare costs), and so the elasticities should be estimated separately for the two types of employment states and separately for married and single mothers. They find that the childcare price elasticity of full-time employment is −0.71 for married mothers and −1.22 for single mothers, and the elasticity for part-time employment is −0.08 and −0.37 for married and single mothers, respectively. These elasticities show that single mothers' full-time and part-time employment decisions are influenced more by changes in childcare prices than are married mothers' decisions. While estimates are not available separately by income level, the bulk of the single mothers are also low-income so these results provide an indication of the likely behavior of low-income working families.

Connelly and Kimmel (2002a) focus on low-income mothers who are at risk of welfare recipiency. They run simulations to examine the importance of childcare subsidies and find that a 50 percent childcare subsidy for low-income single mothers would reduce welfare recipiency by 10 percent and increase employment by 25 percent. As discussed later in this chapter, problems of inadequate subsidies and limited availability of care hinder the potential success of welfare reform.

Justifications for Intervention in the Market for Childcare

What are the justifications for intervention in the childcare market by the state or federal government? Economists tend to justify market intervention when market mechanisms fail to work properly. When a market works properly, the outcome is efficient. Efficiency implies that the quantity that producers are willing to supply is exactly equal to the quantity buyers wish to purchase at a single equilibrium price, and that no individual can be made better off by some other outcome unless someone else is made worse off by that different outcome. Efficient outcomes result from the perfectly competitive markets that economists often reference as somewhat representative of many real-world markets. When a market does not operate efficiently, the quantity supplied may be inadequate at the equilibrium price, the equilibrium price may be too high to be affordable, or quality may suffer. Previous sections of this chapter described some of these problems, namely childcare that may be too expensive for low-income families, insufficient supply of childcare, and inadequate quality care even for higher income families.

James Walker (1991) focuses on the efficiency concerns in the market for childcare. Three significant factors might cause the market outcome to be an inefficient allocation of resources: imperfect competition, externalities, and public goods (see Walter Nicholson 2000). The childcare market is subject to all three of these failures.[7]

In addition, markets can also operate improperly with respect to equity considerations; that is, when the equilibrium price and quantity do not permit sufficient distribution of the good at a reasonable price. While discussions of equity turn on normative arguments, still there is room for economists to enter the discussion. In the childcare market, much as is true for 5 through 18 year old education, a sufficient supply of affordable quality care is desirable due to two facets of fairness: for the family as a unit and the individual child. For the family, childcare transfers are redistributional, raising the overall standard of living. For low-income families, childcare simply cannot be fit into the limited family budget, making it impossible for these families to achieve financial independence through market work. For the child, quality care plays an important role in the child's quality of life. Also, to the extent that the positive effects of quality childcare persist through adulthood, improving the availability of this care serves to improve that child's own life prospects. Quality childcare helps to give a more equal start to every child.

Issues of redistribution and equal opportunity are particularly relevant for recent welfare leavers. With the economic expansion of the 1990s, federal welfare reform waivers granted to states, and finally the 1996 federal welfare reform that imposed a maximum 5-year lifetime federal welfare eligibility limit, more and more very low-skilled single mothers with very little work experience are entering the workforce. These women receive very low incomes and therefore confront serious childcare affordability problems. For welfare reform to be successful, these families will have to be able to afford quality childcare. Otherwise, our society might create as many problems as we are solving with the recent welfare reform.

Current Federal and State Childcare Policies

Currently, the government is involved in the childcare market in numerous ways.[8] A significant portion of the government's involvement is designed to make childcare more affordable. The Dependent Care Tax Credit benefits mostly the middle class and cost the federal government approximately $2.2 billion in the year 2000 (Committee on Ways and Means, Green Book 2000). The credit is not refundable so that families with low earnings that face limited, if any, federal tax burden do not benefit from this policy. There are also childcare subsidy funds targeted to low-income families and ex-welfare recipients. These are monies made available through the Child Care and Development Block Grant (CCDBG), and block-granted to the states as a result of the 1996 federal reform of welfare. The federal government allocated 3.6 billion dollars in fiscal year 2000 for these funds. But these funds were made available only to approximately 15 percent of the families who meet the federal income eligibility limit, so that only the poorest of the poor families receive any support (U.S. Department of Health and Human Services 1999).

These subsidies have the intended consequence of making childcare more affordable and might also increase the quality of care consumed. As not all forms of childcare are eligible for the subsidies (particularly unlicensed, informal care arrangements), these subsidies also may have the consequence of altering the choice of mode of care. For example, even if family day-care homes are preferred by the parents, since licensed providers are not in as great supply as unlicensed providers, parents who prefer such care might be forced to choose center-based care in order to be eligible for a childcare subsidy. It is not clear if this is a good or bad outcome because while some parents might feel they are being forced to forego their first choice of care arrangements, center-based care is often of higher quality.

Finally, the availability of work-based childcare subsidies might encourage more parents (particularly mothers) to enter the workforce. In general, there is a benefit from enabling mothers to choose freely between caring for their children full-time themselves and purchasing part-time or full-time care in the market. When women have this choice, their labor force participation rates rise, thereby enhancing the overall productive potential of our society, and making it possible for women to work in a broader array of occupations, some of which do not permit short- or long-term work interruptions. Society benefits when both men and women can work as doctors, scientists, entrepreneurs, as well as nurses, teachers, and day-care providers. The National Association of Child Advocates' (2000) examination of childcare evaluation research tell us that quality out-of-home childcare education programs are the best way to improve child outcomes. Thus we should not avoid childcare policies that also tend to encourage work because the result can be an increased reliance on pre-kindergarten education programs. In particular, lower-income children benefit the most from quality care. Recent evidence shows us that these benefits can be both short- and long-term, lasting well into young adulthood. (See, for example, *Early Learning, Later Success: The Abecedarian Study*, 2000.)

The government is also involved with policies designed to improve the quality of care or the availability of care. All states have some set of licensing standards (some not particularly binding, though) that establish quality standards for licensed care providers. These standards include maximum allowed child to staff ratios (for example, 4 : 1 for infants) as well as required staff training. Also, some states have programs that subsidize childcare worker training and provide bonuses for workers with specific training or relatively long tenures with the same childcare provider. The federal Head Start program is probably the largest and most well known program that is designed specifically to affect quality and availability simultaneously. Head Start provides 2 years of half or full-day pre-kindergarten to children living in low-income families, and is expected to cost the federal government $3.9 billion in fiscal year 2000 (Committee on Ways and Means, Green Book 2000).

Government intervention in the quality of care by licensing providers and setting quality standards for licensed care can have the intended consequence of improving the quality of care provided in licensed family day-care homes or center-based care. Unfortunately, it can also have the unintended consequence of raising the price of such care, as well as increasing the numbers of providers choosing to forego the licensing process entirely. Currently, it is estimated that nearly 90 percent of family day-care homes are not licensed. These providers do not break any laws by operating without a license (which is akin to a professional credential), and they avoid the hassles and costs of meeting state standards.

Solutions to the Childcare Problems Facing Low-income Families

Probably the most important change in policy would be to make the childcare tax credit refundable, which would provide reimbursements for childcare expenditures for the lowest income workers. This increased subsidy eligibility is consistent with the notion of childcare subsidies as redistributive, in-kind transfers designed to improve the living standards of lower-income families. A second important change would be to extend kindergarten from the half-day program that is available currently in most localities throughout the country to a full-day program that follows the same time schedule as the rest of elementary school. This extension would improve children's readiness for first grade and also ease the childcare burden for working parents of transporting kindergartners from one program to another at mid-day. Part of this change would also extend after-school care availability for older children as well.

A third important change would be to fully fund Head Start so that all eligible low-income children could attend. Currently, only about 35 percent of eligible children are enrolled (Janet Currie 2001). Also, Head Start should be expanded to a full-day full-year program nationwide. Finally, a policy change that is not income-based could be considered. Local school districts could extend the availability of 1 year of free full-day prekindergarten school. Many districts already have a young-fives program for children who are nearly old enough for kindergarten but just not emotionally or academically ready. Providing this free year of prekindergarten would improve the kindergarten-readiness of at-risk children in particular, and help to put all children on a more equal footing at the start of kindergarten. This would be a largely middle-class subsidy, however, and place an even greater burden on already-challenged public schools, without the federal oversight of Head Start.

The advisability of increased regulation in the childcare market is unclear. Certainly, those states that lack sufficient standards on child: staff ratios for center-based care and family day-care homes should adjust those standards to meet the average standards across states. But there is some concern about the impact of standards on the overall availability of care and the willingness of unregulated family day-care providers to enter the licensed market. Blau (2001) offers a broad prescription for the current childcare problems that includes offering financial incentives for parents to seek out quality care. Yet, the ability of state and local governments to identify quality providers and monitor their care is limited at best. It does seem reasonable that the states with the most lax standards improve those standards.

Overall, there is a lack of knowledge about the operation of the childcare market affecting low-income families. President Clinton's Council of Economic Advisors (1997) called for more research for this particular group. Much research is ongoing, however, particularly for those families affected by the 1996 federal welfare reform. As a consequence, many research holes will be filled in over the course of the next few years.

NOTES

1 The 1996 federal legislation that replaced AFDC (Aid to Families with Dependent Children, the previous version of cash welfare) with the largely state-run TANF (Temporary Assistance for Needy Families) was titled the Personal Responsibility and Work Opportunity Reconciliation Act, or PRWORA.

2 I use the expression low-income to refer to families whose income levels are at or below twice the federal poverty threshold, and higher-income for those whose income is above this cut-off value.

3 To put these costs in perspective, consider a recent report by Karen Schulman (2000) that showed for 4 year old children living in urban areas, the average annual cost of care exceeds the average annual cost of tuition at a public college in all but one state.

4 See Rachel Connelly and Jean Kimmel (2002b) for a discussion of married versus single mothers' childcare situations.

5   See, for example, David Blau and Philip Robins (1988), Connelly (1992), David Ribar (1992), and Kimmel (1998).

6   Because the examined outcome is the employment state (employed or not employed), it is modeled as a 0–1 dependent variable. The employment equation is estimated with a probit model, which transforms the discrete observed yes/no employment outcome into a continuous, latent measure of paid work preferences. These most simple models rely on many unrealistic assumptions, including the notion that an individual's available time (24 hours in a day) is divided into paid market work or leisure. Unpaid work in the home is ignored. The employment probit is formulated as any general regression; that is, with a dependent variable on the "left hand side" (namely, the 0–1 employment measure), and a series of independent variables on the "right hand side" of the equation, including family income, a measure of the potential hourly wage, and other factors that help to explain why some individuals choose to work and some choose not to work. For a brief introduction to regression analysis, see chapter 11 by Irene Powell in this volume.

7   Imperfect competition and externalities are discussed in chapter 7 in this volume by Julie Nelson.

8   See Blau (2000) for a comprehensive discussion of childcare subsidy programs.

REFERENCES

Acs, Gregory, Katherin Ross Phillips, and Daniel McKenzie. 2000. *On the Bottom Rung: A Profile of Americans in Low-Income Working Families*. The Urban Institute New Federalism Project, Series A, No. A-42, October.

Blau, David M. 2000. "Child Care Subsidy Programs." National Bureau of Economic Research Working Paper 7806, July. http://www.nber.org.

——. 2001. *The Child Care Problem: An Economic Analysis*. New York: Russell Sage.

Blau, David M. and Philip K. Robins. 1988. "Child-Care Costs and Family Labor Supply." *The Journal of Political Economy*, 106(1): 104–46.

Collins, Ann M., Jean I. Layzer, J. Lee Kreader, Alan Werner, and Fred B. Glantz. 2000. *National Study of Child Care for Low-Income Families: State and Community Substudy Interim Report*. Prepared for the U.S. Department of Health and Human Services, Administration for Children and Families, November.

Committee On Ways and Means, U.S. House of Representatives. 2000. *2000 Green Book: Background Material and Data on Programs Within the Jurisdiction of the Committee on Ways And Means*.

Connelly, Rachel. 1992. "The Effects of Child Care Costs on Women's Decision-Making," in David M. Blau (ed.) *The Economics of Child Care*, pp. 87–118. New York: Russell Sage Foundation.

Connelly, Rachel and Jean Kimmel. 2001. "Marital Status and Full-time/Part-time Work Status in Child Care Choices." W. E. Upjohn Institute for Employment Research Working Paper No. 99–58, updated July 2001.

——. 2002a. "The Effect of Child Care Costs on the Labor Force Participation and Welfare Recipiency of Single Mothers." in *Southern Economic Journal*, previously circulated as W. E. Upjohn Institute for Employment Working Paper No. 01–69, 2001.

——. 2002b. "Marriage, Paid Employment and Child Care," in Shoshana Grossbard-Shechtman (ed.). *Marriage and the Economy*, Cambridge, Massachusetts: Cambridge University Press.

Council of Economic Advisors. 1997. The Economics of Child Care. CEA White Paper, December. http://www.whitehouse.gov/WH/EOP/CEA/html/childcare.html#econ.

Currie, Janet. 2001. "Early Childhood Education Programs." *Journal of Economic Perspectives* 15(2): 213–38.

Early Learning, Later Success: The Abecedarian Study. 2000. Chapel Hill, North Carolina, http://www.fpg.unc.edu/~abc.

Ehrle, Jennifer, Gina Adams, and Kathryn Tout. 2001. "*Who's Caring for Our Youngest Children? Child Care Patterns of Infants and Toddlers.*" Occasional Paper Number 42, Assessing the New Federalism, Urban Institute, January.

Fuller, Bruce, Susan Holloway, and Xiaoyan Liang. 1996. "Family Selection of Child-Care Centers: The Influence of Household Support, Ethnicity, and Parental Practices." *Child Development* 67: 320–37.

Giannarelli, Linda and James Barsimantov. 2000. *Child Care Expenses of America's Families.* Occasional Paper Number 40, Assessing the New Federalism, Urban Institute, December.

Kimmel, Jean. 1995. "The Effectiveness of Child Care Subsidies in the Welfare to Work Transition of Low-Income Single Mothers." *American Economic Review* 85(2): 271–5.

——. 1998. "Child Care as a Barrier to Employment for Married and Single Mothers." *The Review of Economics and Statistics* 80(2): 287–99.

National Association of Child Advocates. 2000. *Making Investments in Young Children: What the Research on Early Care and Education Tells Us.* Washington, DC: National Association of Child Advocates, December.

Nicholson, Walter. 2000. *Intermediate Microeconomics and its Applications.* Eighth edition, New York: The Dryden Press.

Ribar, David. 1992. "Child Care and the Labor Supply of Married Women: Reduced Form Evidence." *Journal of Human Resources* 28(1): 134–65.

Schulman, Karen. 2000. *The High Cost of Child Care Puts Quality Child Care Out of Reach For Many Families.* Children's Defense Fund.

Temporary Assistance for Needy Families (TANF) Program: Second Annual Report to Congress 1999; Executive Summary; U.S. Department of Health and Human Services, Administration for Children and Families, Office of Planning, Research and Evaluation, August.

U.S. Department of Health and Human Services. 1999. HHS Annual Report to Congress, 1999.

Vandell, Deborah Lowe and Barbara Wolfe. 2000. *Child Care Quality: Does It Matter and Does It Need to be Improved?* U.S. Department of Health and Human Services, ASPE.

Walker, James R. 1991. "Public Policy and the Supply of Child Care Services," in David M. Blau (ed.) *The Economics of Child Care*, pp. 51–77. New York: Russell Sage Foundation.

APPENDIX

The four figures in this appendix show the impact of childcare costs on the mother's hours worked. The figures rely on indifference curve analysis. The initial situation is displayed in figure A1, with the individual facing indifference curve I_0 and the wage rate shown by the slope of the diagonal portion of the budget constraint (shown by line ABC). The tangency point

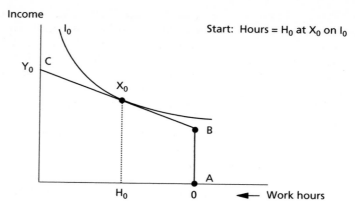

Figure A1 Starting position

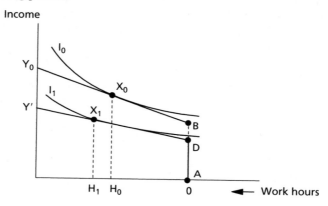

Figure A2 Person 1

(given by X_0) of the indifference curve on the budget constraint shows the equilibrium hours worked at H_0.

I treat childcare costs as both variable (as paid by the hour) and quasi-fixed (due to transportation costs and the common minimum weekly childcare fee required even for low-hours users of care). The variable cost component to childcare costs causes a flattening of the diagonal portion of the budget constraint. The fixed cost component causes a discontinuous shift downward in the budget line. The new budget constraint is given by ADY' (for those who work, and point B for those who do not work.

Figure A2 shows the outcome for Person 1, for whom the childcare costs cause an increase in hours worked to H_1. For this person, the income effect dominates the substitution effect (not shown). Figure A3 shows the outcome for Person 2, who reduces hours worked to H_2. For this person, the substitution effect (driven by the lower effective wage) dominates the income effect. Finally, Person 3 is shown in figure A4. This person initially worked very few hours, and so the imposition of childcare costs causes such a reduction in hours worked that the individual drops out of the labor force.

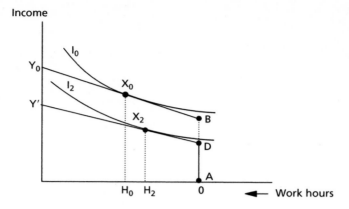

Figure A3 Person 2

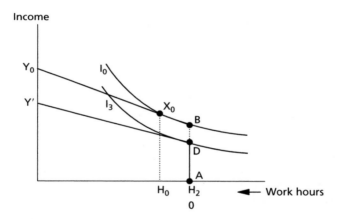

Figure A4 Person 3

The Gender Gap in Earnings

Chapter 9

The Human Capital Explanation for the Gender Gap in Earnings

Joyce P. Jacobsen

The preeminent puzzle for economists interested in gender issues is why women earn less than men do. Remarkably, this fact holds firm across time and space. Abstracting from differences in labor force participation – many women do not do any market work, and many women work fewer hours than most men – the question becomes why women who do market work receive lower hourly earnings on average than do men.

This chapter describes and considers the human capital explanation for this gender gap in earnings. Human capital refers to productivity-related attributes that people develop over time, such as those gained during the formal education process, from training (whether on-the-job or in other programs), and from the experience of working in various firms, occupations, and industries. It also refers to physical and mental health to the extent that healthiness increases productivity. Generally, people with more human capital would be expected to be more productive and therefore to earn more per unit of time than people with less human capital, all else equal. Different forms of human capital, however, may lead to different earnings rates.

While many economists believe that there are other causes of the gender gap in earnings as well as differences in the amounts and types of human capital held by women and men, they also generally believe that human capital differences are an important partial explanation of the gender gap. One important question is therefore how gender may affect human capital investment decisions, thereby leading to different investments by gender. Another question is how much of the gender gap in earnings can be explained by gender differences in human capital.

In this chapter, I first define and flesh out the concept of human capital. I then consider the evidence regarding differences in amounts and types of human capital by gender, along with considering the various mechanisms that could lead to these differences. Then I present and evaluate evidence regarding the contribution of human capital gender differences to the gender pay gap. I round out the discussion by considering alternative explanations (to the neoclassical economic one) both for why "human capital" would vary by gender, and for why the pay gap might occur.

What is Human Capital?

The concept of human capital is quite old. Serious references to it are found in economics writings back to 1676 (Sherwin Rosen 1987: 682). The modern rendition of human capital theory is commonly dated to the writings of Jacob Mincer (1958), Theodore Schultz (1961), and Gary Becker – who wrote a book entitled *Human Capital* (1964; 1993). Human capital theory blossomed in the 1970s into a research program, or, more accurately, as Mark Blaug (1992a: 207) states, into "a subprogram within the more comprehensive neoclassical research program . . ."[1]

Many economists use the term "human capital" following the meaning in Adam Smith, in which a worker chooses to acquire talents "during his education, study, or apprenticeship," which "as they make a part of his fortune, so do they likewise of that of the society to which he belongs" (Adam Smith 1776 II.I.17, 1991). The definition is expanded in some renditions to include anything that can translate into higher productivity, including physical fitness and healthiness. For instance, one labor economics textbook gives the definition of human capital as: "The accumulation of prior investments in education, on-the-job training, health, and other factors that increase productivity" (Campbell McConnell, Stanley Brue, and David Macpherson 1999: 614). An even more general definition is given in another labor textbook: "All acquired characteristics of workers that make them more productive" (Daniel Hamermesh and Albert Rees 1988: 63).

Any parallels between human capital and physical capital (for example, buildings, equipment, and other assets that a business might consider as productive assets) are wholly intentional. In particular, in conventional neoclassical economic theory, the decision as to whether or not to invest in human capital is considered to be one made by a rational economic agent seeking to maximize some function, generally utility, but in a more reductionist form, income, just as decisions regarding investment in physical capital are generally considered to be made by firms seeking to maximize profit. In addition, both firms and individuals might rationally consider whether it is better on the margin to direct funds into human capital investment or physical capital investment, so that the two are directly comparable in terms of the monetary return that an additional dollar of investment would generate. Finally, both forms of capital may be subject to depreciation over time.

A differentiation is often drawn between "general" and "specific" forms of human capital. Clearly human capital types can fall along a spectrum, wherein some forms are useful only in particular firms or jobs (that is, specific), while other forms are useful in a broad range of situations (that is, general). Here, the distinction between general and specific human capital becomes important. Employers are generally unwilling to provide workers with general human capital investments, such as remedial education, because they are concerned that the workers they train will leave the firm soon after training and the firm will receive no return on this training investment. This leads to the prediction that most general human capital will be provided through formal education rather than through on-the-job training or work experience. On the other hand, little specific capital will be provided in formal educational settings, instead being developed on the job through training and experience. Firms may also be hesitant to make specific human capital investments in persons who they think will be leaving the firm. Workers will not, however, be willing to make specific capital investments without guarantee of future employment that will provide a return on these investments. The greater risk associated with investment in specific human capital leads to the prediction that risk-averse workers will require a higher rate of return on specific than on general human capital.

Gender Differences in Human Capital

Human capital theory leads to several explanations for why women earn less than men do. First, women may have less human capital than men have. Secondly, women could have the same amount of human capital as men, but it could vary in type in the following four ways: (1) women may be more likely to invest in human capital that has high non-market return; (2) women may be more likely to invest in human capital that increases satisfaction with time spent in market work, non-market work, or leisure, while men may invest in human capital with a high return in wages but little increase in satisfaction; (3) women may invest in human capital that depreciates less rapidly than the human capital that men invest in; and (4) women may be less likely to invest in specific human capital. In all four cases, women's monetary return on a given amount of human capital investment will therefore be lower than men's.

We must go back a step to ask why any two people would vary in the amounts and types of human capital that they have at any point in time when they are of the same age. Human capital investment generally involves at least one scarce resource – time – and generally the second scarce resource of money. Public schooling is often free, but nonetheless may involve purchase of related items such as textbooks and uniforms. Hence persons (and families) with less money may be less likely to acquire human capital than wealthier persons (and families). Second, decisions regarding human capital investment are not always in the person's hands. Investment decisions can be affected by parents' (and other interested parties, including governmental bodies) choices as to how to allocate resources across their children. In many countries, children may be viewed as viable laborers at early ages; hence the choice to send the child to school involves weighing the opportunity cost of their foregone production, either in the market sector or in the household or family business, as well as the potential

Table 9.1   Measures of educational attainment by gender, developing, and developed countries

	Women	Men	Women/men ratio
Developing countries			
Average years of schooling, 2000			
Persons 25 years and older	4.03	5.74	0.70
Persons 15 years and older	4.33	5.92	0.73
Literacy rate, persons 15 and older, 1998	64.50	80.30	0.80
Developed countries			
Average years of schooling, 2000			
Persons 25 years and older	9.55	10.06	0.95
Persons 15 years and older	9.53	10.01	0.95
Rate of bachelor's degree recipients			
Persons of typical graduation age, 1996	25.30	21.10	1.20

Sources: Barro and Lee (2000: Table 5); United Nations Development Programme (UNDP) (2000: Table 1); NCES (United States National Center for Education Statistics 1999: Table 415). Number of countries in the sample varies depending on data availability.

payoff to the family of the human capital investment in the child. The different outcomes from this comparison process can lead to very different investment decisions for individuals that are in other ways quite equal, but are in very different familial situations.

These decisions may of course be conditioned by gender of the child. Indeed, it is quite clear that across a wide range of developing countries, women receive a much lower level of formal education than do men. The first part of table 9.1 illustrates this educational attainment gap. On average across developing countries, women receive less than three-quarters of the amount of men's formal schooling. While the gap is closing slightly among the younger generation (as can be seen by the slightly higher ratio among those 15 years and older as compared to those 25 years and older), this difference is still substantial. Literacy rates, which could be taken as a minimum measure of education, are also unequal by gender, with less than two-thirds of women reaching this qualification level, as compared to two-thirds of men. These differences could be explained within the neoclassical framework as either involving a higher opportunity cost for educating women rather than men, or leading to a higher payoff from educating men rather than women, or higher out-of-pocket costs for educating women rather than men. All of these factors have been cited in various studies as contributing to this educational attainment differential (Anne Hill and Elizabeth King 1995: 33–6).

Potentially, this bias towards providing more formal education for men may be offset by a bias towards providing more informal human capital attainment, for women.

In particular, female children may receive more training, provided generally by family members, in skills that are of use in household production and/or in other forms of unpaid labor, including childraising skills. This is not a question that we are able to answer definitively at this time, given the nature of available data. While it is true that household time use surveys generally show that female children spend more time in household chores than do male children, this time may be mostly spent not in developing new skills, but in utilizing the skills that they already have.

While we might almost stop here and assume that the main explanation for the gender difference in earnings has now been shown, it turns out that these explanations of lower investment in female children do not apply clearly to developed countries. As shown in the bottom half of table 9.1, women and men in developed countries have roughly comparable mean years of formal education (although women still lag behind men by about half a year of formal schooling). Indeed, women have several favorable characteristics relative to men in these countries, including a higher rate of bachelor's degree attainment, as shown in table 9.1. They are less likely to drop out of school; for example, the dropout rate in the United States – defined as the percentage of those aged 16 to 24 who are not enrolled in school and who have not received a high school diploma or its equivalent – is 10 percent of women and 13 percent of men (U.S. National Center for Education Statistics (NCES) 1999: Table 108). In several countries, including Canada, the United States, Australia, and Sweden (NCES 1993: Table 397), they are more likely to go on to college and even to graduate. For example, in the United States, 56 percent of those enrolled in college are female (NCES 1999: Table 177).

When we turn to measures of type of human capital, as well as amounts of other forms of human capital than formal education and health, gender differences that favor men reappear. Men are more likely to go on to receive professional degrees. Across developed countries, about 40 percent of the bachelor's degree holders are women (NCES 1996: Table 13) and about a third of graduate degrees are awarded to women (NCES 1993: Table 397). For example, in the United States, the proportion of women drops from 61 percent of those earning associate (two-year) degrees, to 56 percent of those earning bachelor's degrees. It then rises to 57 percent of those earning master's degrees, but falls to 42 percent of those earning professional degrees and 41 percent of those earning doctoral degrees (NCES 1999: Table 249).

In addition, at each level of post-secondary education, men are more likely to receive degrees in higher-paying fields. For example, in the United States in 1997, men earned 73 percent of computer science bachelor's degrees and 83 percent of undergraduate engineering degrees, both high-paying fields, while women earned 75 percent of undergraduate education degrees, a low-paying field. Women earned 77 percent of master's degrees in education, while men earned 72 percent of master's degrees in computer science and 82 percent in engineering. One of the best-paid doctoral degrees is economics (!), of which men received 77 percent of the awarded degrees (NCES 1999: Table 258).

Table 9.2   Measures of work history by gender, US workers

Category	Women	Men	Women/men ratio
Proportion who took skill improvement training while in their current job, 1991	41.0	40.0	1.02
Average years worked at current firm	6.5	8.9	0.73
Average years of work experience	18.0	20.4	0.88
Percentage of workers with one or more work interruptions	47.0	13.2	3.63
Percentage of potential work-years spent away from work	14.7	1.6	9.19

Sources: United States Department of Labor (1992: Table 38); Jacobsen and Levin (1998: Table 1); United States Department of Labor (1987 Current Population Reports Series P-70, no. 10 Tables A, C, E). Non-training data are from the Survey of Income and Program Participation, 1984, 1985, and 1987 panels (all three used for tenure and work experience; 1984 only for interruptions and work-years). Workers are ages 21 to 64. Potential work-years is defined as age minus years of schooling minus 6 years.

Educational attainment, much of which occurs before a person has entered into full-time employment, is only part of the story; however, the other major category of human capital that likely contributes to earnings is human capital accumulated during employment. Table 9.2 illustrates a number of these "worktime" human capital measures for the United States workforce, one of the few countries for which an extensive amount of such data are available. Notably, training rates are quite comparable across women and men, although the type and quantity of training received may be quite different. This is borne out by other studies that corroborate the relative equality of total training rates, but show different sources of training by gender, with women more likely to attend vocational and technical institutes and attend seminars outside of work, while men are more likely to participate in apprenticeships and company training (Jonathan Veum 1993: Table 1).

Women have lower mean years of time at their current employer and lower mean years of total work experience. They also have much higher rates of intermittent labor force attachment, that is, gaps in their work experience record – a factor that relates to their lower tenure and experience, but can also potentially relate to higher depreciation rates of human capital for women. The net effect of these factors is that, aside from training, the female workforce apparently has a substantially smaller amount of these forms of worktime human capital than does the male workforce. Given the narrowness of the educational attainment differential in developed countries, and indeed the higher levels of formal educational attainment for women relative to men in several countries, we might expect these differences in worktime human capital to be critical determinants internationally of the gender wage gap in the twenty-first century.

The Impact of Gender Differences in Human Capital on the Gender Gap in Earnings

You have now seen some broad measures concerning differences by gender for factors such as educational attainment and health that can lead to monetary return. The evidence is fairly conclusive that women do not have as much human capital as do men, at least of a form that returns a high monetary payoff in the formal work sector. This section considers how we might measure the impact of these different amounts of human capital on the gender gap in hourly earnings, and reviews the evidence for the proportion of the gender gap accounted for by these differences.

We might well consider that the sizeable differentials in such factors as educational attainment are explanation enough for the gender wage difference. We might also assume that the gender wage difference would be much greater in developing countries, where the human capital gender gap appears widest, than in developed countries. But human capital, or lack thereof, affects not only wages, but also labor market participation. Hence it is logically possible that women might have lower average human capital, in particular lower market-relevant human capital, yet earn at an equal or even higher level than men. This result could be driven by the very different participation rates in paid work. If only those women with very high levels of human capital enter the paid labor sector, while a wider range of men enter into paid labor, the overall gender wage ratio will be comparing two groups with very different average human capital attainment. Hence the degree of gender difference in *actual* earnings will underestimate the degree of gender difference in *potential* earnings (which might be the measure of more interest in considering the full effect of lower human capital on women's productivity).

The effect will be potentially exacerbated if women are more likely to participate in informal labor markets, which tend to pay less well, either because they have lower levels of human capital, or because they are barred from participating in the formal labor market. For one or both of these reasons, this does appear to be the case. Earnings data collected in developing countries are likely to be non-representative of the labor force as a whole. In particular, if these surveys reflect earnings for larger, generally better-paying firms, which are more likely to be included in surveys in any country, doubt is cast on their representativeness. This would again lead to a potential underestimate of the degree of gender difference in potential earnings. On the other hand, if such firms discriminate more (that is, pay women less than men at any given level of human capital, all else equal) than firms overall, and potentially even more than positions in the informal labor market sector, the measured ratios will overestimate the degree of gender difference in earnings for the society as a whole.

Both of these phenomena appear to occur to some degree, but in particular the selection bias appears to work in the direction of underestimating disparity. Notably, gender wage ratios are remarkably similar between developed and developing countries. Even in countries where overall female labor force participation is low, the wage

Table 9.3 Non-agricultural hourly earnings ratios, developed, and developing countries

Country	Women/men	Country	Women/men
Iceland	0.93	Botswana	0.97
Sweden	0.90*	Turkey	0.97*
Australia	0.89	Myanmar	0.96*
Norway	0.88*	El Salvador	0.95*
Denmark	0.83	Kenya	0.94
New Zealand	0.83	Philippines	0.90
France	0.82	Cook Islands	0.89
United Kingdom	0.80	Sri Lanka	0.85
Finland	0.79*	Egypt	0.81
Belgium	0.79	Costa Rica	0.79
Netherlands	0.77	Mexico	0.76
United States	0.76	Brasil	0.75
Ireland	0.75*	Paraguay	0.74
Germany	0.74	Thailand	0.72
Luxembourg	0.70	Swaziland	0.64
Austria	0.69	Cyprus	0.64
Switzerland	0.67	Malaysia	0.63*
South Korea	0.64	Eritrea	0.58
Japan	0.64	Macau	0.56*

* For manufacturing only.

Sources: All countries except United States – International Labour Office, *Yearbook of Labour Statistics* (1994–99) (Table 5). United States – 2000 median weekly earnings for year-round full-time workers, United States Department of Labor 2001, *Employment and Earnings* 48, no. 1 (January): Table 37. Data are from 1989–2000.

ratio is quite comparable to countries where the participation rate is higher, and in some cases countries with low female participation rates have above-average gender wage ratios. Table 9.3 displays some recent data on gender wage ratios. The average level across the represented countries is 0.79. The average across the developed countries, of 0.78, is not significantly different from the average across the developing countries in the table, of 0.79. The range in the table is from 0.56 to 0.97. This is a notably narrower range than for female formal labor market participation, which ranges from a low of 8 percent in Algeria to 92 percent in Burundi (Joyce Jacobsen 1998).

This pattern also reinforces the importance of comparing the actual wage gap to that which would occur if women and men did have equal quantities of human capital. This second, or adjusted, wage ratio, would essentially net out the effects of human capital differences on the wage gap, leaving the remainder to be explained by other causes, including differences in preferences by sex (that is, for non-pecuniary aspects of work), and various discriminatory mechanisms, including pure prejudice (that is, paying equally-qualified women less than men).[2]

For United States data, studies designed to measure the net effect of these differences on the wage gap generally report that some 30 to 50 percent of the gender wage difference is attributable to gender differences in human capital (Jacobsen 1998). These studies generally include at a minimum a control for different levels of education, and then vary in their ability to include other human capital measures. Some measure of actual or potential work experience is also quite commonly included.

Such studies have also been performed for other developed countries using identical techniques. These studies find a roughly comparable proportion of the difference to be attributable to differences in human capital-related characteristics between women and men. This conclusion has been modified, however, by interesting research into how different institutional structures in the labor market can moderate the effect of human capital on relative earnings. In an important series of papers, Francine Blau and Lawrence Kahn (1992; 1996) have demonstrated that the contribution to the gender earnings gap of the wage structure, including the lack of decentralized wage-setting and the greater level of wage inequality, is greater in the United States than in the other countries. They conclude that the United States gender earnings gap would be similar to that in Sweden and Australia, the countries with the smallest gaps (as seen in table 9.3), if the US had their lower level of pay inequality. This would occur because the jobs that women tend to occupy are lower-paid than those that men tend to occupy, but the earnings gap between these different jobs is smaller in other countries. Therefore, even though US women's work qualifications are high relative to those of men, they fare worse relative to men than women in other countries.

There are fewer studies yet for less-developed countries in which an attempt is made to unearth the causes of the earnings gap, and they have led to divergent results. A study of workers in Rawalpindi City, Pakistan (Javed Ashraf and Birjees Ashraf 1993), shows that for this sample, in which the gender earnings ratio is 0.60, about 40 percent of the gap is attributable to differences in characteristics between male and female workers; an older study of Cyprus (William House 1983) found that 38 percent of the gap (with a ratio of 0.55) was attributable to differences in characteristics. These results are roughly in line with results for the United States and other industrialized countries, indicating that employed women in undeveloped countries may not encounter worse discrimination with respect to pay than do women in developed countries. For six other countries where such studies have been carried out (Argentina, Colombia, Haiti, Kuwait, Malaysia, and Venezuela), differences in worker characteristics accounted for between 4 and 25 percent of the earnings gap; notably, the gender earnings ratios were higher in these samples, ranging from 0.64 in Kuwait to 0.87 in Haiti (Katherine Terrell 1992: 393; Nasra Shah and Sulayman Au-Qudsi 1990; Bruce Chapman and J. Ross Harding 1985). Finally, a study using 1977 data from Tanzania (John Knight and Richard Sabot 1982) found that the entire gap was attributable to human capital differences!

These studies are always subject to a variety of critiques regarding their ability to model actual processes in the workplace. Two problems that every study must address are (1) how representative are the data used in the study; and (2) questions about what potentially relevant human capital measures were excluded, usually because they were not available in the data set. The first question has been addressed at length above, and statistical correction techniques are often used to deal in particular with the problem that women who work are not necessarily representative of women as a whole in the population.

The second question can be addressed in part by comparing results from different studies, as studies generally differ in exactly what human capital measures they include. For example, most studies do not consider detailed measures of education, but generally include years of schooling as the measure of this form of human capital. Given that years of schooling vary little by gender for developed countries, this measure is unlikely to lead to a notable adjustment in the gender wage ratio. But, as discussed above, college major patterns are quite different by gender. Hence, it would be interesting to see if a study that controlled carefully for differences in what is studied during college can lead to a larger adjustment in the gender wage ratio. Catherine Weinberger (1998) performs just such a study for a US sample of recent college graduates. She finds that the unadjusted wage ratio for the sample is 0.82, while adjusting for these human capital differences leads to an adjusted wage ratio of 0.85 to 0.90, depending on the type of adjustment and the group considered (white, black, Asian, or Hispanic) – a range of 17 to 44 percent of the gender earnings gap for this sample. This implies that if such controls were used in all studies, that a greater percentage of the gender earnings gap would in general be explained.

One danger in adding additional controls into the adjustment process, however, is the difficulty of interpreting what one is controlling for. Blau and Kahn (2000) report using a representative sample of full-time workers for the US in 1988, in which they systematically adjust the wage ratio first for the "standard" human capital variables of years of education and years of work experience (along with race), and then add controls for workers' industry, occupation, and union status. The unadjusted wage ratio was 0.724; the wage ratio adjusted for education, experience, and race was 0.805 (where the gender difference in their sample of 4.6 years of work experience on average accounted for almost all of the adjustment); and the wage ratio adjusted for all variables was 0.882. Hence, augmenting the set of controls in this way increased the explained portion of the gender wage gap from 29 percent to 57 percent. The interpretation of industry, occupation, and union differences as being indicative of differences in the types of human capital held by workers is problematic however. There are a number of alternative explanations for why different sectors of the labor market pay different wage levels, and for why women might systematically be found in the lower-paying sectors.

Nonetheless, the relative consistency across a large number of studies in finding that use of human capital-type controls do yield narrower gender wage gaps has led to a general consensus among economists that the theory has predictive value.

In particular, the consistent result across a number of studies that differences in work experience matter greatly in determining the gender wage gap is an important finding. In conclusion, there is strong empirical evidence that systematic differences in male and female human capital stocks do account for part of the wage gap. While the specific portion of the gap attributable to differences in human capital varies over time and space, and the gap is rarely totally attributable to these differences, it is in general a significant factor in determining gender differences in hourly earnings.

Critiques of the Human Capital Explanation for the Gender Gap in Earnings

We have now seen that women and men differ in their amounts and types of human capital, and also that these differences have a measurable effect on the gender wage gap. Assuming for the moment that human capital investment choices are freely made (rather than determined by our parents or by other social forces), why would men and women differ in their investment strategies regarding human capital?

Neoclassical economic theory can again be invoked to consider why rational persons would differ in their investment decisions. Preferences for types of return on human capital may differ, in this case systematically by gender, with women preferring types of human capital that generate non-monetary returns (including potentially increased household production). Another set of reasons relates to the observed pattern of women's spending less time in the labor force. If women anticipate spending less total time in paid labor, their total monetary return is reduced relative to that of men's. Even if they anticipate as many total years of paid work, if they anticipate intermittent labor force attachment, it could lead to their choosing less-rapidly depreciating forms and less firm-specific capital, both of which would tend to have lower returns than more risky capital.

If we assume that agents are rational, but that labor markets are not perfectly competitive, then discrimination against women may occur, but would be anticipated by women, who would take actions to mitigate its effects on them personally. Discrimination against women in the labor market in either hiring or pay has the result of providing them with a lower rate of return on human capital. Anticipating discrimination, women might therefore invest less in market work-related human capital.

Discrimination in access to human capital attainment may also occur, creating a barrier to women's achieving their desired level of investment. In the case of on-the-job training, this could be partly due to the perception on the part of employers to make specific human capital investments in women if they anticipate lower tenure on their parts (that is, statistical discrimination). In the case of formal education, the gatekeepers of educational institutions serve as the discriminating agents.

It appears that discrimination in access to education, training, and labor markets was the critical determinant of women's lower human capital investments in historical periods. Discrimination also continues to be the major explanation for women's lower human capital investments in developing countries. It has been more difficult, however, to design satisfactory tests for the hypotheses mentioned above for developed countries, even using recent and reasonably comprehensive data sources (Jacobsen 1998). The issue of whether or not women choose occupations that require less-rapidly depreciating human capital has not been resolved, with researchers finding opposing results. There is evidence that women's expectations regarding childrearing and labor force intermittency can affect their formal education options, such as college major, and their acquisition of on-the-job training. There is also evidence that women value the non-monetary aspects of work relatively more than do men. These expectations, however, may themselves be formed by realizing that access to lucrative forms of employment is curtailed for women, making it difficult to argue that discrimination has not played an indirect part in shaping women's choices at this critical phase.

One of the main critiques of human capital theory has been its narrow focus on labor market activity, which has tended to ignore interactions with marriage markets and choices made prior to entry into the prime labor market years. For example, while the discussion above assumed free choice on the part of all persons in making human capital investment decisions, critics have argued that women's choice to spend less time in labor force participation is not freely made. If there are social norms and customs governing choice, then free choice is an oxymoron. Ability and/or desire to acquire various forms of human capital, which may vary systematically by sex, may be shaped by such norms and customs, which ascribe different activities to women and men. In particular, to the extent that the double day/second shift is automatically assigned to women, women may choose forms of human capital that are compatible with this requirement. Additionally, parents, husbands and other persons may make the choices regarding human capital investment for the woman. Clearly, the feedback issues regarding society's expectations of women's roles becoming self-fulfilling have not been carefully modeled, nor is this issue readily tractable given current empirical and theoretical tools. This is a major area for further research in economics.

This critique of the neglect of explicit modeling of feedback has been particularly trenchant and well-founded with regard to the empirical literature on wage differentials, nearly all of which is based on the human capital model of wage determination. As discussed in the previous section, researchers try to control for all human capital-related measures in order to explain differences in wages between two groups. They then ascribe the unexplained component to a combination of omitted variables and discrimination, providing an apparent upper bound on the percentage of the wage gap that can be ascribed to discrimination against one of the groups. To the extent that the less-favored group has less human capital because of experiencing discrimination or constrained choice in one of the ways mentioned above, this effect cannot be separated from freely choosing to invest in less human capital.

Another critique of human capital theory is that, in its atomistic focus on the individual's decision, it ignores the effects of other agents' actions on that decision. This is true not only in the senses described in the two preceding paragraphs, but also when incorporating ideas from crowding theory. To the extent that women are only allowed into a narrow range of occupations, the rate of return on human capital in the female-dominated occupations is reduced below what it would be in a freely-operating labor market. Also, if occupations differ in terms of the wage differential paid to women and men of equal productivity, women will be more likely to invest in specific human capital for the less discriminatory occupations. This creates a different occupational choice process for women than for men. In particular, occupations that are lower-paid but less discriminatory are relatively more attractive to women than they would be in a world with no discrimination.

A third critique, voiced by a wide range of labor market theorists, including Marxist and institutionalist scholars, is that all of the phenomena reported above are also compatible with alternative models of wage determination (see Blaug 1992b: Part II). Education may serve as a screening device to determine who is more or less able rather than as a way to increase ability, or as a method of acculturating workers to the capitalist production mode and segmenting them so as to inhibit formation of worker coalitions (Samuel Bowles and Herbert Gintis 1975). Rising wages as an individual persists with a firm over time could be a pure function of linking wages to seniority, rather than evidence of increased productivity through accrual of more human capital.

Expanding these lines of thought into a feminist critique would attribute the differences between returns to men's and women's human capital to the desire to maintain patriarchy. In particular, it may be the case that determination of what forms of human capital are particularly valuable in the society is made in part based on which gender is likely to obtain the human capital. These types of dynamics mean that actions intended to increase women's human capital holdings, particularly holdings of types that have currently higher return, would have lower-than-expected returns. Therefore we might imagine that if women are successful in, say, achieving entry into the academy, that the patriarchal order will be maintained by reducing access to another area and reordering wages so as to privilege this area instead. Returns to, say, holding a college degree or even a particular postgraduate degree, would systematically fall as more women received these forms of advance training, while returns would rise in other areas that remain male-dominated or become newly masculinized. Occupational segregation and labor market segmentation theorists, particularly those focusing on the apparent relationship between lower earnings and higher percentage female, have pointed out that occupations that have become feminized appear simultaneously to undergo reduced relative status and reduced relative earnings (Barbara Reskin and Patricia Roos 1990). Projected returns to increasing women's human capital endowments may also be overestimated if glass ceiling effects persist – that is, subtle discrimination which prevents women from achieving equal returns to those of men as they reach the higher levels of human capital within a given occupation or industry (Joyce Jacobsen and Lawrence Levin 2000).

A final critique is whether people really make the types of forward-looking calculations assumed by the theory (which, as generally implemented, does not consider incomplete information or uncertainty). For instance, one study found that young women systematically underestimate the number of work years and therefore under invest in human capital (Steven Sandell and David Shapiro 1982). The degree of uncertainty introduced by changes in marriage market workings (for example, rising divorce rates during the 1970s, lower rates of ever-marrying in the 1980s) might lead to a rejection of the principles of human capital calculation, or alternatively a risk-reduction strategy of overinvestment in human capital, leading to lower returns than those predicted in a riskless world. Additionally, uncertainty regarding future payoffs might lead to differential behavior by gender regarding human capital investment if men and women differ systematically in risk-aversion and/or appraisal.

Conclusion

Human capital theory, taken together with supporting evidence, provides an important piece towards solving the puzzle of why women earn less than men do. Analysis of the arguments behind human capital theory, however, raises a number of questions as to whether or not increasing the level of human capital of women relative to men will automatically lead to a narrowing of the gender earnings gap. This is a topic on which more research remains to be done, particularly regarding the nature of the feedback mechanisms from discrimination in the labor market to human capital investment decisions. The human capital paradigm has served, and continues to serve, as an important spur to research, some in support and some in opposition to its conclusions.

NOTES

1   See Rosen 1987 for a thorough statement of the conventional neoclassical formulation.
2   I provide a description for this technique in the appendix. For a brief explanation of regression analysis, see chapter 11 by Irene Powell in this volume.

REFERENCES

Ashraf, Javed and Birjees Ashraf. 1993. "Estimating the Gender Wage Gap in Rawalpindi City." *Journal of Development Studies* 29(2): 365–76.
Barro, Robert J. and Jong-Wha Lee. 2000. "International Data on Educational Attainment Updates and Implications." National Bureau of Economic Research Working Paper No. 7911.
Becker, Gary S. 1993. *Human Capital: A Theoretical and Empirical Analysis, with Special Reference to Education, Third Edition*. Chicago: University of Chicago Press.
Blau, Francine D. and Lawrence M. Kahn. 1992. "The Gender Earnings Gap: Learning from International Comparisons." *American Economic Review* 82(2): 533–38.
——. 1996. "Wage Structure and Gender Earnings Differentials: An International Comparison." *Economica* 63(Supplement): S29–S62.
——. 2000. "Gender Differences in Pay." *Journal of Economic Perspectives* 14(4): 75–99.

Blaug, Mark. 1992a. *The Methodology of Economics, Second Edition*. Cambridge: Cambridge University Press.

—— (ed.). 1992b. *The Economic Value of Education: Studies in the Economics of Education*. Aldershot and Brookfield: Edward Elgar.

Bowles, Samuel and Herbert Gintis. 1975. "The Problem with Human Capital Theory – A Marxian Critique." *American Economic Review* 65(2): 74–82.

Chapman, Bruce J. and J. Ross Harding. 1985. "Sex Differences in Earnings: An Analysis of Malaysian Wage Data." *Journal of Development Studies* 21(3): 362–76.

Hamermesh, Daniel S. and Albert Rees. 1988. *The Economics of Work and Pay, Fourth Edition*. New York: Harper & Row.

Hill, M. Anne and Elizabeth M. King. 1995. "Women's Education and Economic Well-Being." *Feminist Economics* 1(2): 21–46.

House, William J. 1983. "Occupational Segregation and Discriminatory Pay: The Position of Women in the Cyprus Labour Market." *International Labour Review* 122(1): 75–93.

International Labour Office. 1994–99. *Yearbook of Labour Statistics*. Geneva, Switzerland, International Labour office.

Jacobsen, Joyce P. 1998. *The Economics of Gender, Second Edition*. Cambridge: Blackwell.

Jacobsen, Joyce P. and Lawrence M. Levin. 1998. "Tenure and Experience: Relative Returns by Race and Sex." Working Paper, Wesleyan University.

——. 2000. "Looking at the Glass Ceiling: Do White Men Receive Higher Returns to Tenure and Experience?" in Robert Cherry and William M. Rodgers III (eds.) *Prosperity for All? The Economic Boom and African Americans*, pp. 217–44. New York: Russell Sage Foundation.

Knight, John B. and Richard H. Sabot. 1982. "Labor Market Discrimination in a Poor Urban Economy." *Journal of Development Studies* 19(1): 67–87.

McConnell, Campbell R., Stanley L. Brue, and David A. Macpherson. 1999. *Contemporary Labor Economics, Fifth Edition*. Boston: Irwin/McGraw Hill.

Mincer, Jacob. 1958. "Investment in Human Capital and Personal Income Distribution." *Journal of Political Economy* 66(4): 281–302.

Reskin, Barbara F. and Patricia A. Roos. 1990. *Job Queues, Gender Queues: Explaining Women's Inroads into Male Occupations*. Philadelphia: Temple University Press.

Rosen, Sherwin. 1987. "Human Capital," in John Eatwell, Murray Milgate, and Peter Newman (eds.) *The New Palgrave: A Dictionary of Economics*, pp. 681–90. London: Macmillan.

Sandell, Steven H. and David Shapiro. 1982. "Work Expectations, Human Capital Accumulation, and the Wages of Young Women." *Journal of Human Resources* 15(3): 335–53.

Schultz, Theodore. 1961. "Investment in Human Capital." *American Economic Review* 51(1): 1–17.

Shah, Nasra M. and Sulayman S. Au-Qudsi. 1990. "Female Work Roles in a Traditional, Oil Economy: Kuwait." *Research in Human Capital and Development* 6: 213–46.

Smith, Adam. 1991. *Wealth of Nations*. Buffalo: Prometheus Books. Originally published 1776.

Terrell, Katherine. 1992. "Female-male Earnings Differentials and Occupational Structure." *International Labour Review* 131(4–5): 387–404.

United Nations Development Programme (UNDP). 2000. *Human Development Report*. http://www.undp.org/hdro/statistics.html.

United States Department of Labor. 1987. "Male-Female Differences in Work Experience, Occupation, and Earnings: 1984." Current Population Reports Series P-70: *Household Economics Studies*, No. 10.

United States Department of Labor. 2001. *Employment and Earnings* 48(1), January.

United States Department of Labor, Bureau of Labor Statistics. 1992. "How Workers Get Their Training: A 1991 Update." Bulletin 2407.

United States National Center for Education Statistics. 1993. *Digest of Education Statistics, 1993.*

——. 1996. *Education Indicators: An International Perspective.* http://nces.ed.gov/pubs/eiip/.

——. 1999. *Digest of Education Statistics, 1999.* http://nces.ed.gov/pubs2000/Digest99/.

Veum, Jonathan R. 1993. "Training Among Young Adults: Who, What Kind, and For How Long?" *Monthly Labor Review* 116(8): 27–32.

Weinberger, Catherine J. 1998. "Race and Gender Wage Gaps in the Market for Recent College Graduates." *Industrial Relations* 37(1): 67–84.

APPENDIX

Using the statistical technique of regression analysis, equations can be estimated separately for women and men that relate the amount of various human capital measures held by each group to the wage levels experienced on average by each group. A regression of wage W on personal characteristics can be estimated of the form $W = \sum_n \beta X$, where X is a set of n characteristics and β is the corresponding set of n coefficients for a set of persons. Regressions have the characteristic that evaluating them at the mean values for all independent variables yields the mean wage for the group. So, if separate equations are estimated for men and women, the mean wages for men and women can be calculated as $\overline{W}_m = \sum_n \beta_m \overline{X}_m$ and $\overline{W}_w = \sum_n \beta_w \overline{X}_w$, where the subscript m denotes male values, the subscript w denotes female values, and a bar over the variable denotes the mean value for that variable. Thus the unadjusted gender wage ratio can be calculated as:

$$U = \frac{\overline{W}_w}{\overline{W}_m} = \frac{\sum_n \beta_w \overline{X}_w}{\sum_n \beta_m \overline{X}_m}.$$

An adjusted wage ratio can be calculated in one of two ways, using either the male mean characteristics: $\sum_n \beta_w \overline{X}_m / \sum_n \beta_m \overline{X}_m$ or the female mean characteristics: $\sum_n \beta_w \overline{X}_w / \sum_n \beta_m \overline{X}_w$.

The former answers the question: what would the gender wage ratio be if men had the human capital levels of women? The latter answers the question: what would the gender wage ratio be if women had the human capital levels of men? There is no way to predict which will produce a larger adjustment; many studies calculate both adjusted wage ratios and take an average of the two. We might consider the latter adjustment to be the more relevant one, as women appear to be increasing their human capital levels at a faster rate over time than are men. The adjusted wage ratio, however calculated, may then be compared to the unadjusted wage ratio to see in particular if the adjustment for different levels of human capital has brought the adjusted wage ratio closer to 1.

Chapter 10

Occupational Segregation Around the World

Debra Barbezat

If you are reading this paper as part of a school assignment, consider the makeup of your classes. If you are taking an economics class, an educated guess would be that two-thirds of your classmates are male. The proportions would be reversed, however, if you happen to be studying sociology.[1] Does a student's choice of major vary by educational setting? Apparently so since economics is one of the most popular under-graduate majors at women's colleges. Moreover, some women's colleges that have moved toward coeducation have witnessed a decline in the popularity of economics among female students.[2] Once students graduate they will find the same lack of integration between men and women in the workplace. Most women work in occupations that are almost exclusively female while the majority of men work alongside men. By way of illustration, table 10.1 presents a breakdown of the six major occupational groups in the United States, noting all occupations that are less than ten percent or greater than 90 percent female.

The tendency for men and women to be employed in different occupations is known as occupational segregation by sex, and it is one of the most distinctive features of labor markets in the United States and abroad. To quote Richard Anker, a specialist on this topic: "Occupational segregation by sex is extensive in every region, at all economic development levels, under all political systems, and in diverse religious, social, and cultural environments" (1997: 315). The primary goal of this paper is to review the extent of occupational segregation by sex both in the United States and other countries. In preparation for this task, we first examine various statistical measures of occupational segregation. Next, we review theoretical explanations of occupational segregation in order to understand why this common characteristic of labor markets is as persistent as it is pervasive. Finally, we discuss the relationship between segregation measures and other key economic variables.

Table 10.1   US occupations with relatively low and high female representation in 2000

Managerial and professional specialty

	% Female		% Female
Construction inspectors	9.5	Registered nurses	92.8
Engineers	9.9	Occupational therapists	91.4
		Pre-kindergarten and kindergarten teachers	98.5

Technical, sales, and administrative support

	% Female		% Female
Surveying and mapping technician	7.4	Dental hygienists	98.5
Airplane pilots and navigators	3.7	Licensed practical nurses	93.6
Sales workers, parts	8.9	Secretaries, stenographers, typists	98.0
		Receptionist	96.7
		Financial records processing	91.8
		Teachers' aides	91.0

Service occupations

	% Female		
		Childcare workers	97.5
Firefighting and fire protection	3.8	Cleaners and servants	94.8
Pest control occupations	5.0	Dental assistants	96.4
		Hairdressers/cosmetologists	91.2
		Family childcare provider	97.7
		Early childhood teacher's assistants	95.2

Precision, production, craft and repair

	% Female		% Female
Mechanics and repairers	5.1	Dressmakers	92.7
Construction trades	2.6		
Extractive occupations	1.9		
Plant and system operators	5.4		

Operators, fabricators, and laborers

	% Female
Mixing and blending machine operators	8.1
Separating, filtering, and clarifying machine operators	3.7
Furnace, kiln, and oven operators (except food)	5.8
Welders and cutters	4.9
Truck drivers	4.7
Transportation occupations (except motor vehicles)	3.5
Material moving equipment operators	5.4

Table 10.1   Continued

Construction laborers	3.8
Garbage collectors	3.8
Garage and service station	7.7
Farming, forestry, and fishing	
	% Female
Supervisors	9.3
Groundskeepers and gardeners (except farm)	7.4
Forestry and logging Occupations	8.4

Source: *Employment and Earnings*, Bureau of Labor Statistics, January 2001, Table 11, pp. 178–83.

The importance of this topic is underscored by the number of authors who have found that higher levels of occupational segregation by sex are associated with larger earnings gaps between men and women. In fact, Jerry Jacobs and Suet Lim (1992: 451) argue that "sex segregation is of interest largely because of its connection with the gender gap in wages." While there is no doubt that the occupational distribution of men and women explains some portion of the earnings gap, this relationship, as we will see later, is not as reliable as some might assume. Moreover, there are numerous other reasons to be concerned about the unequal distribution of men and women across occupations and industries. One obvious concern is that barriers to entry and restrictions on the use of labor prevent labor inputs from being used in an optimal way, thereby reducing national output. Whether considering unions, unemployment insurance systems, or the immobility of male and female workers across occupational categories, it is well established that labor market rigidities are associated with higher rates of unemployment and a reduced ability of the economy to adjust to changing economic conditions.[3] Anker reminds us as well that beyond equity and efficiency concerns, occupational segregation "has an important negative effect on how men see women as well as how women see themselves by reinforcing and perpetuating gender stereotypes" (1998: 6–7). These stereotypes may have detrimental effects on women's economic position, including women's choices regarding training and other human capital investment.

Explaining Occupational Segregation

Leading economic theories of occupational segregation may be grouped as either supply-side or demand-side explanations. Supply-side explanations tend to attribute different labor market outcomes to women's deliberate and voluntary choices with regard to education, training and occupation. This is an important distinction from other theories with different implications for public policy. As Andrea Beller (1982) notes:

> If more than half the population is denied access to 60 percent of the occupations, being crowded into a few at lower earnings, equality of opportunity does not exist. But if women freely choose to enter only a third of all occupations and those occupations pay less, then women's lower earnings may not be a fundamental social problem. The major issue is whether the dramatic differences in the occupational distributions of the sexes result from different choices made by each, given equal opportunities, or from unequal opportunities to make similar choices. (p. 372)

What Paula England et al. (1988) so aptly perceived, however, is that separating competing theories becomes an even more difficult task when "discrimination creates accommodation to limited options that may appear as preferences" (1988: 546).

According to a supply-side explanation, women differ from men in the productivity-related characteristics, and some might add, the preferences, they bring to the labor market. For example, human capital theory predicts that if women anticipate a shorter total duration in the labor force, the present value of the future returns to human capital will be lower and, *ceteris paribus*, women are less likely to invest. The same factors would cause women to acquire less training once in the labor market. One early justification for the unequal distribution of men and women across jobs was that women, who are responsible for the greater share of household labor the world over, would by necessity withdraw from the labor market at points in their lives. Time out of the labor force is associated with skill atrophy and lower wages upon reentering the market. In order to minimize this cost, women rationally choose to enter occupations in which the financial penalty associated with intermittency is relatively small. It has also been argued that women would prefer jobs with relatively high starting salaries over those with low starting salaries and greater future returns to experience (referred to as "appreciation") since they expect a shorter time in the labor market.

A number of researchers have failed to find empirical support for the supply-side explanation of segregation. One of the first critics, England (1982), demonstrates empirically that the financial penalty associated with withdrawal was as large in predominantly male occupations as in female occupations. Moreover, women who spend more post-school years out of the labor force are no more likely to be in female occupations than women who had been continuously employed. Women's labor force commitment has certainly grown over time. In 1999, the labor force participation rate for married women, husband present, with children under the age of 3 years old was an impressive 61.8 percent in the US. Fifty-six percent of the bachelor's degrees awarded in 1997 went to women as did 41 percent of doctorate degrees, 41 percent of medical degrees and 44 percent of law degrees.[4] Occupational segregation has declined in the US in recent decades, but we could question whether the declines are commensurate with women's greater commitment to work outside the home and their acquisition of human capital.

Even if women and men were to receive equal amounts of human capital, discrimination might cause women to receive a lower return for their productive characteristics, whether in the form of reduced wages, a lower likelihood of promotion, or a disadvantage in gaining entry to particular jobs. Several theories of discrimination exist and all of them contribute to our understanding of women's unequal distribution across occupations. Because these models often ascribe discriminatory behavior to employers, we collectively refer to them as constituting a "demand-side" explanation for women's unequal distribution across occupations.[5]

According to the Becker discrimination model (Gary Becker 1971), employers who have a personal prejudice against a minority group view the cost of hiring a minority worker as higher than the worker's market wage, with the additional cost reflecting the employer's psychic disutility from interacting with the worker. The ratio of the minority to majority wage in the labor market depends on the supply of minority labor as well as the extent of psychic disutility exhibited by employers. Segregated workplaces are a prediction of the Becker model. Once the wage differential emerges, Becker predicted that workplaces would tend to be segregated with employers whose psychic disutility was lower than the difference in the minority and majority wage, hiring only minority workers. Employers whose psychic disutility was so large that it exceeded the discounted cost of minority workers, would tend to hire majority workers. Xin Meng's (1998) recent study of occupational segregation in Shandong Province, China underlines the applicability of Becker's approach. Meng attributes differences in occupational segregation between rural and urban areas to differences in employer preferences in the two areas. She also notes that, to some extent, Communist ideology did mitigate the detrimental effects of personal prejudice. Local authorities in the rural industrial sector, for example, were required to enforce egalitarian government ideology when making job assignments (Meng 1998: 750).

Because information on employees is scarce and expensive to acquire, employers may supplement their incomplete information by considering characteristics of the group with which a prospective employee is affiliated. Statistical discrimination, the practice of ascribing group characteristics to an individual member of that group, may arise if the mean level of some productive characteristic is unequal between two groups. For example, employers will prefer to hire men if, on average, they have a higher level of education or a lower turnover rate. Female employees who have higher levels of education than the men's mean, or turnover rates that are below the men's average, will nevertheless face discrimination as employers attempt to improve their selection process.[6] William Bielby and James Baron (1986) found statistical discrimination to be a significant determinant of occupational segregation, although the motive for this behavior, according to the authors, was primarily stereotypical views about appropriate work for men versus women rather than any incentive to reduce costs. Feedback effects may accompany statistical discrimination, as indicated in this example from Francine Blau et al. (2001: 228):

> [I]f employers' views of female job instability lead them to give women less firm-specific training and to assign them to jobs where the costs of turnover are minimized, women have little incentive to stay and may respond by exhibiting exactly the unstable behavior that employers expect. Employers' perceptions are confirmed and they see no reason to change their discriminatory behavior. Yet, if employers had believed women to be stable workers and had assigned them into positions that rewarded such stability, they might well have been stable workers!

Richard Anker and Catherine Hein (1985) present a number of case studies of Third World countries, showing that statistical discrimination against female workers is linked to higher labor costs originating from, among other factors, relatively high birth rates, protective legislation, and mandatory maternity leave benefits. Similarly, William House (1986) finds that employers in Cyprus, Ghana, India, Mauritius, Nigeria and Sri Lanka frequently perceived women as being more costly workers and less productive, on average. In a more detailed study of Cyprus, House finds that while negative employer attitudes contributed to occupational segregation, employer perceptions regarding the quality and continuity of female labor force participation were often inaccurate.

Finally, neoclassical economics also includes institutional approaches for explaining occupational segregation by sex. These models typically examine situations in which institutions such as unions, monopsonistic employers, and large firms hold power in the labor market, resulting in a lack of competition that is detrimental to some groups of workers. According to the monopsony model, employees may be distinguished by their elasticity of labor supply.[7] Workers with relatively elastic labor supply, which could be men or women (depending upon the circumstances), receive lower wages and experience lower employment levels. Peter Doeringer and Michael Piore (1971) develop the theory of dual labor markets, which argues that the labor market is divided into relatively high-paying, stable jobs in the primary sector and less desirable jobs located in the secondary sector. The primary jobs tend to be associated with large, unionized enterprises, and, often, the presence of internal labor markets. If there are gender differences in initial job assignment, a combination of factors makes it difficult to move from the secondary to the primary sector.

There are various extensions of labor market segmentation models. As summarized by Blau, et al. (2001), some researchers note that employers benefit from segmenting the labor market since it prevents workers from gaining power and seeing their common interests. Another approach is to emphasize how patriarchy leads male workers, employers, and their unions to foster continued segregation by gender.[8] In the words of Anker, a basic premise of what he calls feminist/gender theories is that "women's disadvantaged position in the labour market is caused by, and is a reflection of, patriarchy and women's subordinate position in society and the family" (1997: 324). The unequal and selective division of responsibilities between work at home and market work creates stereotypes and societal expectations leading to gender differences in schooling and the acquisition of human capital. Occupational choices reinforce these gender stereotypes.

Measuring Occupational Segregation

Many researchers have noted the tendency of men and women to be employed in different occupations and there exists several approaches to measuring the degree of segregation. One basic approach is simply to document the changing representation of men and women in selected "male-dominated" and "female-dominated" jobs. The majority of researchers, however, prefer to analyze summary statistical measures of segregation. The most widely used segregation index has been the index of dissimilarity developed by Otis Duncan and Beverly Duncan in 1955. The index, also referred to as the ID index, takes on values from 0 (complete integration) to 100 (complete segregation). By way of illustration, the index is calculated below for two groups of workers:

$$\text{Duncan index} = 100 \times \sum_{i=1}^{n} \frac{\left| \dfrac{X_i}{X} - \dfrac{Y_i}{Y} \right|}{2}$$

There are N occupations and X_i is the number of persons of a group in occupation i. X represents the total number of persons in this first group. Y_i represents the number of persons in a comparison group in occupation i, and Y is the total number of persons in the comparison group.[9] One reason that the majority of segregation studies have used the Duncan index is its intuitive interpretation. An index value of, say, 40 is often interpreted as meaning that 40 percent of women (or men) would have to change occupations in order for men and women to be distributed in the same manner across occupations. Unfortunately, this interpretation, contained in many textbooks and research articles, is incorrect (Zafiris Tzannatos 1990; Janet Siltanen et al. 1995). According to Anker, the correct interpretation of the Duncan index is "the proportion of male workers plus the proportion of female workers who would need to change occupations in order to have the same proportion of women in every occupation (and the same proportion of men in every occupation, but with a different value)" (1998: 90).

We need to exercise caution when using the Duncan index to examine changes in concentration over time. Consider an economy that consists of only two occupations: production workers, which is 80 percent male, and professional workers, which is 50 percent female. If the Duncan index value decreases between two time periods, the decline may have been caused by women moving into production jobs thus further integrating that occupation. It is also possible that desegregation did not occur within that occupation, but instead that there was a decline in the size of the production occupation relative to the professional category. For this reason, researchers also calculate a standardized Duncan index that allows the researcher to estimate the degree of sex segregation within occupational categories while controlling for the size of occupations over time. A standardized index allows researchers to discern what the

Table 10.2   Duncan values over the time based on 1-, 2-, and 3-digit occupational classifications for five study countries. Copyright © International Labour Organization 1998

Country/year	Duncan values		
	1 digit	2 digit	3 digit
Netherlands			
1973	0.462	0.639	0.671
1979	0.448	0.622	0.654
1990	0.381	0.556	0.588
Japan			
1970	0.257	0.448	0.526
1980	0.284	0.450	0.529
1990	0.256	0.458	0.529
France			
1982	0.379	0.613	0.636
1990	0.393	0.586	0.607
Switzerland			
1970	0.304	0.584	0.667
1980	0.293	0.573	0.654
Kuwait			
1975	0.508	0.732	0.743
1985	0.499	0.733	0.743

The five countries included in this table met the following conditions: (i) data were available for two or three years, (ii) data were available at the three-digit level and were relatively easy to aggregate to the one- and two-digit levels.
Source: Figures excerpted from Table 6.9, *Gender and Jobs*, Richard Anker, 1998.

trend in occupational segregation would have been had the relative size of occupations remained constant over the time period.

Another important characteristic of the Duncan index is that its value varies according to the number of occupational categories used. Specifically, the magnitude of the index tends to rise as the number of occupational categories employed rises.[10] Studies that rely on relatively broad occupational classifications, therefore, produce smaller measures of occupational segregation than studies that employ a greater number of occupational categories. Using the standard industrial classification (SIC) categories for occupation, one-digit data are highly aggregated whereas three-digit data contain the most variation.[11] Table 10.2 illustrates how the Duncan index rises with number of occupations considered.[12]

Trends in Occupational Segregation in the US

Segregation indexes have been calculated for the United States beginning with 1900 census data. Using decennial census data, Nancy Bertaux (1991) showed that the Duncan index, estimated to be 70 to 71 percent in 1870, declined to a value of 63 to 64 percent in 1900. Bertaux attributed this decline to widespread industrialization. Interestingly, while the occupations available to women were substantially different in 1870 and 1900, they did not change substantially after 1900, causing the author to conclude that "the roots of today's 'women's jobs' can be clearly seen in the occupational shifts experiences in the late 19th century" (Bertaux 1991: 458).

Consistent with this comment, researchers who calculate the Duncan index for the period 1900 through 1970 find almost no variation in occupational segregation by sex. Barbara Reskin and Heidi Hartmann's (1986) study is typical of the literature. The authors conclude that "the [Duncan] index of segregation computed for three-digit occupational classifications for each decennial census has fluctuated between 65 and 69 between 1900 and 1970" (Reskin and Hartmann 1986: 23). The seventies were a watershed period in terms of reducing occupational segregation. Using both census and CPS data, Beller (1984) finds that the Duncan index declined monotonically from a value of 68.14 in 1971 to 64.15 in 1977. The decline over the seventies was confirmed by other researchers, including Suzanne Bianchi and Nancy Rytina (1986) who estimate a 7.4 percentage point decline in the Duncan index between 1972 and 1982. The studies conclude the reduction in measured segregation stemmed from a "composition" rather than a "mix" effect. In other words there was a substantial change in the sex composition within specific occupations, as exemplified by women's entry into professional and managerial positions, rather than any substantial change in the relative size of occupations.

Despite declines, the Duncan index still indicates the presence of a substantial degree of occupational segregation by sex and this index only dropped below 60 percent during the 1980s. As David Cotter et al. (1995) comment, the 1980s was known as a relatively conservative era, so the question becomes whether the conservative climate impeded the progress made in the 1970s, or, was the momentum built up in the previous decade "self-perpetuating"? All evidence points to the latter conclusion. Blau et al. (1998) use census data and a consistent set of occupations to document a decrease in the Duncan index of 8.43 percentage points over the 1970s and a substantial, if somewhat smaller decline of 6.27 percentage points over the 1980s. Also using census data, Jacobsen (1994; 1997) calculates Duncan index values of 59 percent in 1980 and 53 percent in 1990. Comparable figures from Cotter et al. (1995) show a decline of 6.5 percentage points among full-time year-round workers in that decade. In short, the consensus is that the decline in segregation continued at a somewhat slower pace during the 1980s. The majority of the decrease has been tied to the changing gender distribution of occupations and a smaller role attributed to changes in occupational mix.

Finally, Thomas Wells (1999) demonstrates that, by the 1990s, women's ability to integrate male-dominated occupations may have lessened, causing little further decline in the Duncan index. Based on CPS data and a fixed set of 497 occupational categories, the standardized Duncan index was 54.6 in 1990 and 53.1 in 1997. Researchers await results from the 2000 census in order to substantiate these findings. Comparing results from Bertaux and Wells, we can assess progress in reducing occupational segregation over many years of US history. While recognizing all the difficulties involved with measuring this concept over time, we might conclude that the Duncan index has fallen no more than 17 percentage points over 127 years. As shown in the next section, the persistence of this phenomenon is not limited to the US.

International Trends in Occupational Segregation

According to our review, at least 53 percent of men and women would need to change jobs in order for men and women to be similarly distributed across occupations in the United States as of 1997. How does this level of segregation by sex compare with estimates for other countries? Did other countries experience similar declines in segregation over time? Are there differences between developing and industrialized countries? We turn next to these questions. There are numerous studies of individual countries and regions of the world, but our focus will be on studies that apply a common statistical method to data collected from several countries.[13]

Early work in this area is plagued by non-comparability of databases, particularly inconsistent time periods and occupational definitions. Many of the earlier studies were based, by necessity, on very aggregated job categories.[14] Most authors examine a selection of one-digit occupational classifications, which results in a dozen or fewer occupations. Again, the broad occupational groupings impart a downward bias to the Duncan measure. Examining data for the 1960s, Elise Boulding et al. (1976) find that Latin America had the highest Duncan index at 49 percent. By region, North America and Europe had index values of 37 percent, which was lower than North Africa and the Middle East but higher than Africa and Asia. Donald Treiman and Patricia Roos (1983) examine data from the 1970s for 9 countries using 14 occupational classifications. The Duncan index was highest, 60 percent, in Sweden and lowest, 38 percent, in Austria. Rachel Rosenfeld and Arne Kalleberg (1990) employ seven occupational categories across four countries (US, Canada, Norway, and Sweden) to derive an index for the early 1980s. Again, Sweden had the highest Duncan index value (40 percent) and the United States had a value of 30 percent. Blau and Kahn (1992) offer additional estimates for the 1980s: values of the Duncan index ranged from 32 percent for Switzerland to a high of 81 percent for Australia.

Jacobs and Lim (1992) calculate the Duncan index for 39 countries across three years: 1960, 1970, and 1980. Findings show that ten of 13 countries in North, Central and South America experienced a decrease in occupational segregation from

1960 to 1980, with the highest 1980 levels found in Latin America. Results for Asia and Europe were mixed. For eight of 14 European countries, the Duncan index rose between 1960 and 1980, with Denmark having the highest Duncan value, 0.497. In Asia, Kuwait and Australia had the highest Duncan values (0.529 and 0.471 respectively). Thailand, Singapore, Malaysia, the Philippines, Japan, India and Korea all had Duncan values of 0.25 or below. As measured by the Duncan index, occupational segregation fell in 7 of the 12 Asian countries between 1960 and 1980. In addition to the Duncan index, the authors calculate a size-standardized measure of segregation, which holds the size of occupations constant over time. The size-standardized indexes indicate that if the relative size of occupations had remained the same, occupational segregation would have declined in all but 8 study countries.

There are some common findings in these previous studies, most notably, the fact that considerable sex segregation in the workplace exists in virtually all countries. Several authors noted the small Duncan values in Asia, average levels in the United States and many European countries, and the relatively high level of segregation in Latin America and Scandinavian countries. Nevertheless, these early studies were limited by aggregated occupational data and a small set of study countries.

In recent years, the definitive work on cross-national comparisons of sex segregation has become Anker's *Gender and Jobs: Sex Segregation of Occupations in the World* (1998). Anker's study is based on data collected by the International Labour Organization with the express purpose of calculating cross-national measures of occupational segregation. The study employs detailed occupational classifications (an average of 175 occupations per country studied). It includes data for 41 countries and regions, with time series data for 32 countries. The material in the rest of this section is drawn from Anker's very comprehensive 1998 book.

Before calculating statistical measures of segregation, Anker examines six non-agricultural occupations in detail in order to get an overview of how men and women are represented within these broad classifications for all study countries.[15] In 49 of the 56 countries or areas, he finds that women are over-represented in the professional and technical category. Throughout the world, women are also concentrated in clerical and service occupations. In 50 of the 56 countries or areas, women were overrepresented in the clerical occupation category. The six exceptions, however, were important because, as Anker notes, they represent about half of the world's population (China, India, Pakistan, Haiti, Nigeria, and Ghana). The stereotype of the female secretary or assistant, therefore, does not apply in much of the world. In 51 of the 56 countries, women were also overrepresented in the service category. In four of the countries where this was not the case, Islam was either the prevalent or, an important religion, which would have limited women's interactions with others. Women's disproportionate representation in services has been observed for the United States as well. In fact, continued growth in the service sector has afforded women increased employment opportunities over time.

By contrast, for all study regions, women's representation in administrative/ managerial as well as production occupations is well below their representation in the labor force. Women's representation in administrative and managerial occupations is highest in the United States, Canada, and Egypt, and lowest in the Asia/Pacific region. While women are underrepresented in production occupations, the largest major occupational group, the degree of underrepresentation is lower in Asia. In China, India and Pakistan, for example, women's share of production employment parallels their representation in the labor force. In Japan, Malaysia, and the Republic of Korea women's share of production employment is double that in the OECD countries (Anker 1998). Anker cites export-based industrialization as playing a major role in employing women in Asian countries, while spinners/weavers and tailors/dressmakers employ many women in Malaysia and India.

Anker's results indicate a great contrast in the gender composition of sales occupations across the world. In the majority of OECD countries and much of Latin America and Africa, women are overrepresented in sales occupations. Yet, women tend to be underrepresented in North Africa and the Middle East. The public contact between men and women typically required in sales positions most likely makes such jobs socially unacceptable for women in many countries, particularly India, Pakistan, the Middle East, and North Africa.

Table 10.3 presents some of Anker's key findings with regard to the measurement of occupational segregation across countries. The Duncan index is calculated based on two- and three-digit occupational data, such that on average, 175 occupations are used in constructing the index. Because the number of occupational categories varies for each country, the Duncan75 variable equals the Duncan index value calculated for the same 75 occupations across all countries. All indexes are based on the most recently available data.[16] The total, unweighted, average using a fixed set of 75 occupations is 0.58, which suggests a high degree of occupational segregation by sex across countries. The Duncan index based on a varying number of occupations suggests that 60 percent of men and women in the world would have to change occupations in order for them to be distributed across occupations in a manner that is consistent with their representation in the labor force. There also exist large differences across regions. The Duncan75 index varies from 0.48 in Asia/Pacific countries to 0.68 in the Middle East and North Africa. Yet, within regions, there is little variation in index values, despite socio-economic and labor market conditions that do differ across the region. These results indicate the importance of cultural factors in the determination of occupational segregation by gender.

Similar to time-series estimates for the United States, Anker finds that occupational segregation by sex declined throughout the world during the 1970s and 1980s, with the notable exception of China, Hong Kong, and Japan. Standardized estimates of the Duncan values also indicate that the majority of the decline worldwide stemmed from increased integration of men and women within occupations rather than changes in the relative size of occupations (Anker 1998). In fact, researchers studying the broader occurrence of sex segregation arrive at many of the same conclusions. Throughout the world, women's occupational choice is much more limited than

Table 10.3   National values of the Duncan index, latest available year. Copyright ©
International Labour Organization 1998

Region/country/area	Duncan index	Number of non-ag. occup.	Duncan75 (adjusted to 75 non-ag. occup.)
OECD			
Australia	0.615	279	0.581
Austria	0.597	64	0.607
Canada	0.509	44	0.541
Cyprus	0.634	376	0.570
Finland	0.673	264	0.616
France	0.607	433	0.556
Germany (West)	0.600	268	0.523
Italy	0.517	231	0.449
Luxembourg	0.586	71	0.589
Netherlands	0.588	150	0.567
New Zealand	0.618	281	0.582
Norway	0.646	291	0.573
Spain	0.570	77	0.569
Switzerland	0.654	452	0.581
Sweden	0.604	49	0.630
United Kingdom	0.638	509	0.567
United States	0.548	461	0.463
OECD average (unweighted)	**0.600**	**253**	**0.563**
Asia/Pacific			
China	0.443	277	0.363
Fiji	0.600	75	0.603
Hong Kong	0.490	73	0.493
India	0.492	423	0.446
Japan	0.529	259	0.502
Korea, Republic of	0.402	56	0.432
Malaysia	0.490	76	0.489
Asian average (unweighted)	**0.492**	**177**	**0.476**
Other developing			
Angola	0.652	67	0.656
Costa Rica	0.566	55	0.598
Ghana	0.710	75	0.710
Haiti	0.669	75	0.669
Mauritius	0.586	70	0.593
Netherlands Antilles	0.645	76	0.644
Senegal	0.577	80	0.573
Average (unweighted)	**0.629**	**71**	**0.635**

Table 10.3   Continued

Region/country/area	Duncan index	Number of non-ag. occup.	Duncan75 (adjusted to 75 non-ag. occup.)
Transition economies			
Bulgaria	0.507	43	0.541
Hungary	0.585	118	0.558
Poland	0.677	361	0.592
Former Yugoslavia	0.602	206	0.540
Average (unweighted)	**0.593**	**182**	**0.558**
Middle East and North Africa			
Bahrain	0.635	86	0.627
Egypt	0.586	74	0.587
Iran, Islamic Rep.	0.638	21	0.681
Jordan	0.769	61	0.776
Kuwait	0.743	268	0.733
Tunisia	0.663	55	0.695
Average (unweighted)	**0.672**	**94**	**0.683**
Total average (unweighted)	**0.597**	**179**	**0.577**

Source: Reprinted with permission from Table 9.1, *Gender and Jobs*, Richard Anker, 1998.

men's. Women tend to occupy positions that correspond to their social roles and these jobs offer lower rewards in terms of compensation and career advancement.

Vertical Segregation and the Earnings Gap

It is widely accepted that a reduction in occupational segregation will increase the earnings of working women relative to working men. It is similarly expected that an increase in women's labor force participation will cause desegregation across jobs. Unfortunately, the relationship between occupational segregation and other labor market variables is not this consistent. One of the first US studies to suggest a strong relationship between occupational segregation and pay gaps is Erica Groshen (1991) who examines the origins of the gender gap in five industries. Groshen concludes that "the largest source of the female/male wage gap is the association between wages and the proportion female in occupations, which accounts for up to two-thirds of the gap..." (p. 469). Nevertheless, many other researchers, especially those investigating labor markets outside the US, have found no statistically significant relationship between segregation measures and earnings gaps. Several studies document a positive association between the ratio of female to male earnings and segregation indexes.[17]

To illustrate the point, in Nordic countries, women's labor force participation has historically been higher than in most OECD countries and above the comparable rate for the US. This feature may be one result of a long history of public policies to promote gender equality. The female–male pay ratio has also been relatively high in Nordic countries (averaging between 78 percent and 89 percent from 1991–93). But despite an overall labor market picture that seems to be a model for other countries, various segregation indexes for 1970, 1980 and 1990 document a level of occupational segregation that is substantially higher than that found in OECD countries.[18] Similarly, Anker (1998) finds the lowest average level of occupational segregation in the Asia/Pacific region, an area that is known for relatively low female–male pay ratios.

How do we explain the lack of correlation between occupational segregation and women's relative earnings? So many other factors come into play that occupational segregation is almost, as Cotter et al. (1995) puts it, "an independent dimension of gender inequality" (p. 4). For instance, centralized wage setting (associated with lower female–male pay gaps), enterprise size (salaries tend to be higher in large enterprises), and the general level of pay differentials in the country all contribute to levels of wage inequality by gender (Anker 1998). In our earlier example, Nordic countries are characterized by a low overall level of wage inequality that undoubtedly contributes to the higher female–male earnings ratio. Finally, one of the most important factors to consider is vertical segregation. Vertical segregation refers to how within occupations, there is a hierarchy of jobs and women tend to be overrepresented in the lower-paying, less prestigious jobs. Because women tend to hold disadvantaged positions within occupations, increasing the representation of women in a male-dominated occupation does not necessarily raise women's relative earnings. In fact, several researchers have concluded that gender differences in pay are as large within occupational groups as they are across occupations.

Examples of vertical segregation are plentiful. Blau et al. (2001) document the substantial growth of women in professional employment. But, 41 percent of the women holding professional jobs in 1995 were in five relatively low-paying categories: dietician, librarian, nurse, pre-kindergarten and kindergarten teacher, and elementary school teacher (Blau et al. 2001: 139). In the year 2000, 41 percent of female professional workers were still located in those five occupations.[19] Women have continued to enter the academic profession, but their representation in the highest-paying jobs is still below their representation in the profession as a whole. Within the field of economics, women earned 28 percent of new PhDs during academic year 1997–8 and this figure has been above 20 percent since, at least, the 1980s.[20] Nevertheless, the Committee on the Status of Women in the Economics Profession, which conducts annual surveys of economics departments across the United States, found that in 1999 only 4.8 percent of full professors holding tenure at the top 20 PhD-granting departments were women. The comparable figure for the top 10 departments was 3.9 percent, a total of seven women.[21]

Vertical segregation may be evident in very narrowly defined occupations. Returning to table 10.1, we notice that only 8.9 percent of workers who sell parts are women. But, women comprise 50 percent of all sales occupations. In addition to parts, men are more likely to sell motor vehicles and boats (11 percent female), televisions and appliances (27 percent female), hardware and building supplies (22 percent female). Median weekly earnings for these full-time sales positions were: $676, $519 and $454 respectively in 2000. Women are most likely to sell apparel, which is 77 percent female. Since the average earnings for apparel sales people is only $307 per week (full-time), the resulting earnings gap by gender would be substantial in the sales occupation.[22]

Even when women reach the top of an occupational hierarchy, vertical segregation may reduce their relative pay. In a 2001 paper by Marianne Bertrand and Kevin Hallock, the authors examine ExecuComp salary data. This data set includes compensation information for the five highest paid executives in a large group of US firms. Bertrand and Hallock find that over the period 1992 to 1997, women tripled their representation in the top executive ranks. Nonetheless, women in the sample earned approximately 45 percent less than their male colleagues. Part of the explanation for their lower pay was the firms in which women were employed. For example, women were more likely to manage smaller companies. Vertical segregation regarding positions was also evident.[23] The top four executive positions are CEO, Chair, Vice Chair and President. In each of these categories, women held less than 1 percent (in the case of President, 1.7 percent) of the positions. Such examples are mirrored in other countries. While Japanese women have increasingly been able to find employment in large corporations, women are largely excluded from management positions in the career, or, "sogoshoku rank." The result is a substantial earnings gap even while more women accept employment with large corporations (Anker 1998: 35).

Conclusion

One-half of all workers in the world are in jobs that are either female-dominated (defined as more than 80 percent women) or male-dominated (more than 80 percent of the workers are male) (Anker, 1998). So, the gender differences that are already apparent in the classroom are repeated, if not magnified, in the labor market. A gender-linked choice will also have financial implications in the market. The median annual earnings of economists was approximately $48,330 in 1998. Other social scientists, with the exception of psychology, had a median annual earnings of $38,990 in 1998.[24]

Our review of cross-national studies of occupational segregation reflects that there are many sources of occupational segregation and there is probably support for both supply-side and demand-side theories of segregation. Given the similarity in measured discrimination within specific sub regions of the world, as well as the stereotyping of occupations in a way that reinforces typical social stereotypes of women, feminist theories of segregation also contribute to our understanding of this widespread phenomenon. Cross-national comparisons are important in helping us understand which occupational features are variable and which seem common to all countries. While there are regions of the world in which women constitute a relatively large proportion of miners, production workers, and scientific/technical specialists, there is still great overlap in the types of jobs most women perform. To fully understand the source of occupational segregation, economists need to go beyond market behavior to consider non-market factors (for example, religious and cultural factors) as well as pre-market behavior.

This review also provides evidence that the extent of segregation has declined over time in the US and in many parts of the world. While this is a positive trend, the prevalence of vertical segregation means that further integration of women into men's jobs, or, vice versa, does not always improve women's relative pay or status. Even equal pay policies will do little to improve women's economic position if women are relegated to the bottom of the job hierarchy. Comparable worth policies seem to accept the persistence of segregation by sex and attempt, instead, to pay workers in female-dominated jobs wages that are equivalent to workers who are employed in "comparable" male-dominated jobs. In addition to other criticisms of comparable worth, some claim that improving the pay of women in female-dominated jobs simply serves to maintain their concentration in a limited number of occupations. The fact that the decline in segregation has been greatest in the US may suggest that affirmative action and anti-discrimination laws have been effective in reducing segregation. The most recent Duncan estimates for the US 52.6 according to Wells (1999) and 54.8 according to Anker (1998), suggest that we need to look further for policies that will continue to address this problem.

NOTES

1   The *Digest of Education Statistics*, reports that for academic year 1997–8, 69 percent of BAs awarded in sociology were to women 32 percent in economics (2000, Table 257).
2   See "Bucking the Trend, Wellesley Students Flock to Economics" and "Women in Economics" by Schuss (2001). Schuss reports that Wheaton College, formerly a women's college, claimed economics as its most popular major in the late 1980s. Since admitting men, however, 41 percent of economics majors in a recent semester were women, despite the fact that women constituted 63.7 percent of the student body at that time.
3   The desirability of flexible labor markets is documented in "Working Man's Burden" (*The Economist*, 1999).
4   Figures are from the *Statistical Abstract of the United States*. 2000: Tables 654, 317, 321, and 322.
5   For a more detailed discussion of the economic theories of discrimination, see chapter 11 by Irene Powell in this volume.

6   Risk averse employers will also engage in statistical discrimination when the mean values of productive characteristics are equal, but the standard deviation of the distribution is larger for one group.

7   More elastic labor supply suggests greater responsiveness to wage changes.

8   These theories are discussed in Chapter 7 of Blau et al. (1998).

9   Description of the index is taken from Joyce Jacobsen (1998), Chapter 6.

10 Given the mathematical formula for the Duncan index, as one broad occupation is subdivided into several occupations, the index value must rise unless the percentage female is exactly the same across all the occupational subdivisions (see Anker 1998: 95).

11 The international equivalent coding scheme is the ISCO.

12 While the Duncan index remains the most commonly used index in the United States and Great Britain, there are many alternative measures, beginning with the original Gini coefficient. The marginal matching index (MM) was developed by Siltanen et al. in a 1995 ILO publication. In 1980, the OECD proposed using the WE index. The Department of Employment in the United Kingdom also has a preferred index known as the sex ratio index (SR). Anker (1998), Siltanen et al. (1995), and Blackburn et al. (1995) provide detailed discussion of the merits of various indexes.

13 For a summary of individual country studies as of the early nineties, see Barbezat (1993).

14 These early studies include Boulding et al. (1976), Treiman and Roos (1983), and Roos (1985). More recent studies of occupational segregation across countries include Rosenfeld and Kalleberg (1990), and Blau and Kahn (1992). Anker (1998), table 3.1, presents a table of numerous cross-national studies.

15 All reported results for the six occupational areas are contained in Anker (1998) Chapter 8.

16 Approximately 50 percent of the national data were for the 1990s. Three-quarters of the data came from 1985 or later (Anker 1998: 174).

17 See Barbezat (1993) and Anker (1998) for reviews of this literature. Lewis and Shorten (1991) and Rimmer (1991) provide two examples of situations in which a reduction in segregation would reduce women's relative earnings.

18 Nordic countries include Denmark, Finland, Iceland, Norway, and Sweden. All information on Nordic countries is from Melkas and Anker (1998). In explaining these results, the authors emphasize a number of factors, including the fact that the overall level of wage inequality is quite low in Nordic countries, which contributes to women's higher relative wages. They also stress the large scale "monetization of household work" whereby a relatively large proportion of female workers are engaged in child and elderly care, cooking, cleaning, and other activities that are similar to traditional household labor.

19 *Employment and Earnings*, January 2001, Table 11.

20 *Digest of Education Statistics*, 2000, Table 257.

21 These figures are contained in Committee on the Status of Women in the Economics Profession's 1999 Annual Report, Tables 2 and 3.

22 Figures are from *Employment and Earnings*, January 2001: Tables 11 and 39.

23 For an interesting discussion of what the authors call women's "hollow victory" in entering the professions, see Michael Carter and Susan Carter's article "Women's Recent Progress in the Professions Or, Women Get a Ticket to Ride After the Gravy Train has Left the Station" (1981).

24 Figures are from *Occupational Outlook Handbook*, 2000–01 edition, Bureau of Labor Statistics, pp. 148–56.

REFERENCES

Anker, Richard. 1997. "Theories of Occupational Segregation by Sex: An Overview." *International Labour Review* 136(3): 315–39.

——. 1998. *Gender and Jobs: Sex Segregation of Occupations in the World.* Geneva: ILO.

Anker, Richard and Catherine Hein. 1985. "Why Third World Employers Usually Prefer Men." *International Labour Review* 124(1): 73–90.

Barbezat, Debra A. 1993. "Occupational Segmentation by Sex in the World." IDP Working Paper, Geneva: ILO.

Becker, Gary S. 1971. *The Economics of Discrimination: Second Edition.* Chicago: University of Chicago Press.

Beller, Andrea H. 1982. "Occupational Segregation by Sex: Determinants and Changes." *Journal of Human Resources* 17(3): 371–92.

——. 1984. "Trends in Occupational Segregation by Sex and Race, 1960–1981," in Barbara F. Reskin (ed.) *Sex Segregation in the Workplace: Trends, Explanations and Remedies,* pp. 11–26. Washington, DC: National Academy Press.

Bertaux, Nancy E. 1991. "The Roots of Today's 'Women's Jobs' and 'Men's Jobs': Using the Index of Dissimilarity to Measure Occupational Segregation by Gender." *Explorations in Economic History* 28(4): 433–59.

Bertrand, Marianne and Kevin Hallock. 2001. "The Gender Gap in Top Corporate Jobs." *Industrial and Labor Relations Review* 55(1): 3–21.

Bianchi, Suzanne M. and Nancy Rytina. 1986. "The Decline in Occupational Sex Segregation During the 1970s: Census and CPS Comparisons." *Demography* 23(1): 79–86.

Bielby, William T. and James N. Baron. 1986. "Sex Segregation Within Occupations." *American Economic Review* 76(2): 43–7.

Blackburn, Robert M., Janet Siltanen, and Jennifer Jarman. 1995. "The Measurement of Occupational Gender Segregation: Current Problems and a New Approach." *Journal of the Royal Statistical Society* 158(Part 2): 319–31.

Blau, Francine D. and Lawrence Kahn. 1992. "The Gender Earnings Gap: Some International Evidence." National Bureau of Economic Research, Working Paper No. 4224, December.

Blau, Francine D., Marianne A. Ferber, and Anne E. Winkler. 2001. *The Economics of Women, Men, and Work: Fourth edition.* Upper Saddle River, NJ: Prentice-Hall.

Boulding, Elise. 1976. *Handbook of International Data on Women.* New York: Wiley.

Carter, Michael J. and Susan Boslego Carter. 1981. "Women's Recent Progress in the Professions Or, Women Get a Ticket to Ride After the Gravy Train Has Left the Station." *Feminist Studies* 7(3): 477–503.

Committee on the Status of Women in the Economics Profession (CSWEP), 1999 Annual Report.

Cotter, David A., Joann M. DeFiore, Joan M. Hermsen, Brenda Marsteller Kowalewski, and Reeve Vanneman. 1995. "Occupational Gender Segregation in the 1980s." *Work and Occupations* 22(1): 3–21.

Digest of Education Statistics. 2000. Washington DC: U.S. Department of Health, Education, and Welfare, National Center for Education Statistics.

Doeringer, Peter B. and Michael J. Piore. 1971. *Internal Labor Markets and Manpower Analysis.* Lexington, MA: D. C. Heath and Company.

Duncan, Otis Dudley and Beverly Duncan. 1955. "A Methodological Analysis of Segregation Indexes." *American Sociological Review* 20: 210–17.

The Economist. 1999. "Working Man's Burden." February 6: 84.

Employment and Earnings. 2001. Washington DC: US Department of Labor, Bureau of Labor Statistics, January.

England, Paula. 1982. "The Failure of Human Capital Theory to Explain Occupational Sex Segregation." *Journal of Human Resources.* 17: 358–70.

England, Paula, George Farkas, Barbara Stanek Kilbourne, and Thomas Dou. 1988. "Explaining Occupational Segregation and Wages: Findings from a Model with Fixed Effects." *American Sociological Review* 53: 544–58.

Groshen, Erica L. 1991. "The Structure of the Female/Male Wage Differential: Is It Who You Are, What You Do, or Where You Work?" *Journal of Human Resources* 26(3): 457–72.

House, William J. 1986. "The Status and Pay of Women in the Cyprus Labour Market," in Richard Anker and Catherine Hein (eds.) *Sex Inequalities in Urban Employment in the Third World.* London: Macmillan.

Jacobs, Jerry A. and Suet T. Lim. 1992. "Trends in Occupational and Industrial Sex Segregation in 56 Countries, 1960–1980." *Work and Occupations* 19(4): 450–86.

Jacobsen, Joyce P. 1994. "Trends in Workforce Segregation, 1960–1990." *Social Science Quarterly* 75(1): 204–11.

——. 1997. "Trends in Workforce Segregation: 1980 and 1990 Census Figures." *Social Science Quarterly* 78(1): 234–5.

——. 1998. *The Economics of Gender: Second edition.* Malden, Massachusetts: Blackwell Publishers.

Lewis, Donald E. and Brett Shorten. 1991. "Occupational Segregation, Labour Force Participation and the Relative Earnings of Men and Women." *Applied Economics* 23: 167–77.

Melkas, Helina and Richard Anker. 1998. *Gender Inequality and Occupational Segregation in Nordic Labour Markets.* Geneva: ILO.

Meng, Xin. 1998. "Gender Occupational Segregation and its Impact on the Gender Wage Differential Among Rural-Urban Migrants: A Chinese Case Study." *Applied Economics* 30(6): 741–52.

Occupational Outlook Handbook. 2000–01 edition. Washington DC: U.S. Department of Labor, Bureau of Labor Statistics.

Reskin, Barbara F. and Heidi I. Hartmann, (eds). 1986. *Women's Work, Men's Work: Sex Segregation on the Job.* Washington DC, National Academy Press.

Rimmer, Sheila M. 1991. "Occupational Segregation, Earnings Differentials and Status among Australian Workers." *The Economic Record,* September: 205–16.

Roos, Patricia A. 1985. *Gender & Work: A Comparative Analysis of Industrial Societies.* SUNY Press.

Rosenfeld, Rachel A., and Arne L. Kalleberg. 1990. "A Cross-national Comparison of the Gender Gap in Income." *American Journal of Sociology* 96(1): 69–109.

Schuss, Deborah. 2001. "Women in Economics." *The Boston Globe,* February 4: C5.

——. 2001. "Bucking the Trend, Wellesley Students Flock to Economics." *The Boston Globe,* February 4: C5.

Siltanen, Janet, Jennifer Jarman, and Robert M. Blackburn. 1995. *Gender Inequality in the Labour Market: Occupational Concentration and Segregation.* Geneva: ILO.

Statistical Abstract of the United States. 2000. 120th edition. U.S. Census Bureau 2000. Washington DC: Government Printing Office

Treiman, Donald J. and Patricia Roos. 1983. "Sex and Earnings in Industrial Society: A Nine-Nation Comparison." *American Journal of Sociology* 89(3): 612–50.

Tzannatos, Zafiris. 1990. "Employment Segregation: Can We Measure it and What Does the Measure Mean?" *British Journal of Industrial Relations* 28(1): 105–11.

Wells, Thomas. 1999. "Changes in Occupational Sex Segregation during the 1980s and 1990s." *Social Science Quarterly* 80(2): 370–80.

Chapter 11

Labor Market Discrimination: A Case Study of MBAs

Irene Powell

Economists generally argue that differences in earnings between individuals result from differences in productivity (a supply-side explanation). Factors that affect the supply of labor are worker preferences, and productivity factors such as education, labor market experience, and other worker attributes. When discussing earnings differences between demographic groups, or between men and women, however, another possible explanation is discrimination (a demand-side explanation).

Economists define labor market discrimination as the differing treatment in the labor market of two equally qualified individuals solely on the basis of their gender (or race, age, sexual orientation, and so on). Thus, the difference in treatment must be unrelated to productivity differences. Such differential treatment could occur either in wages or in access to jobs and promotions. That is, women's access to particular occupations – *occupational segregation* by gender – could result from either discrimination or differing productivity and preferences.[1] For example, occupational discrimination could result from: (1) women having education and experience that qualifies them for certain occupations, such as nursing or teaching (a supply-side effect); (2) women having preferences that lead them into nursing or teaching (a supply-side effect); or (3) employers being more likely to employ women in nursing and teaching jobs, and less likely to employ them in, for example, construction or engineering, *for reasons other than productivity differences* (a demand-side effect). These same demand-side and supply-side factors could also affect *wages*, even for men and women in the same occupations. Rather than focus on the possible connection between discrimination and occupational segregation, this chapter will focus primarily on *wage* discrimination, that is when two equally qualified individuals in the same occupation are paid different wages because of the group to which they belong.

Many studies have examined the evidence on the existence of wage discrimination. For example, Francine Blau and Lawrence Kahn (1997) estimated the average wage gap between men and women using data from a large, nationally representative sample.[2] They calculated a wage gap of 28 percent between men and women who were full-time workers aged 18 to 65. That is, the women's wage was 72 percent of the men's.

We cannot, however, conclude that this 28 percent measures the degree of wage discrimination that exists in the United States. Wages vary across individuals because of differences in characteristics such as skills, experience, and education, that is, differences in what economists call human capital.[3] Therefore, an average gender wage gap of 28 percent might result for reasons *other than discrimination* if, for example, women have fewer years of experience than men. Blau and Kahn, in the same study cited above, found that women in their sample had 12.8 years of full-time work experience compared to men's average of 17.4 years. Thus, a more careful analysis of men's and women's human capital and other characteristics is needed to reach a conclusion about the existence and extent of wage discrimination.

This chapter presents the major neoclassical theories of how discrimination could occur in a market economy, and describes the primary statistical method economists use to identify gender discrimination. Then, as an example of this method, the results of one such study, Mark Montgomery and Irene Powell (2001), are presented.

Theories of Discrimination

Neoclassical theories that attempt to explain the existence of discrimination primarily fall into two categories, taste for discrimination models and statistical discrimination models. These models will be explained briefly below. More detailed explanations of the theories can be found in Joyce Jacobsen (1998) and Francine Blau et al. (2001).

The taste for discrimination

Nobel-prize winning economist Gary Becker first presented the taste for discrimination model in his PhD dissertation. In this theory, discrimination occurs because individuals have a personal prejudice against workers from a particular group(s), causing these prejudiced individuals to have a "taste for discrimination." Becker (1971) developed three related models for three possible market actors who could have a taste for discrimination: employers, coworkers, and customers.

In the employer model, prejudiced employers are willing to trade profits for the ability to avoid hiring workers from the disfavored group. These employers are willing to pay a wage premium to the favored group to avoid hiring workers from the disfavored group. Prejudiced employers perceive an additional cost of hiring workers from a particular group, or perhaps, as in the case with women, into certain non-traditional jobs. Employers would perceive the cost of a male worker in such a job to be his wage, but would perceive the cost of a female worker to be her wage plus the psychic cost of having her in the non-traditional job. Thus, employers will only hire a woman if they can pay her a lower wage than an equally qualified man, and will hire men at a higher wage.

Some interesting implications derive from this theory of discrimination. The prejudiced employers are sacrificing profits in order to be able to indulge the taste for discrimination. Thus, *non-discriminating* employers could hire equally qualified women at a lower wage than men, but at a higher wage than the *discriminating* employers would pay the women. In this case the non-discriminating employers will have lower production costs, and, in competitive markets, be able to drive the prejudiced employers out of business. Some neoclassical economists would argue, then, that market forces would tend to eliminate this type of discrimination over time.

Becker also considered taste for discrimination models in which the prejudiced actors were fellow workers. In the simplest theory, prejudiced employees (men) will require a higher wage to cover the psychic costs of having coworkers from the disfavored group (women), at least if the latter are in non-traditional jobs. Complicating matters is the implication that men who are forced to work with women in certain jobs may cause the women to be less productive, by, for example, harassment, non-cooperation, exclusion from mentoring, and informal networking. In the presence of such harassment, we also would predict that men would be paid more than their equally qualified female counterparts.

This type of discrimination on the part of fellow employees could take many forms. For example women may not be hired into supervisory jobs, and if they are, might receive lower wages if they are less productive supervisors because male workers (and/or female workers) do not wish to be supervised by women. Blau et al. (2001) cite a 1996 Gallup Poll finding that 37 percent of women and 54 percent of men prefer male bosses. Many studies report accounts by women of harassment by co-workers in blue-collar jobs, such as in construction and heavy manufacturing.[4] Employee discrimination also could take the form of sexual harassment. Evidence from sexual harassment court cases abound (see Blau et al. (2001) for a discussion). Very little statistical research exists that analyzes the empirical evidence on employee discrimination. The evidence from these statistically more sophisticated tests of the theory is mixed (see Jacobsen (1998) for a discussion of this evidence).

An interesting implication of the employee taste for discrimination model is that this type of discrimination would not be as easily eliminated by competition over time because employers are actually maximizing profits given the presence of the behaviors and attitudes of the prejudiced workers. Even in this case, however, the market presumably would favor male workers who did not cause this problem; that is, the employment of non-discriminating workers would allow firms to hire the most productive workers regardless of gender. This ability to hire the most productive workers would presumably result in higher productivity and lower costs. So again, we would expect market forces to eliminate over time the ability of male workers to indulge their taste for discrimination.

The final case Becker analyzed was that in which *customers* have a taste for discrimination. In this case, customers prefer to buy from firms who do not employ the disfavored group in non-traditional jobs. Thus, they may avoid hospitals with women as physicians, or auto dealerships with female sales staff. As a result, firms will pay workers from the disfavored group (women) less then otherwise equally qualified men in order to make up the lost revenue from employing them in the non-traditional job. A *New York Times* article (Lewin, 2001), for example, reports on a possible case of *reverse* customer discrimination in which a male obstetrician/gynecologist charged a medical practice of sex discrimination his salary and eventual dismissal. He charges that he was dismissed from the practice because women prefer female obstetricians/gynecologists. Customer discrimination against women has been suggested in other medical specialties and jobs like car sales and professional sports. Empirical studies have found evidence of customer discrimination in the prices of baseball cards.

Note, however, that in many industries firms that hire women in the objectionable jobs anyway would pay them a lower wage, and thus have lower production costs and be able to charge a lower product price. Non-prejudiced customers would be able to pay lower prices than the prejudiced customer. Again, market forces could well be expected to work against this type of discrimination over time.

Clearly, the more prevalent the taste for discrimination, both across and within employer, employee, and customer groups, the longer it would take for market forces, even in competitive markets, to eliminate the resulting gender wage discrimination. Moreover, as Becker (1971) pointed out, not all markets are perfectly competitive. For example, for various reasons competitive market forces do not operate very effectively in health care markets. This characteristic might help insulate patients and medical practices from negative impacts from the type of customer discrimination described above. Thus, the length of time it would take for gender wage discrimination to be eliminated by market forces might be quite long.

Statistical discrimination

Statistical models of discrimination developed by Edmund Phelps (1972) and Dennis Aigner and Glen Cain (1977) attempt to explain gender wage differences in the *absence* of prejudice. These economists argue that unbiased employers may face uncertainty in judging qualifications and predicting future performance of prospective employees. This uncertainty results in costs associated with screening potential employees. Thus, rather than undertake extensive testing and interviewing to precisely predict employee productivity, employers will use easy-to-observe personal attributes as "signals" about productivity. An example of a signal is a college diploma. Even if the job requires no advanced education directly, the diploma shows that the job applicant is intelligent and diligent enough to complete a degree. In addition, if there are actual differences in some productivity-related characteristic between two groups of workers, the employer will use membership in a particular group as a signal about future performance. For example, historically women have been more likely, on average, to leave the labor force during childbearing years. The statistical discrimination model predicts that profit-maximizing employers will use these average differences in labor force attachment between men and women as a signal of the likelihood of losing the prospective employee. A higher likelihood of quitting will involve extra costs for hiring and training replacement workers. Thus, employers will use gender as a signal of the likelihood of incurring the extra costs, and will pay women a lower wage than an equally qualified man, by an amount commensurate with the expected extra costs. A gender wage gap will occur, *even for women who will not leave the labor force to raise children.*

Large numbers of studies have been published that test for, and estimate the magnitude of, gender wage discrimination (see Dale Belman and John Heywood 1991; Randy Albeda et al. 1997; Jacobsen 1998; and Blau et al. 2001 for reviews of this literature). Also, several studies have tested for the existence of hiring behavior consistent with signaling. Most of the latter studies examine the "sheepskin effect," the wage returns to having a college degree – not the education and skills, just the degree. The author's brother, for example, dropped out of college in April of his senior year of college. Clearly he had approximately the same education and skills as similar students who graduated. Yet in a case such as this, the possession of the "sheepskin," the college diploma, might be taken as a signal of relatively difficult to measure characteristics such as motivation and sense of responsibility. Any difference in wages would be the result of the college degree acting as a positive screening signal.

In this chapter, utilizing a study by Montgomery and Powell (2001), I address the following question: Can a "positive" signal, such as the receipt of an advanced degree, counteract the "negative" signal of being female? That is, might a woman with a lot of education be regarded as "atypical" of her sex, and arouse less discrimination among prospective employers? The results discussed here examine this question using a longitudinal survey of registrants for the Graduate Management Admission Test (GMAT).[5] The question is analyzed by comparing the gender wage gap for a group of GMAT registrants who completed the MBA with another group who did not.

Testing the Theory

Bivariate regression

Probably the first statistical method that comes to mind for establishing whether gender wage discrimination occurs is to compare the average wages of men and women and calculate the gender wage gap. To illustrate, let's consider the difference in hourly wages between the 854 men and women in our GMAT sample who completed the MBA. The hourly wage of male MBAs is $19.59; the hourly wage for women MBAs is $16.52, showing a wage gap of $3.07 per hour. The ratio of the women's wage to that of the men in this sample is 0.84. Thus, women who have completed the MBA earn 84 cents for every dollar earned by men, or $3.07 less in wages per hour.[6]

Table 11.1   Descriptive statistics for GMAT registrants by sex and whether completed MBA

Variable	Completers of MBAs			
	Women		Men	
	Mean	SD	Mean	SD
Hourly earnings on primary job	16.52	8.28	19.59	10.82
Independent variables:				
Age	25.90	5.41	27.03	5.90
Married	0.44	0.40	0.53	0.42
Number of kids at home	0.19	0.37	0.18	0.22
Tenure on current job (yrs)	2.78	9.91	3.08	8.49
Worked 1 to 3 years prior to test	0.30	0.46	0.29	0.47
Worked 3 to 7 years prior to test	0.23	0.36	0.29	0.21
Worked >7 years prior to test	0.17	0.41	0.23	0.37
GMAT score	493	88	529	95
Undergraduate GPA	3.04	0.42	3.16	0.39
% at less selective coll.	38.80	30.02	41.23	31.90
Humanities major undergraduate	0.11	0.23	0.06	0.32
Soc. science major undergraduate	0.13	0.40	0.20	0.33
Science major undergraduate	0.21	0.44	0.26	0.40
Confidence index	27.89	4.94	28.12	5.10
Family very important	0.87	0.34	0.86	0.34
Career very important	0.70	0.49	0.64	0.47
% Women in 3-digit occupation	48.42	14.17·	43.82	16.10
Sample size	340		514	

Economists, however, use a different method for examining the existence of the gender wage gap. The basic statistical method used to test for the existence of a relationship between two variables is bivariate regression analysis. For example, given data for individuals on their wages and sex, we could estimate the relationship between wage and sex:

$$\text{Wage}_i = a + b(\text{FEMALE}_i) + e_i.$$

FEMALE is a dummy variable that would equal 1 if the individual is a woman, 0 if a man. And b, the coefficient on the FEMALE variable, would measure the effect of being female on wages. Interestingly, the coefficient "b" in this type of bivariate regression of wage on a dummy variable with two categories, men and women, will give us an equivalent measure to the average difference in wages between the men and women in the sample.

Again using our sample of 854 completers of the MBA, the results of a bivariate regression is shown below and in column 1 of table 11.2.

$$\text{Wage}_i = 19.59 - 3.07(\text{FEMALE}_i) + e_i.$$

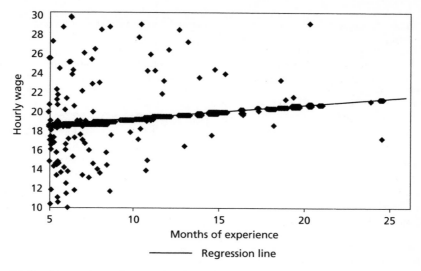

Figure 11.1   Scatterplot and regression line of wage and experience

We can see that the "constant" (the "a" coefficient) is 19.59, and the coefficient on the FEMALE dummy variable (the "b" coefficient') is −3.07. These estimates mean that the men in the sample had an average hourly wage of $19.59, and that the women average $3.07 per hour less than the men. The results of the bivariate regression correspond exactly to the simple difference between the two means.

In order to better visualize the relationship between wage and another variable, and to visualize what a bivariate regression tells us, let us consider the relationship between wage and years of experience, as measured by the number of months spent on the current job. Figure 11.1 plots the data points for wage and years of experience for the individuals in the GMAT sample who completed the MBA.

Next, similar to the bivariate regression between wage and sex, the relationship between wage and years of experience is estimated. The estimated regression for the 854 completers of the MBA is given below, in column 2 of table 11.2, and is plotted on the graph above.

$$Wage_i = 18.02 + 0.12(Experience_i) + e_i.$$

We can see that the "constant" (the "a" coefficient) is 18.02, and is plotted on the y-axis where years of experience would be equal to zero. The constant tells us the average wage for individuals with zero years on the current job. The coefficient on the experience variable (the "b" coefficient) is 0.12. This coefficient represents the slope of the regression line plotted on the graph, and measures the average increase in wage for each additional month of experience on the current job. In this case, we estimate that the hourly wage increases by 12 cents for every additional month of experience.

Table 11.2   Example: bivariate and multivariate regression results for completers of the MBA

Variable	Column 1 coefficients	Column 2 coefficients	Column 3 coefficients	Column 4 coefficients	Column 5 coefficients	Column 6 coefficients
Constant	19.42	18.02	19.07	16.07	18.82	23.00
Female	−3.08*		−3.04*	−2.87*	−2.77*	−2.53*
Experience		0.12*	0.12*	0.12*	0.12*	0.12*
GMAT				0.74*	0.82*	0.79*
Confidence index					−0.09**	−0.09**
% Female in occupation						−0.08*
Sample size	854	854	854	854	854	854

* Indicates statistically significant at the 10% level or better in a two-tailed test.
** Indicates statistically significant at the 10% level in a one-tailed test.

We also can perform a hypothesis test to determine whether the measured effect is "statistically significant." If we find the estimated effect to be statistically significant, we can conclude that the estimated effect exists in our sample because there truly *is* an effect of experience on wage, and not because of the particular sample of individuals we happen by chance to be analyzing.[7] The coefficient for experience is statistically significant, and thus we conclude that experience does affect the wage.

Furthermore, the coefficient on FEMALE in the bivariate regression between wage and sex is also statistically significant (and negative). We may conclude that a gender wage gap favoring men exists. With this type of result, we might be tempted at this point to conclude that discrimination has caused the difference in wages.

The problem with bivariate regression analysis (a regression between *two* variables) is that there surely are other factors that affect the wage earned by individuals. Not only might we want to estimate the effect of these other variables, but omitting to do so *at the same time* that we estimate the effect of being female will cause our estimate of the gender gap to be biased, that is, to be consistently wrong as calculated from repeated samples. We already have considered, for example, job experience as another factor that is likely to explain differences in wages across individuals. Also, women, due to childbearing, have fewer years of experience than men on average (in our sample of completers, women's experience is 2.78, versus men's 3.08). In this case, estimating the effect of being female, *without holding experience constant*, will mean that the FEMALE variable measures the negative effect on women's wages of the difference in experience. The estimate of the gender wage gap is biased downward, that is, the estimated effect on wages of being female is likely to be more negative than the true effect of being female, holding other effects constant. Remember the definition of wage discrimination: a difference in wages for *equally qualified* individuals. Thus, to test for the existence of discrimination, we need to estimate the effect of being female, holding constant, or controlling for, other qualifications such as months of job experience.

Multivariate regression

Fortunately, the statistical method of multivariate regression (a regression between *more* than two variables) allows us to estimate the effect of one variable, holding constant the other variables included in the regression. So, to test for the existence of discrimination, we might estimate the following model using multivariate regression for a sample of individuals:

$$Wage_i = a + b_1 FEMALE_i + b_2 \, Experience_i + e_i,$$

The estimated coefficient on the variable FEMALE, b_1, would measure the effect of being female on the wage, *holding constant job experience*. That is, the multivariate regression method allows us to pretend that we are comparing the average wages of two groups of individuals, one of females and one of males, who are otherwise identical in their years of experience. If being female is estimated to have a negative and statistically significant effect on wages, we might conclude that discrimination exists.

Again, this method is illustrated using the GMAT sample of completers of the MBA. Column 3 of table 11.2 presents the results of a multivariate regression in which experience and sex are used to explain differences in the wage. In this regression the effect of experience on wage is still estimated to be 0.12, and is statistically significant. The effect of being female is negative and still statistically significant; women are, on average, being paid a lower wage than men who are equally qualified in terms of experience. The effect on wages of being female, however, is now −$2.77; being female lowers the hourly wage by $2.77, holding experience constant. Thus, the estimated effect of being female is smaller ($2.77, instead of $3.07) when we control for experience.

Finally, we can control for other factors that might affect wages. Again, we illustrate this method using the GMAT sample of completers of the MBA. Columns 3 to 6 of table 11.2 present the results of multivariate regressions in which certain variables are added one at a time to the regression to explain the differences in wages. These explanatory variables are:

1 experience on the current job, equal to the number of months on the current job for each individual in our sample (Experience);

2 total score received on the GMAT, a measure of education and ability (GMAT);

3 a measure of the motivation and attitudes of each worker, measured with a confidence index that is based on self-evaluated confidence[8] (CONFIDENCE); and

4 a measure of the degree to which the person's occupation is traditionally female, equal to the percent of workers in each worker's occupation who are women (OCC percent FEMALE).

Looking at the results in column 6, we observe a positive effect of experience and GMAT score, as we would expect. For example, the coefficient of 0.12 for the variable Experience indicates that individuals with one more month of experience on the current job earn 12 cents more per hour, holding the other variables constant. Being in an occupation that is a more "female" job, one that has more women as a percent of its workforce, *decreases* earnings. Specifically, the coefficient of −0.08 on OCC percent FEMALE indicates that a 10 percentage point increase in the percent of workers who are female decreases the average wage by 80 cents per hour, holding other variables constant. All of the coefficients in column 6 are statistically significant.

More important, these results show that the effect of being female gradually decreases as we control for additional factors affecting productivity. The estimated effect on the wage of being female decreases from $3.07 without controls for other characteristics, to $2.53 when other productivity variables are included. That is, the results indicate that being female decreases the hourly wage by $2.53 for women with similar experience, ability, confidence, and occupations as that of men. We expect that $2.53 is a more accurate measure of discrimination, either statistical discrimination or discrimination due to prejudice, than the $3.07 gap we observe in average wages; part of the $3.07 wage gap is due to differences between men and women in characteristics such as experience, occupation, and test scores.

Estimating a multivariate regression with a female dummy variable included to measure wage discrimination does not allow us to estimate differences in returns to characteristics by gender. For example, it may be that an additional year of experience has a different effect on wages for women than for men. Or, being in an occupation that is "more female" may have a different effect on wages for men than for women. To allow for different returns to characteristics by gender, we must estimate regressions separately for men and women, thus allowing both the intercept and slope coefficients to change. A summary measure of discrimination is then estimated that utilizes the full effects of group differences. Such estimates are not included in the current study; however, see Montgomery and Powell (2001) and chapter 9 by Joyce Jacobsen in this volume for an explanation of the methodology and a discussion of results obtained from various studies in which discrimination is estimated in this way.

One final complication in testing for the existence of discrimination, and estimating the magnitude of the gender wage gap, is the existence of other omitted variables and "unobservables." There may be other factors that affect wages that are left out of the regression. For example, individuals may have different college majors, have gone to different quality schools, be married or not, have children or not, and so on. If some of these omitted factors are also different for men or women, then our estimate of the gender wage gap, and of discrimination, will still be biased. Basically we want to include as many determinants of wage differences as are measurable in order to improve our estimate of discrimination. To the extent that some determinants are not easily observed or measured, critics will be able to ascribe the existence of a gender wage gap to differences in these unobservables, rather than to discrimination.

Evidence: Does Receipt of an MBA Serve as a Signal that Counteracts Statistical Discrimination?

Description of the model and data

As described above, Montgomery and Powell (2001) address the question: Can a "positive" signal such as advanced education overcome a "negative" signal such as being female? The GMAT Registrant Survey is a longitudinal study that surveyed 7400 individuals who registered to take the GMAT on test dates between June 1990 and March 1991. The analysis concentrates on the 4285 individuals who actually took the test and returned the questionnaire. The registrants were surveyed three times between 1991 and 1994. Data from the survey questionnaire were supplemented with information from GMAT registration and test records and with measures of educational quality from Barron's *Profiles of American Colleges* and *Profiles of American Business Schools* (1991).

The survey of GMAT registrants is uniquely suited for addressing potential bias in comparing the gender gap for two groups with different education levels. First, by looking at takers of the GMAT test the authors focus on a population that is reasonably homogeneous with respect to pre-MBA human capital and career goals. Second, when matched with GMAT test scores and other registration data, the survey provides information about determinants of wages missing from most other gender gap studies. These characteristics include measures of innate ability, the quality of the education received, and attitudes toward work and family. Most previous studies were unable to control for so many elements of worker productivity and preferences that affect the supply of labor.

The regression might still suffer from the role of further unobservables. Educational credentials are correlated with hard-to-observe personal traits like ability and motivation, and the correlation between education and other variables can confound the comparison of the wage gap. Suppose we observe, for example, a smaller gender wage gap among those with an advanced degree. The smaller wage gap could imply that the degree reduces discrimination, or it could merely reflect additional unobserved and unmeasured differentials in ability or motivation at the higher educational level. In the regression results discussed below, the authors have calculated estimates corrected for the "sample selection" problem that exists in regressions that compare the wages and characteristics of individuals who completed a degree to those who did not.

The dependent variable in the analysis is the *logarithm* of the hourly wage on the current primary job (as of 1994, the date of the Third Wave GMAT Survey[9]). By taking the log of the wage as the dependent variable, the estimated regression coefficients measure the *percentage change* in the hourly wage – instead of a dollar change – that would result from a change in the explanatory variables. This concept is illustrated in the discussion of results below. For salaried employees (the majority of the sample) hourly earnings are computed by dividing weekly (monthly) earnings by the number of hours worked in a typical week (month).

The explanatory variables (those variables that are hypothesized to affect wages) include standard demographic characteristics such as marital status and age, work experience variables, measures of ability, measures of the quality of the undergraduate education, occupation, and some indicators of attitude and motivation. The variables are as follows.

Explanatory variables

Work experience variables:
- Tenure = number of months on the primary current job
- Occupation = percent of workers who are female in the individual's occupation
- Experience = total labor market experience measured by four categories:
  - (a) Less than 1 year of work experience prior to registering for the GMAT
  - (b) 1 to 3 years of prior work experience
  - (c) 3 to 7 years of prior work experience
  - (d) More than 7 years of prior work experience

Measures of ability and education:
- GMAT Test Score
- Undergraduate GPA
- Competitiveness of the undergraduate school attended by the individual, equal to the percentage of GMAT registrants who attended a less selective under-graduate school (as ranked by Barron's) than the individual
- Undergraduate major measured by four categories: Humanities, Social Science, Science and Math, and Business

Attitude variables:
- Importance of family and children = 1 if the individual responded that family and children were "very important" at the time of registration for the GMAT, 0 if not "very important"
- Importance of career and work = 1 if the individual responded that career and work were "very important" at the time of registration for the GMAT, 0 if not
- Confidence index = measure of the extent to which respondents thought they had each of 16 characteristics and skills that would be considered important in "becoming a successful business manager or executive"[2]

Other demographic variables:
- Children = number of children less than age 18 living at home
- Married = 1 if the individual is married or living with a partner, 0 if not married
- Black = 1 if the person is African-American, 0 if not
- Asian = 1 if the person is Asian-American, 0 if not
- Age = age at the time of the Third Wave GMAT Survey, 1994

Table 11.3 Multivariate regression results corrected for sample selection

Variable	Completers of MBAs		Non-completers of MBAs	
	Coef.	T-stat	Coef.	T-stat
Female	−0.08	−0.89	−0.13	−3.08
Married	0.07	0.83	0.04	1.14
Number of children at home	0.02	0.21	0.02	0.66
Age	0.004	0.31	0.001	0.21
Asian	−0.010	−0.098	−0.02	−0.28
Black	0.03	0.21	−0.09	−1.65
Tenure on current job (mos)	0.02	2.47	0.02	8.09
Tenure squared (mos/100)	−0.01	−2.25	−0.01	−9.86
Worked 1 to 3 years prior to test	0.24	2.18	0.13	2.20
Worked 3 to 7 years prior to test	0.40	3.15	0.19	3.06
Worked > 7 years prior to test	0.49	2.53	0.25	3.03
GMAT score	0.16	2.51	0.18	8.05
Undergraduate GPA	0.16	1.79	0.01	0.30
% at less selective college	0.002	1.71	0.001	1.52
Humanities major undergraduate	−0.13	−0.89	−0.10	−0.77
Social science major undergraduate	−0.18	−1.74	0.07	1.20
Science major undergraduate	−0.01	−0.10	−0.07	1.43
Family very important	0.26	2.41	0.12	2.25
Career very important	0.06	0.78	0.01	0.31
Confidence index	0.02	2.01	0.04	1.89
% Women in 3-digit occupation	−0.33	−0.87	−0.31	−3.27
Sample size	854		3431	

Results

Table 11.3 reports the result of the multivariate regression using the variables described above, corrected for the sample selection of completing or not completing the MBA.[10] Again, the coefficient on the FEMALE dummy variable represents our indicator of the gender wage gap. Measured in this way, the gender wage gap could result from either a taste for discrimination, or statistical discrimination, or both. If this measured gender wage gap is lower for recipients of the MBA, then we can conclude that at least part of the gap is the result of statistical discrimination that is lessened by the positive signal of the MBA.

The evidence supports the key hypothesis: the effect of being female is different for those registrants who completed the MBA and for those who did not. For completers of the MBA, being female has a statistically *insignificant* effect on the wage of 8 percent.

That is, the estimated effect of being female is small enough that it probably exists just in the sample being observed, and not in the population in general. Therefore, Montgomery and Powell conclude that there is not a gender wage gap for recipients of the MBA. For non-completers, however, being female has a highly significant negative effect on earnings of roughly 13 percent. That is, even holding the measured supply-side effects constant, non-MBA women earn 13 percent lower wages than equally qualified non-MBA men.

Interestingly, being in a more "female occupation" has a negative and statistically significant effect on the wage for non-completers, but is not statistically significant for completers. The coefficient in the regression for non-MBAs implies that moving from an all-male to an all-female occupation would lower the wage by 31 percent. The lack of statistical significance for the completers implies that being in female occupations is not a factor that explains wage differentials for MBAs.

Table 11.3 also contains a number of interesting results about other variables in the model. First, the results for the dummy variable for being African American are consistent with the hypothesis that obtaining an MBA exposes one to less discrimination. In the regression for completers, the coefficient on the dummy, Black, is small and statistically insignificant, but for non-completers, the African-Americans are estimated to earn 10 percent less than equally qualified whites, an effect that is statistically significant.

Second, work experience and tenure on the current job have the expected large, positive, and significant effects on earnings. The coefficient on the GMAT score is significant and positive for both completers and non-completers. A 100-point increase in GMAT score increases the wage by about 17 percent for both MBAs and for non-MBAs, holding other variables constant. Educational quality of the undergraduate school also has an effect on wages. The competitiveness of the undergraduate school has a positive and statistically significant effect for both MBAs and non-MBAs. On the other hand, the college major variables are statistically insignificant in most of the regressions, holding constant other factors such as ability, experience, and attitude.

Attitude variables are estimated to be important determinants of the wage. The confidence index has a positive and statistically significant effect on wages for both groups of registrants. For example, an MBA holder who claimed she "very much" had all 16 person attributes in the index would have 32 percent higher wages than someone who only claimed to have these traits "somewhat." A surprising result, however, is that reporting family to be very important had an unexpected and statistically significant positive effect on wages. Perhaps commitment to family, rather than representing a career constraint, is indicative of positive attributes such as a strong sense of responsibility and caring for others. Considering career very important had a positive but statistically insignificant effect on earnings for both groups in all models.

Conclusions and Summary

Neoclassical economic theory says that lower wages for women are caused by differences in the supply of and demand for women's labor versus men's labor. The relatively more conservative of neoclassical economists, such as Gary Becker, argue that wage differences between men and women are primarily a supply-side phenomenon resulting from differences in productivity. They further argue that to the extent that prejudice, operating through a "taste for discrimination," is temporarily responsible for part of the gender wage gap, it will be eliminated by market forces over time.

Other neoclassical economists suggest that the gender wage gap may be caused, at least in part, by statistical discrimination that operates on wages through the demand-side of the labor market. Being female may be used as a negative signal to employers about lower labor force attachment and higher turnover. Barbara Bergmann (1986) points out that statistical discrimination, like any discrimination, is illegal under US anti-discrimination laws. Nevertheless, because using gender as a signal in this way is profit-maximizing, there is no reason to believe that a gender wage gap resulting from statistical discrimination will be eliminated by market forces. According to neoclassical theory, the only way for statistical discrimination to disappear is for the signal to no longer be accurate, that is, for women to no longer be different from men in labor force attachment, turnover, and so on.[11]

Less conservative neoclassical economists argue that discrimination might take a very long time to be eliminated by market forces. If the "taste for discrimination" is widespread throughout society, exists among employers, co-workers, *and* customers, and is present in product and labor markets that are not always competitive, then the market might be slow to work against it, especially if it operates along with statistical discrimination. These economists point to statistical studies that show that wage discrimination exists, based on evidence that a wage gap persists even after productivity and other characteristics are controlled for (see, for example, Robert Wood et al. 1993).

Relatively more conservative neoclassical economists are unlikely to be convinced, however, even by this type of evidence of discrimination. They argue that whatever gender wage gap remains after controlling for other factors is the result of further "unobservable" differences in productivity. The statistical studies also are typically unable to distinguish between a wage gap caused by statistical discrimination and one caused by a taste for discrimination.

The study by Montgomery and Powell (2001) discussed above sheds some light on this issue. The evidence suggests that the gender wage gap still exists among registrants for the GMAT who did not complete the MBA, even after controlling for ability, attitudes, educational quality, and traditional measures of work experience. The study also finds, however, that the signal provided by the advanced degree, the MBA, offsets the signal of being female and eliminates the gender wage gap. At least among this relatively well-educated type of worker, the evidence suggests that statistical discrimination plays a definite role in explaining the difference in wages between men and women, and that it can be offset by earning an advanced degree.

NOTES

1   See chapter 10 by Debra Barbezat in this volume.
2   Their data were from the Panel Study of Income Dynamics, survey data on individuals in the US in 1988.
3   See chapter 9 by Joyce Jacobsen in this volume.
4   See for example, Schroedel (1985) cited in Jacobsen (1998) and Bergmann (1986).
5   These data were collected by the Battelle Memorial Institute for the Graduate Management Admissions Council (GMAC), Seattle, Washington State.
6   Descriptive statistics for all variables used in the following regression analyses are located in table 11.1.
7   The hypothesis test utilizes an estimate of the potential variation of the coefficient b over repeated hypothetical samples. If this measure of variation, the standard error, is large, then we would expect our coefficient b to be a less accurate measure of the true effect of sex, or experience, and so forth, on the wage. If "b" is large relative to its standard deviation then we conclude that it is not statistically significant. As a general rule, if the ratio of b : standard error is greater than 1.64, then we say the coefficient is statistically significant, that is, not equal to zero.
8   The confidence index is equal to the sum of the self-rated presence of 16 characteristics/ skills that would be considered important in "becoming a successful business manager or executive." A higher total score is taken to indicate the degree of self-confidence of the individual, and the score can vary from 16 to 48.
9   Full information on the GMAT Surveys can be found in Grady et al. (1995).
10 Individuals who complete the MBA may have different ability and motivation than those who do not complete. If we have not included variables that fully measure these differences and therefore, if part of the differences in ability and motivation are "unobserved," then estimates of differences in discrimination for completers and non-completers will be biased. The following results correct for this sample selection bias.
11 Indeed, studies are beginning to indicate that college women's turnover behavior has become similar to college men's (see, for example, Kristin Keith and Abigail McWilliams 1995).

REFERENCES

Aigner, Dennis and Glen Cain. 1977. "Statistical Theories of Discrimination in the Labor Market." *Industrial and Labor Relations Review* 30: 175–87.
Albeda, Randy, Robert Drago, and Steven Shulman. 1997. *Unlevel Playing Fields: Understanding Wage Inequality and Discrimination*. New York: McGraw-Hill.
Barron's Educational Series (ed). 1991. *Profiles of American Colleges* and *Profiles of American Business Schools*. Barron's Educational Series, July.

Becker, Gary S. 1971. *The Economics of Discrimination: Second Edition*. Chicago: University of Chicago Press.

Belman, Dale and John S. Heywood. 1991. "Sheepskin Effects in the Returns to Education: An Examination of Women and Minorities." *The Review of Economics and Statistics*. 720–4.

Bergmann, Barbara R. 1986. *The Economic Emergence of Women*. New York: Basic Books.

Blau, Francine D., Marianne A. Ferber, and Anne E. Winkler. 2001. *The Economics of Women, Men, and Work: Fourth Edition*. Upper Saddle River, New Jersey: Prentice Hall.

Blau, Francine D. and Lawrence Kahn. 1997. "Swimming Upstream: Trends in the Gender Wage Differentials in the 1980s." *Journal of Labor Economics* 15: 1–42.

Grady, William, Terry Johnson, Mary Kay Dugan, and Nazli Bayda. 1995. "Program and Gender Differences In Progress Through The MBA Pipeline: Wave III Of The GMAT Registrant Survey." *The Magazine of the Graduate Management Admission Council*, Autumn, 31–9.

Keith, Kristin and Abigail McWilliams. 1995. "The Wage Effects of Cumulative Job Mobility." *Industrial and Labor Relations Review* 49: 121–37.

Lewin, Tamar. 2001. "Women's Health Is No Longer a Man's World." *New York Times*, February 7, Section A, p. 1, Column 2.

Montgomery, Mark, and Irene Powell. 2001. "Does A Woman with an Advanced Degree Face Less Discrimination? Evidence from MBA Recipients." Working paper, October.

Phelps, Edmund. 1972. "The Statistical Theory of Racism and Sexism." *American Economic Review* 62: 659–61.

Schroedel, J. R. 1985. "Alone in a Crowd: Women in the Trades Tell Their Stories. Philadelphia, PA: Temple University Press, in Jacobsen, Joyce P. 1998. *The Economics of Gender: Second Edition*. Malden, MA: Blackwell Publishers.

Wood, Robert G., Mary E. Corcoran, and Paul N. Courant. 1993. "Pay Differences among the Highly Paid: The Male-Female Earnings Gap in Lawyers' Salaries." *Journal of Labor Economics* 11: 417–41.

Chapter 12

Employment Discrimination, Economists, and the Law

Joni Hersch

On average, women earn less than men. Women and men also tend to concentrate in different occupations. When are these differences due to employment discrimination? And when are they simply due to preferences and choices? Although narrowing, an earnings gap by gender persists even with women's rising labor force participation and continuity. The female–male ratio for usual weekly wages has increased from 0.56 in 1969 to 0.74 in 1999.[1] In addition, most occupations are disproportionately of one gender, and indices of occupational segregation persistently show an unequal distribution by gender across occupations. Occupations with a larger share of female employees have lower average earnings, and to a large extent the gender gap in pay is due to the concentration of women in lower paying jobs.

But whether any unexplained pay gap arises from discrimination is far from obvious. There are two competing possibilities: the gap is potentially explicable by gender differences in observed or unobserved characteristics that affect earnings and/or arise from differences in choice; versus the gap is due to discrimination. Similarly, any observed occupational structure may be due to differences in characteristics or choice, or may result from illegal refusal to hire or promote qualified women into certain jobs.

Disappointingly, economic theory does not provide unambiguous guidance to whether discrimination is responsible for unexplained pay or occupational disparities. A student taking principles of microeconomics might be persuaded by the notion that competitive market forces will eliminate discrimination. After taking intermediate microeconomics, however, the argument becomes more nuanced. Markets are not always perfect, and market power, tastes for discrimination among coworkers and potential customers, and so forth, give rise to the possibility that discrimination can exist. While there is little direct empirical evidence on the various theories of discrimination, the large number of successful discrimination suits suggests that it is unlikely that market forces have eliminated employment discrimination of all kinds.

Economists have long debated whether such disparities result from discrimination without reaching consensus. Of course, endless abstract debates do not resolve whether any specific individual has been a victim of employment discrimination. This chapter discusses the laws prohibiting employment discrimination and the methods used in litigation to establish a legal finding of discrimination, drawing the link between economics and the legal context.

How Lawyers and Economists View Discrimination

Lawyers and economists both use the term discrimination to refer to adverse treatment of individuals on the basis of their membership in a group. But this is where the commonality of approach ends. The most obvious difference is that lawyers deal with specific cases, asking whether a specific employer has discriminated against specific individuals or groups. In contrast, economists rarely have information on specific cases, and indeed prefer to look at the big picture by examining statistical evidence from large samples of workers. Instead of asking "Were this individual's civil rights violated by her employer?" economists ask, "Are women systematically paid less than men with equal qualifications?"

A second difference pertains to the rules of the game. Lawyers must identify the specific laws that are violated and present supporting evidence, where the standards of evidence vary according to the nature of the alleged violation. As we will see soon, the legal framework constrains what evidence is permissible and what is identified as discrimination. In contrast, the main constraint on economists in analyzing discrimination is data availability. If we adequately control for all sources of hiring or pay differentials, we could then isolate whether any outcome is caused by unlawful decisions motivated by the sex of the individual rather than by legitimate differences in work related characteristics. Economic data falls far short of this ideal. Ironically, lawyers, who typically have far better information about individual workers than do economists, are often restricted by the legal environment to make use of much of this information.

The Role of Economists

While economists who study discrimination pay limited attention to the legal environment in specifying their economic models, lawyers value economists highly for their statistical prowess, since in many discrimination cases the evidence is primarily statistical. Many claims allege that a firm hired, promoted, or retained disproportionately few women or minorities, or paid women and minorities less than comparable men. To demonstrate discrimination in employment outcomes, economists present statistical evidence based on labor market data showing a difference in observed outcomes for members of the protected class relative to what we would expect in the absence of discrimination.

In addition to providing statistical analysis of the labor market, economists provide estimates of compensatory damages arising from the adverse employment decision. For example, if a woman charges that her job has been wrongfully terminated, an economist would calculate how much she would have earned in the remaining time she would have been expected to hold her original job, offsetting this by what she earns on future jobs.

Economists also provide the important function in litigation of educating judges and juries about statistical evidence. Judges who typically have little training in econometrics decide the credibility of the statistical analysis, either directly or as the "gatekeeper" in allowing evidence to be presented in trial. Likewise, juries must interpret the statistical evidence to reach a decision. It is vital that economic experts explain complex statistical concepts in a manner that can be readily understood by persons without formal training in statistics so that the appropriate legal outcome results.

Federal Equal Employment Opportunity Laws

Employment discrimination refers to adverse treatment of workers based on their membership in a group. Equal Employment Opportunity (EEO) laws have evolved over the years and there are a number of statutes and amendments that comprise the federal laws. The centerpiece of federal employment discrimination law is Title VII of the Civil Rights Act of 1964 (Title VII), which prohibits employment discrimination by employers, unions, and employment agencies on the basis of race, color, religion, sex, or national origin.[2] Sexual harassment, which includes demands for sexual favors as well as workplace conditions that create a hostile environment, is also prohibited under Title VII.

New legislation and amendments have increased the number of workers covered by the laws and have added protection against discrimination on the basis of age, disability, and pregnancy. In particular, the Pregnancy Discrimination Amendments to Title VII ruled that sex includes "pregnancy, childbirth or related medical conditions," and requires that employers treat pregnancy and childbirth the same as any other condition similarly affecting the ability to work.

Other laws of particular relevance to women are the Equal Pay Act of 1963 (EPA) and the Family and Medical Leave Act of 1993 (FMLA). The EPA requires that men and women who perform equal work within a particular establishment receive equal pay unless justified by a system of seniority, a merit or production system, or "any other factor other than sex."[3] The FMLA allows employees of firms with more than 50 employees up to 12 weeks of unpaid leave in a 12-month period for birth or adoption of a child, to care for a family member, or for own health.

There are two situations in which employers can legally make decisions on the basis of group membership: when group membership is essential for job performance and as part of an affirmative action plan. First, an employer can make employment decisions on the basis of sex, religion, or national origin (but not on the basis of race) if this qualification is "reasonably necessary to the normal operation of that particular business or enterprise." These are known as "bona fide occupational qualifications (BFOQ)." This condition is interpreted narrowly and must go to the essence of the employer's business. It is not enough for the employer to claim they would make more money by discriminating, or that customer preference or customer discrimination forces them to discriminate.

Whether sex was a BFOQ was the issue in many cases involving airlines. Until challenged in the courts throughout the 1970s, most airlines hired only unmarried women as flight attendants. To justify their policies, airlines claimed that sex was a BFOQ. For example, in Diaz v. Pan American World Airways, Inc. (1971), Pan Am argued that business needs required them to hire only women flight attendants since they provide a soothing atmosphere preferred by male air travelers. In Wilson v. Southwest Airlines Co. (1981), Southwest Airlines likewise claimed that it was necessary for business purposes for their flight attendants to be dressed in provocative uniforms. The courts found neither of these explanations to justify sex as a BFOQ.

Affirmative action programs likewise specifically use race or sex in the employment process. There are three legally distinct forms of affirmative actions plans. First, Executive Order 11246 of 1965 (EO 11246) requires employers holding federal contracts to have a written affirmative action plan, which requires setting goals and timetables to correct underutilization of minorities. Second, courts can, and typically do, order affirmative actions plans as a remedy for prior discrimination. Third, employers can voluntarily institute affirmative action plans.

The Equal Employment Opportunities Commission (EEOC) was established by Title VII to enforce the EEO laws, establish equal employment policy, provide education, information, and technical assistance, to approve litigation, and to file suits in certain circumstances. Under Title VII, employees who feel they have been discriminated against are not permitted to simply file a suit. They must first file a charge with the EEOC (or with the corresponding state agency) within specified time periods. In FY 2000, 31.5 percent of the 79,896 charges filed with the EEOC were charges of sex discrimination.[4] After receiving the charge, the EEOC investigates and determines whether there is "reasonable cause" to believe that Title VII has been violated. At this point the EEOC either dismisses the charge or attempts to resolve the charge by settlement or mediation. If this is unsuccessful, the EEOC may sue, or may issue a "right to sue" notice allowing the charging party to file a private lawsuit. The charging party may also file a private suit even if the EEOC dismisses a charge.

In addition to charges brought by individuals who believe that their employment rights have been violated, individuals, organizations, or agencies may file on behalf of another person. The vast majority of discrimination allegations involve a single individual. Class actions allow a representative to sue on behalf of numerous similarly situated individuals, such as all women employees. The EEOC can also file suits alleging a "pattern and practice" of discrimination on behalf of a class even without identifying specific individuals who believe they have been discriminated against.

Legal Theories of Discrimination

Title VII discrimination claims are filed under one of two theories of discrimination: disparate treatment (also known as intentional discrimination) or disparate impact. As the Supreme Court wrote in Teamsters v. United States (1977), disparate treatment is the most easily understood type of discrimination. The employer simply treats some people less favorably than others because of their race, color, religion, sex, or national origin. Proof of discriminatory motive is critical, although it can in some situations be inferred from the mere fact of differences in treatment. The Supreme Court distinguished disparate treatment from disparate impact by noting that disparate impact claims involve employment practices that are facially neutral in their treatment of different groups but in fact fall more harshly on one group than another and cannot be justified by business necessity. Proof of discriminatory motive is not required under a disparate impact theory.

As noted earlier, economists use labor market data to compare employment outcomes of members of the protected class to what we would expect in the absence of discrimination. A statistically significant disparity can thereby provide evidence that this is a pattern and practice of employer behavior rather than a decision affecting only specific individuals for reasons not necessarily related to discrimination. In most Title VII lawsuits, the central issues are the strength of the statistical evidence, and how employers can justify their business practices. In short, if plaintiffs produce statistical disparities, the defendant employer has two options: rebut the statistical evidence directly, or show the employment practices are job-related and serve reasonable business purposes. If the defendant successfully argues that the practice served reasonable business purposes, the plaintiff still can prevail at trial by showing that an alternative policy with lesser discriminatory effects would be as effective.

Generally, class actions alleging pattern and practice of discrimination are disparate impact claims, while individual cases are disparate treatment. Until recently, both types of discrimination carried the same legal remedies, and were limited to actions that would make an individual "whole." Making whole refers to restoring the individual to the condition they would have been in but for the discrimination and includes remedies such as back pay, hiring, promotion, reinstatement, and so forth. The Civil Rights Act of 1991 permitted compensatory and punitive damages, as well as jury trials, for intentional discrimination. Compensatory damages include payments for actual and potential monetary losses as well as compensation for mental anguish and inconvenience. In addition, if the employer is found to act with malice, punitive damages could be awarded. In contrast to disparate impact, in which the amount of potential damages will be fairly predictably related to workers' earnings, the possibility of punitive damages increases the financial risk faced by employers in disparate treatment cases. Jury trials, compensatory, and punitive damages are not permitted in disparate impact cases.[5]

Until outlawed by Title VII, disparate treatment was often quite explicit, with help wanted ads commonly stating "men's jobs" and "women's jobs" or "white only." While such explicit discrimination is far more unusual now, a recent example shows that it has not disappeared (Albert Karr 2000). An employment agency recently agreed to stop filling job orders with stipulations such as "no Detroit residents," "males only," and "no applicants with accents."

Disparate impact discrimination occurs via employment practices that have the effect of excluding one group even though the employer had no such intent. An example is height and weight minimums for prison guards, which are met by fewer women than men. This type of discrimination is subtler than disparate treatment, especially since many employment practices, such as height and weight minimums for prison guards, may seem perfectly reasonable and rational.

Many disparate impact cases involve hiring practices that may seem to be neutral. Employers use a variety of methods to advertise their job openings. Much recruitment is done informally, with current employees telling their acquaintances about job openings. From the standpoint of economic efficiency, this procedure may be attractive to employers. Recommendations from current employees may be informative about the quality and suitability of the candidate, and these applicants will have a good idea of the character of the job, which may reduce training costs and turnover. Such a practice, however, may well lead to a workforce that is not representative of the qualified workforce. A number of important cases have resulted from such hiring disparities, and one in particular, Wards Cove Packing Co. v. Antonio (1989), in part led Congress to pass the Civil Rights Act of 1991.

Regression Analysis in Employment Discrimination Cases

Regression analysis is routinely used in employment discrimination cases, particularly class actions, to provide evidence on whether similarly-situated individuals are treated differently for illegal reasons.[6] By using regression models, we control for work-related characteristics such as education and experience that legitimately may cause differences in pay between individuals. It is deceptively easy just to run a regression using canned software, throwing into the model as explanatory variables whatever data are available. The statistical issues that economists tackle include the choice of the relevant sample, the decision of what variables to include, determining whether some variables are themselves the outcome of possible discrimination, and the consequences of excluding relevant variables on evidence or the magnitude of any gender pay disparity.

The consequences of incorrectly specifying the regression equation are well known. Exclusion of relevant variables may mislead researchers to the inference of discrimination, as sex or race serves as a proxy for omitted variables that are correlated with sex or race. On the other hand, inclusion of too many variables, or inclusion of inappropriate variables correlated with sex or race, may result in a misleading inference of no discrimination, as multicollinearity weakens the statistical significance of the group indicator variable. Furthermore, inclusion of tainted variables – those variables that are themselves the outcome of discriminatory practices – may likewise result in a misleading inference of no discrimination. A controversial situation that often arises is whether the regression should control for job level, since promotion decisions might have been made discriminatorily.

Must a regression analysis include all measurable or relevant variables in order to be presented as evidence in the courtroom? The US Supreme Court decided that it is not requisite that every relevant variable be included for a regression analysis to be useful. The Supreme Court stopped short, however, of the impossible task of defining precisely how complete a regression must be in order to be legally valid. In Bazemore v. Friday (1986: 400), the Court stated that:

> While the omission of variables from a regression may render the analysis less probative than it otherwise might be, it can hardly be said, absent some other infirmity, that an analysis which accounts for the major factors "must be considered unacceptable as evidence of discrimination." Normally, failure to include variables will affect the analysis' probativeness, not its admissibility.

One consequence of Bazemore is that defendants generally cannot undermine a regression analysis by simply pointing out that it lacks some variable.

While much effort is involved in including as many variables as validly possible, the legal framework also limits inclusion of certain variables. For example, economists routinely include in wage regressions indicators of marital status and number of children, and in fact there is an active literature examining the widely established male marital wage premium of around 10 to 20 percent (Joni Hersch and Leslie Stratton 2000). Employers, however, are legally prohibited from asking information about marital status and number of children. Often this information is available from employment records such as health and pension benefit forms, but whether it can be used in litigation enters murky grounds.

Not surprisingly, plaintiffs in sex discrimination cases present regression results showing there is a statistically significant disparity by sex in wages or occupation. Defendants then attempt to undermine this evidence. Often defendants start by attacking the regression equation on the basis that it omits so many important variables that it is meaningless. The Sears case, discussed later, is a prominent example in which the plaintiffs' regression analysis was criticized for failing to control for women's interest in commission sales jobs.

In addition to claiming that the regression omits the most important variables, there are several other tricks that can make statistical significance go away. Defendants frequently chop the sample into increasing small and homogeneous groups. By doing so, any gender disparity observed in larger samples is less likely to be statistically significant when the sample size declines or the sample observations become more alike. Other tactics include examining wage growth rather than wage levels, or controlling for starting salary in the regression. Since women will typically have lower starting salaries in those situations resulting in a discrimination suit, starting salary will be highly correlated with gender, weakening the statistical significance of the gender coefficient. Furthermore, precisely because women typically have lower starting salaries, they often have higher wage growth despite continued lower wage levels.

Do not be misled into thinking that all judges are naive victims of clever and persuasive economists. An amusing quote from United States Department of Treasury v. Harris Trust & Savings Bank (1986: 23) demonstrates that judges are often fully aware of the strategies that econometricians and statisticians use:

> Expressed in simplest terms the Plaintiff's goal was to include every negative observation in the data base, while Harris, on the other hand, wished to emasculate the data base as much as possible by removing any damaging data observations. Both sides also manipulated the selection of variables in the statistical equations in such a way as to benefit them. These maneuverings translated into the Government including any female or minority employee, no matter how marginally qualified, in its data base, and Harris excluding any employee, no matter how well qualified, from its studies. The Department also studied the Harris work force in the largest slices possible to increase the statistical significance of its studies. The Bank disaggregated its employees to the maximum extent possible in an attempt to destroy any significant statistical output. Both sides selected or omitted variables for their regression equations which would skew the results of the studies in their favor.[7]

An Overview of the Legal Process

The legal response to anti-discrimination laws has developed over the years as various cases raising complex issues have reached the courts. This section provides an overview of the legal process and discusses some prominent cases.

Disparate treatment claims

Most disparate treatment claims involve individual plaintiffs. The legal process typically begins with the plaintiff alleging that the reason for an adverse employment action was illegal discrimination. For example, a female plaintiff may allege that although she was qualified, she was not hired or promoted because she was female.

Early cases were based on quite explicit discriminatory treatment of women. For example, the employer in Weeks v. Southern Bell Tel. & Tel. Co. (1969: 236) refused to hire the female plaintiff for the job of switchman because it was deemed "strenuous" and required emergency work at night and in locations that might be considered dangerous. The district court judge found this a violation of Title VII, noting:

> [m]en have always had the right to determine whether the incremental increase in remu-neration for strenuous, dangerous, obnoxious, boring or unromantic tasks is worth the candle. The promise of Title VII is that women are now to be on an equal footing.

As anti-discrimination laws became more widely known and enforced, it became less likely that an employer would have explicit discriminatory policies. Many individual disparate treatment claims are therefore based on circumstantial evidence (evidence from which a discriminatory motive may be inferred) rather than on direct evidence. A case of discrimination based on circumstantial evidence proceeds by process of elimination: once non-discriminatory reasons are ruled out, the inference is that the employment decision was motivated by unlawful discrimination.[8] If the defendant does not rebut the plaintiff's case, the plaintiff wins.

Usually, however, the defendant employer will deny that discrimination motivated the decision and offer a non-discriminatory reason for the employment decision. For instance, the employer may claim that the female employee was not promoted because she was incompetent or had weak interpersonal skills. Once the defendant has provided a legitimate, non-discriminatory reason, the plaintiff needs to show that the employment decision was actually due to discrimination, and that the proffered reason is "pretextual," that is, a false or weak reason advanced to hide the actual reason.

What if the plaintiff succeeds in establishing that the employment decision was motivated by illegal discrimination, but the defendant employer asserts that they would have made the same decision for permissible reasons? Mixed motive cases are those in which the employer considered both prohibited reasons (say sex) as well as legitimate factors (say competence) in making an employment decision.

An extremely important case involving mixed motives is Price Waterhouse v. Hopkins (1989). Ann Hopkins sued her employer Price Waterhouse when it refused to offer her partnership. A number of the firm's partners supported her for partnership. Evidence produced at trial indicated that her clients thought very highly of her, and she had been successful in securing for her firm a $25 million contract. Nevertheless, there were numerous concerns and comments about her "interpersonal skills," particularly with staff members, and that "supporters and opponents of her candidacy indicated that she was sometimes overly aggressive, unduly harsh, difficult to work with and impatient with staff." If these were the only grounds for refusing to make her a partner, there would be no case. But other grounds surfaced as the basis for the negative partnership decision. Partners described Hopkins as "macho," and that she "overcompensated for being a woman," and she was advised to "walk more femininely, dress more femininely, wear makeup, have her hair styled, and wear jewelry" to improve her chance for promotion.

The Supreme Court decided that the employer is not liable for discrimination if the employer would have made the same decision under legitimate criteria. Congress, however, did not agree on this point, and amended Title VII in the Civil Rights Act of 1991 as follows: "an unlawful employment practice is established when the complaining party demonstrates that race, color, religion, sex, or national origin was a motivating factor for any employment practice, even though other factors also motivated the practice." That is, Title VII is violated when unlawful discrimination is a motivating factor even if the same result would have been produced under legitimate criteria.

Despite the admirable aims of this legislation, the standards used in different federal circuits have varied, so the legacy of Price Waterhouse is unclear. This is not especially surprising. Multiple motives underlie most employment decisions. How large a motivating factor must sex stereotyping represent to meet the legal standard? Lower courts have used different standards including "discernible factor," "significant factor," and "substantial part," and different outcomes have occurred even among courts nominally using the same standard (Tracy Bach 1993).

Systemic disparate treatment cases are claims of discrimination that affect groups rather than individuals. These issues can be highly controversial as some discriminatory policies may be intended not only to protect groups of workers but also to insulate the employer from tort claims. Consider Johnson Controls, a firm that manufactured batteries. In the manufacturing process workers were exposed to lead, which has been linked to the risk of harm to the fetus and the reproductive abilities of both men and women. In 1982 Johnson Controls shifted from a policy of warning about the hazards of lead exposure to a policy of excluding women of childbearing age from jobs that involved lead exposure. The Supreme Court found this practice to be illegal sex discrimination in United Auto Workers v. Johnson Controls, Inc. (1991). Perhaps the concern over fetal risks of lead exposure was exaggerated – at least OSHA thought so, and stated that "there is no basis whatsoever for the claim that women of childbearing age should be excluded from the workplace in order to protect the fetus or the course of pregnancy."[9]

The centrality of economic and statistical analysis in class action litigation was evident in EEOC v. Sears, Roebuck & Co. (1988). This case is noteworthy for a number of reasons, including the length of the trial, the massive amount of evidence produced, and the extensive and heated scholarly debate that ensued. Sears was the largest employer of women and the majority of its salespersons were women, but relatively few of the higher-paid commission salespersons were female. The EEOC sought to prove that Sears engaged in a national pattern or practice of discrimination by failing to hire and promote women into commission sales jobs on the same basis as men and by paying female management, professional, and administrative employees less than similar males.

The Sears case extended over an astonishingly long period of 15 years. The EEOC filed a discrimination charge in 1973. After settlement and conciliation efforts failed, the EEOC brought suit in 1979. A ten-month trial began in 1984, culminating in a verdict in favor of Sears. This verdict was upheld on appeal in 1988, which observers viewed as a crushing blow to the EEOC.

The EEOC's evidence was almost entirely statistical. The EEOC presented no individual victim testimony, a fact that the court did not fail to notice. To demonstrate discrimination in hiring into commission sales jobs, the EEOC compared the proportion of commission salespersons that were female to the overall proportion of female applicants for any sales job at Sears. The EEOC used regression analyses to demonstrate that disproportionately few women held commission sales positions, controlling for individual characteristics including job applied for, age, education, and three measures indicating experience with sales and commission jobs and with product lines. These regression analyses yielded large statistically significant differences by gender.

Once the EEOC demonstrated statistically significant disparities, Sears could attempt to rebut the statistical evidence directly, which they did with a vengeance. Sears focused on undermining two of the EEOC's key assumptions: that women and men were equally interested in, and qualified for, commission sales positions. The courts accepted the view that women were not interested in commission sales, based on Sears' evidence that commission sales involved risk, unusual working hours, and "a high degree of technical knowledge, expertise and motivation" (EEOC v. Sears, Roebuck & Co. 1988 p. 320). Store managers testified to their inability to convince women to take commission sales jobs, noting that:

> [v]arious reasons for women's lack of interest in commission selling included a fear or dislike of what they perceived as cutthroat competition, and increased pressure and risk associated with commission sales. Noncommission selling, on the other hand, was associated with more social contact and friendship, less pressure and less risk. (p. 320–1)

Although the EEOC's regression analyses controlled for objective measurable work-related characteristics, these analyses were discounted by the court, in noting "[o]ther important factors not controlled for in EEOC's analysis are those characteristics which could be determined only from an interview, not from the written application. These include physical appearance, assertiveness, the ability to communicate, friendliness, and economic motivation." In other words, hiring decisions were based on subjective factors, and who had more economic motivation than male heads of household? Indeed, in contrast to education and years of work experience that can be quantified, it is hard to imagine how we would unambiguously quantify interest and economic motivation.

In his dissent of the appellate court verdict, Judge Cudahy criticized the district and appellate courts' reliance on Sears' stereotypical assumptions of women, stating:

> [t]hese conclusions . . . are of a piece with the proposition that women are by nature happier cooking, doing the laundry and chauffeuring the children to softball games than arguing appeals or selling stocks. The stereotype of women as less greedy and daring than men is one that the sex discrimination laws were intended to address. It is disturbing that this sort of thinking is accepted so uncritically by the district court and by the majority (Dothard v. Rawlinson 1977 p. 361).

Disparate impact claims

Disparate impact cases usually involve groups of workers in a protected class, and frequently arise from hiring practices. Demonstrating disparate impact requires showing that the facially neutral employment practices are not necessary for business purposes and result in a statistical disparity among workers in protected classes. Proof of discriminatory motive is not required. Evidence on whether an employer's hiring practices resulted in disparate impact is necessarily statistical.

As with disparate treatment cases, the issues in disparate impact discrimination can be highly controversial. The issue in Dothard v. Rawlinson (1977) involved height and weight requirements for prison guards employed by the Alabama state penitentiary system. The minimums excluded less than 1 percent of men in the population but over 40 percent of women. Thus, it was easily established that these requirements had a disparate impact on the employment of women. The employer argued, without offering supporting evidence, that height and weight are related to strength, and that strength is essential to job performance. If strength were job related, it could be tested directly – a direct test would satisfy Title VII. Thus, the district court held that the height and weight requirements violated Title VII. Furthermore, although prison guards are in close contact with prisoners, the district court rejected the employer's defense that sex was a BFOQ. The Supreme Court disagreed with this final point, ruling that the employer could hire only male guards in contact areas of maximum-security penitentiaries because more was at stake than the "individual woman's decision to weigh and accept the risks of employment." Sex was found to be a BFOQ since it related to the guard's ability to maintain prison security, referring to the likelihood that inmates will sexually assault women guards.

That the mere presence of women guards undermines prison security is highly speculative, as Justice Marshall pointed out in his dissent. He also noted:

> this rationale regrettably perpetuates one of the most insidious of the old myths about women that women, wittingly or not, are seductive sexual objects. The effect of the decision, made I am sure with the best of intentions, is to punish women because their very presence might provoke sexual assaults. (Dothard v. Rawlinson 1977 p. 345)

A recent case raises similar issues regarding physical standards for police officers. The situation in Lanning v. Southeastern Pennsylvania Transportation Authority (1999) involves a public transportation authority that required that applicants for jobs as transportation police officers run 1.5 miles in 12 minutes. Since relatively fewer women than men are able to meet this standard, the screening test had a disparate impact on employment of women. The trial court found this screening test was validly related to job performance. This finding, however, was reversed on appeal on the grounds that the transportation authority failed to show that meeting this requirement was necessary for successful performance of the job in question. In contrast, in 1994 UPS changed the minimum weight that its truck drivers are required to lift from 50 pounds to 150 pounds. While this new policy undoubtedly has a disparate impact on the employment of women, since UPS accepts for shipment packages weighing up to 150 pounds, this requirement is defensible on the grounds that it is necessary for business purposes.

Affirmative action – reverse discrimination claims

While affirmative action plans have the laudable goal of increasing opportunity and eliminating segregation in the workforce, in practice they are frequently highly controversial. Whites and males have brought Title VII charges arguing that by giving preferential treatment to those in protected classes, they were thereby unlawfully discriminated against.

The Supreme Court has determined that affirmative action plans are permissible if they are designed to remedy "a manifest imbalance" in traditionally segregated jobs and they do not "unnecessarily trammel on the interests" of the majority group members. In order to determine whether a manifest imbalance in a traditionally segregated job category exists, the minority composition of jobholders is compared to their availability in the relevant labor market. The disparity does not have to be as great as required to support a legal presumption of discrimination, so employers can adopt a voluntary affirmative action plan without showing past discrimination on their part.

The seminal Supreme Court case establishing the legal status of affirmative action programs in addressing gender disparities is Johnson v. Transportation Agency (1986). The Agency found that women composed only 22.4 percent of their employees, while the area labor market was comprised of 36.4 percent female. Furthermore, there was a high degree of segregation by sex within job categories. In particular, none of the Agency's 238 workers in the relevant job category "Skilled Craft" were women. These factors established that there was a "manifest imbalance" in the proportion of women in traditionally male jobs. As part of its affirmative action program, the Agency considered the sex of a qualified applicant when making promotion decisions into male-dominated job classifications. A male employee who was passed over for promotion in favor of a woman brought suit, alleging that he had been denied promotion on the basis of sex in violation of Title VII. The Supreme Court found that the voluntary affirmative action plan was legal. Considering sex in making promotion decisions did not trammel on the rights of men since only qualified women were considered for promotion, sex was only one factor in the employment decision, and the plan did not create an absolute barrier to men's promotion.

There have been a number of cases involving university faculty members. Typically the university involved in reverse discrimination litigation had conducted a salary equity study using regression analysis, finding that women were paid less than similar men. The university then instituted an affirmative action program, either voluntarily or by court order, which raised women's pay. Male faculty members then filed suits claiming that these affirmative action programs violated their rights under Title VII, alleging that the salary equity study in question was too flawed to be credible and spuriously indicated a gender pay disparity. By this argument, if there is no actual gender pay disparity, there is no manifest imbalance. And if women's salaries were raised but not men's in the absence of a manifest imbalance, then men's rights were trammeled on.

Smith v. Virginia Commonwealth University (1995) provides a useful example of the complex econometric issues involved. In 1989, Virginia Commonwealth University (VCU) conducted a salary equity study and performed a multiple regression analysis taking into account educational level, tenure status, number of years of VCU experience and number of years of prior academic experience. This study indicated that women faculty members earned on average $1,354 less than their male counterparts. This average gap of $1,354 was multiplied by the number of female faculty members, and this sum of money was distributed to female faculty members with the amount varying according to individual merit.

Male faculty members sued alleging Title VII discrimination, claiming that the regression omitted the most important variables and in doing so erroneously found a gender pay disparity.[9] The male plaintiffs' suit maintained that the regression analysis was invalid because it failed to control for prior experience as an administrator and for performance factors. Administrators were paid higher wages, and faculty members retained this increase in salary when they return to teaching, thus inflating faculty salaries. If indeed women are less productive than men, excluding performance factors will indeed widen the pay gap attributed to sex.

Why didn't VCU take these factors into account? The university explained that their study did not include performance factors, such as teaching evaluations and number of publications, for three reasons: that they are difficult to quantify, because they are included indirectly in the form of academic rank, status, and experience; and because there is no reason to believe that performance differs by gender. VCU's reason for not taking into account a faculty member's prior service as an administrator is that this is likely to be a tainted variable. A disproportionate number of men had prior administrative experience, and the selection of administrators may itself be the outcome of discrimination.

The male plaintiffs in the VCU case never presented estimates from an alternative regression model. Without additional analysis, the consequence of including these additional factors (if appropriate) is by no means certain. Studies have found a gender pay gap among faculty members persists even after publication records are included in the regression (Michael Ransom and Sharon Megdal 1993; Richard Raymond et al. 1988).

Concluding Comments

One legacy of Title VII of the Civil Rights Act of 1964 is that women under age 50 have spent their entire labor market years covered by laws prohibiting employment discrimination on the basis of sex. Since women have been covered by these laws for almost four decades, there should only be litigation under these statutes if there are violations. Many economic theories predict that discriminatory forces should be eliminated over time either through market competition or through learning about gender differences in productivity. This has not, however, occurred. Discrimination litigation is alive and well, and the many suits and settlements favoring women plaintiffs suggest that the end to employment discrimination is not in sight.

Many visible recent cases involve professional women. In the past, few professional women sued, perhaps out of concern that they would be stigmatized and their career would be jeopardized. Over time, however, professional women have become more outspoken. There have been a number of suits charging sex discrimination by women academics. A recent example involves the tenure denial of a woman professor employed at Vassar College, a historically female college, who claimed sex discrimination. Some notable recent cases have involved women employed at several Wall Street firms, including Morgan Stanley, Merrill Lynch, and Smith Barney. In particular, Smith Barney achieved notoriety because of its "boom-boom room" in which women were verbally and physically harassed.

Economists continue to play a central role in society's efforts to eliminate discrimination through litigation efforts. Regression equations are widely used to determine whether there is a pay or occupational disparity attributable to sex rather than to legitimate factors, and the principle battleground continues to be over the proper specification of these equations. The standards for statistical evidence are becoming better defined as lawyers and judges become more experienced with quantitative methods.[10] The continued refinement of economic methods, particularly in labor economics and econometrics, will bolster the role of economists in the courtroom and help achieve society's goal of eradicating discrimination.

NOTES

1 The value for 1969 is provided in Francine Blau (1998), Table 4 and refers to mean earnings for full-time wage and salary workers between ages 25 and 64. The value for 1999 is calculated from U.S. Census Bureau (2000), No. 696, and refers to median earnings for full-time wage and salary workers over age 25.

2 Sex was not included in the initial draft of the act. Ironically, sex was added as a protected class by an opponent of the entire Civil Rights Act, apparently as an (unsuccessful) attempt to defeat the entire bill.

3 An interesting historical note is that in World War II, the War Labor Board mandated "equal pay for comparable work" for men and women. This policy expired when the war ended, and the ensuing administrations were unable to extend this provision. In adopting the EPA, Congress imposed a more stringent standard – "equal pay for equal work" than the War Labor Board policy of "equal pay for comparable work."

4 Source: http://www.eeoc.gov/stats/charges.html.

5 Why do you think the Civil Rights Act of 1991 increased the penalties for intentional discrimination? One possibility is that as our society moves closer to the goal of eliminating discrimination, and the anti-discrimination laws become more ingrained in employers' minds, intentional discrimination is even more blameworthy and should be subject to greater sanctions.

6   For a brief overview of regression analysis, please see chapter 11 by Irene Powell in this volume.

7   The court found that Harris had discriminated against women employees. The complete text is available at http://www.oalj.dol.gov/public/ofccp/decsn/78ofc02e.htm.

8   The seminal Supreme Court case specifying how circumstantial evidence is used in employment discrimination cases is McDonnell-Douglas v. Green (1973). There are four parts to establishing sufficient legally required evidence of discrimination to require rebuttal by the defendant. For example, in a case of hiring discrimination, the plaintiff would need to demonstrate that she is female and therefore a member of a protected class; that she was qualified for a job that she applied for; that she was rejected; and that the position remained open and the employer continued to seek applicants with similar credentials.

9   While this may mitigate the possibility that tort claims from exposed employees would be successful, it does not prohibit claims by injured children. Keep in mind that scientific evidence does not insulate employers from tort actions. Bendectin, a widely used effective treatment for morning sickness, was taken off the market after the manufacturer, Merrell Dow, faced thousands of suits (Foster and Huber 1997). Despite no scientific evidence that Bendectin caused birth defects, multiple juries found the manufacturer liable, although Merrell Dow won on appeal in all but one case.

10 The district court granted summary judgment in favor of VCU, finding that the university properly instituted its affirmative action plan. The male faculty members appealed, and the appellate court found that there was a "genuine issue of material fact," which makes summary judgment for either side inappropriate. The case was thereby remanded to the district court for a complete trial. There is no information regarding VCU available on Westlaw after the 1996 appellate court finding. Presumably this case settled out of court.

11 Law school courses in quantitative methods are becoming more widespread. For example, Harvard Law School instituted a first year course in Analytic Methods for Lawyers in Spring 2000, which was immediately enrolled at capacity.

REFERENCES

Bach, Tracy L. 1993. "Gender Stereotyping in Employment Discrimination: Finding a Balance of Evidence and Causation under Title VII." *Minnesota Law Review* 77: 1251–81.

Blau, Francine. 1998. "Trends in the Well-Being of American Women, 1970–95." *Journal of Economic Literature* 36(1): 112–65.

Foster, Kenneth R. and Peter S. Huber. 1997. *Judging Science: Scientific Knowledge and Federal Courts.* Cambridge MA: MIT Press, p. 4.

Hersch, Joni and Leslie S. Stratton. 2000. "Household Specialization and the Male Marriage Wage Premium." *Industrial and Labor Relations Review* 54(1): 78–94.

Karr, Albert R. 2000. "Court Orders Michigan Employment Agency to End Wholesale Discrimination." *Wall Street Journal*, May 2.

Ransom, Michael R. and Sharon Bernstein Megdal. 1993. "Sex Differences in the Academic Labor Market in the Affirmative Action Era." *Economics of Education Review* 12(1): 21–43.

Raymond, Richard D., Michael L. Sesnowitz, and Donald R. Williams. 1988. "Does Sex Still Matter? New Evidence from the 1980s." *Economic Inquiry* 26(1): 43–58.

U.S. Census Bureau, Statistical Abstract of the United States: 2000 (120th edition) Washington, DC, 2000.

CASES CITED

Bazemore v. Friday, 478 U.S. 385, 106 S.Ct. 3000 (1986).

Diaz v. Pan Am. World Airways, Inc., 442 F.2d 385 (5th Cir. 1971).

Dothard v. Rawlinson, 433 U.S. 321, 97 S.Ct. 2720 (1977).

EEOC v. Sears, Roebuck & Co., 628 F. Supp. 1264 (N.D. Ill. 1986), *affirmed*, 839 F.2d 302 (7th Cir. 1988).

Johnson v. Transportation Agency, 480 U.S. 616, 107 S.Ct. 1442 (1986).

Lanning v. Southeastern Pennsylvania Transportation Authority, 181 F.3d 478 (3rd Cir. 1999), *cert. denied*, 528 U.S. 1131 (2000).

McDonnell-Douglas v. Green, 411 U.S. 792, 93 S.Ct. 1817 (1973).

Price Waterhouse v. Hopkins, 490 U.S. 228, 109 S.Ct. 1775 (1989).

Smith v. Virginia Commonwealth University, 84 F.3d 672 (4th Cir. 1996).

Teamsters v. United States, 431 U.S. 324, 97 S.Ct. 1843 (1977).

United Auto Workers v. Johnson Controls, Inc., 499 U.S. 187, 111 S.Ct. 1196 (1991).

United States Dept. of Treasury v. Harris Trust & Savings Bank, 78-OFCCP-2 (1986).

Wards Cove Packing Co. v. Antonio, 490 U.S. 642, 109 S.Ct. 2115 (1989).

Weeks v. Southern Bell Tel. & Tel. Co., 408 F.2d 228 (5th Cir. 1969).

Wilson v. Southwest Airlines Co., 517 F. Supp. 292 (W.D.Tex. 1981), *later proceedings*, 880 F.2d 807 (5th Cir. 1989).

Index